Located Lives

Located Lives

Place and Idea in
Southern Autobiography

EDITED BY J. BILL BERRY

The University of Georgia Press

Athens and London

© 1990 by the University of Georgia Press
Athens, Georgia 30602
"Writing Upside Down: Voice and Place in
Southern Autobiography" © 1990 by
William Howarth
All rights reserved

Designed by Kathi L. Dailey
Set in 10 on 13 Merganthaler Caledonia
The paper in this book meets the guidelines
for permanence and durability of the
Committee on Production Guidelines for
Book Longevity of the Council on Library
Resources.
Typeset by Tseng Information Systems, Inc.
Printed and bound by Thomson-Shore, Inc.

Printed in the United States of America

94   93   92   91   90   5   4   3   2   1

Library of Congress Cataloging in
Publication Data

Located lives : place and idea in Southern
autobiography / edited by J. Bill Berry.
    p. cm.
    Based on a conference held at Arkansas
State University in April 1988.
    ISBN 0-8203-1217-7 (alk. paper)
    (ISBN 0-8203-1225-8 (pbk: alk. paper)
    1. American prose literature—
Southern States— History and criticism—
Congresses.   2. Authors, American—
Southern States—Biography—History and
criticism—Congresses.   3. Southern States
— Biography—History and criticism—
Congresses.   4. Biography (as a literary
form)—Congresses.   5. Southern States in
literature—Congresses.   6. Autobiography
—Congresses.   I. Berry, J. Bill.
PS261.L7   1990
818'.08—dc20   89-27422
                                      CIP

British Library Cataloging in Publication
Data available

Frontispiece: Too far to walk it, Eudora
Welty Collection, Mississippi Department
of Archives and History.

Contents

Acknowledgments   vii

Introduction   ix

The Interpretation of Southern Autobiography

Writing Upside Down: Voice and Place in Southern
Autobiography   3
WILLIAM HOWARTH

Between Individualism and Community: Autobiographies of
Southern Women   20
ELIZABETH FOX-GENOVESE

The Territory Behind: Mark Twain and His Autobiographies   39
ROBERT ATWAN

Lives Fugitive and Unwritten   52
GEORGE CORE

Autobiographical Traditions Black and White   66
JAMES OLNEY

Eudora Welty's Autobiographical Duet: *The Optimist's
Daughter* and *One Writer's Beginnings*   78
SALLY WOLFF

Healing the Woman Within: Therapeutic Aspects of Ellen
Glasgow's Autobiography   93
MARILYN R. CHANDLER

Autobiography in Southern Journalism   107
ROY REED

Southern Personal Essays

Between Defiance and Defense: Owning Up to the South   119
JAMES M. COX

Uncles and Others   132
GEORGE GARRETT

Mosaics of Southern Masculinity: Small-Scale Mythologies 152
PAT C. HOY II

Class Southerner   167
J. BILL BERRY

Notes on Contributors   188

Acknowledgments

Most of the essays in this collection were originally presented at the 1988 conference, "Backward Glances: Southern Autobiographical Traditions and Perspectives," hosted by Arkansas State University. Elizabeth Fox-Genovese's essay was originally delivered at the 1988 meeting of the Modern Language Association. Sally Wolff's essay appears for the first time in this collection. Bill Berry's "Class Southerner" first appeared in *Virginia Quarterly Review*, and the editor and publisher gratefully acknowledge permission to reprint the essay here.

The editor and the publisher also wish to acknowledge the journals in which some of the essays have appeared since the conference: *Sewanee Review* for James Cox's "Between Defiance and Defense: Owning Up to the South" and Pat Hoy's "Mosaics of Southern Masculinity"; and *Southwest Review* for William Howarth's "Writing Upside Down: Voice and Place in Southern Autobiography."

I wish to thank the following for the parts they played in the conference:

The Arkansas Endowment for the Humanities, Arkansas State University, the Winthrop Rockefeller Foundation, the Arnold Foundation through the Arkansas Community Foundation, Frank and Lou Angelo, Carter and Pat Patteson, and Walter and Mary Ann Trulock for sponsorship and funding.

The Arkansas State University faculty and staff, especially Lyman Hagen and Sally Wolff, who helped plan and coordinate the conference, and Marilyn Brewer, who handled correspondence and countless other details.

Arkansas State University students Laura Burns, Tim Burns, Lisa

Higgins, Laurie Hinck, Pattie Leinenbach, Mark Lewis, Matt Lemmons, Kenneth Neely, Joyce Nuttbrock, Tim Prater, Bryant Taylor, Nhu Nguyen, and Chidong Zhang, for assistance with details of conference activities; particular thanks to Penny Wolfe, who supervised registration.

Robert Atwan, George Core, Pat Hoy, and Phillip Richards, who offered valuable advice in planning the conference.

I also wish to thank Debra Winter who steered the manuscript of this book through the University of Georgia Press and Brenda Kolb, who copyedited the manuscript. A special thanks to Mimi Whistle for thoughtful suggestions about the conference, the manuscript, and my essay, particularly.

Introduction

J. BILL BERRY

France was a land, England was a people, but America, having about
it still that quality of the idea, was harder to utter—it was the graves
at Shiloh and the tired, drawn, nervous faces of its great men, and the
country boys dying in the Argonne for a phrase that was empty before
their bodies withered. It was a willingness of the heart.

F. Scott Fitzgerald

Like a good many other writers, I am myself touched off by place. The
place where I am and the place I know, and other places that familiarity
with and love for my own make strange and lovely and enlightening to
look into, are what set me to writing my stories.

Eudora Welty

I s there a southern autobiographical tradition? Is there a set of
themes or topics that distinguishes southern personal narrative?
Does it make sense to speak of "southern autobiography" at all—to
propose that, despite their considerable diversity, southern narratives
share motives, concerns, and attitudes, a voice and sensibility that differentiate them from those produced elsewhere? Eudora Welty informs
readers of *One Writer's Beginnings* that "especially crossing the line
you couldn't see but knew was there, between the South and the North
—you could draw a breath and feel the difference." Can readers feel
the difference in southern autobiography?

The question of the distinctiveness of southern autobiography is the
most fundamental issue raised by this collection of critical essays and

personal narratives. Not all the contributors feel the difference. One (perhaps two) questions the existence of a tradition. For several, the distinctiveness of southern autobiography is self-evident. Others are less certain, ambivalent—self-divided. The disagreement among contributors reflects the complexity of the question; the tension within individual writers is itself a major key to understanding southern personal narrative.

Autobiography may be the preeminent form of American literary expression. The very word "autobiography" dates from just after the American and French revolutions, when a heightened self-consciousness began to emerge with such figures as Rousseau and Franklin. The Age of Revolution helped to establish the importance of the individual. Without that importance, there would not have been the proliferation of autobiographies that followed close upon the revolutionary period. Since the founding of the Republic, autobiography has both expressed and helped to engender our sense of this country. It has delivered a rich and various—at times divided and divisive—series of answers to Crèvecoeur's question, "What then is this American, this new man?" Autobiography is the true song of ourselves, as Robert Sayre has asserted.[1]

The song has had distinguished singers. Thoreau's *Walden* and Adams's *Education of Henry Adams* rank, by anyone's standards, among the classics of our literature, and James M. Cox would add Franklin's autobiography to his list of the ten major American prose works.[2] American autobiographies impress by their sheer number—ten thousand of them, by one recent estimate. Almost anyone can write personal narrative, especially if one accepts as autobiographies the "as told to" enterprises issuing from the professional athletes and CEOs currently enjoying a richly earned status as American heroes. Both in quantity and in accessibility (for writers and readers), autobiography amply validates William Dean Howells's description of it as "the most democratic province in the republic of letters."[3]

Despite the quantity and quality of autobiographical writing, the serious theoretical and critical literature on personal narrative is, for the most part, of fairly recent origin. Thirty-five years ago, autobiography studies could not be said to exist. Now they are a growth industry. New books appear regularly; literary journals devote special issues to the subject; and, in what is the clearest signal of the maturation of the field, there is now an interesting and increasingly influential journal, *A/B: Auto/Biography Studies*. To date, several excellent, full-length studies and collections of essays have examined American autobiography, black autobiography, and women's autobiography. Individual writers known primarily as autobiographers (Maya Angelou, for instance) have been the subjects of book-length considerations. And established classics such as the autobiographies of Franklin, Thoreau, and Henry Adams have merited frequent and thorough investigation.

For American personal narrative, Franklin's *Memoir*, as he styled it, is critical: this first great American success story is the model for hundreds of figures in American fiction as well as nonfiction. To be sure, American autobiography has models that predate Franklin. Captivity and travel narratives, to mention two important examples, may bear no relation to the *Memoir*; and, especially since World War II, new themes and experimentation increasingly characterize American autobiographical writing. Even so, Franklin looms as "something approaching the archetypal American autobiographer,"[4] defining, more than any other figure, what is American in American autobiography. Since Franklin, American autobiographers have tended to identify with America or some idea that is held to be fundamentally American. Writers as disparate as Thoreau, Whitman, and Adams (and, one might add, Andrew Carnegie, P. T. Barnum, and many others) comment in various ways on autobiographical themes—honesty, the success myth, the ideal of the self-made man, the belief in social progress—classically set forward by Franklin. The popularity of such recent books as the massively earnest *Iacocca*, the very title of Norman Podhoretz's *Making It* (giving a defiant, Brownsville jeer to any who would question the deeply American values Podhoretz believes he represents), testify to Franklin's continuing hold on the American imagination. The *Memoir* embodies what Americans think of themselves as individuals and as a people. That is why D. H. Lawrence called Franklin "the pattern American" and why Robert Sayre pronounced the *Memoir* "a version of the national epic."[5]

In this national epic, however, the American South has participated ambiguously, at times unwillingly. It has produced, from early in its history and because of the very logic (however confused) of its culture, large numbers of people who would have denied that the pattern tailored by Franklin was fit or even possible to imitate. There have been perceptive essays treating individual southern narratives as well as suggestive articles comparing various southern autobiographies, as did William L. Andrews's recent "In Search of a Common Identity: The Self and the South in Four Mississippi Autobiographies."[6] Yet surprisingly little current criticism emphasizes region as a basis for exploring autobiography, despite its being a truism that regionalism is fundamental to American culture. The idea of region cuts across worn paths to reach central questions including race, class, and gender. Further, as William Howarth points out, the abundance and quality of southern poetry, fiction, drama, and essays since the Civil War have made southern literature a major form of national expression. A distinguishing feature of this literature has been its sense of history, its consciousness of the past in the present, as Allen Tate observed of the southern renascence. The writer's sense of the past, his consciousness of history's effects on present identity and achievement, is of the essence of literary autobiography. The richness of southern fiction as well as current interest in autobiography strongly urge close consideration of southern autobiography.

The present collection grows out of a conference held at Arkansas State University during the spring of 1988. The conference attracted an exceptional group of scholars and writers who shared a conviction that southern autobiography merited focused consideration. Most were southerners. The material engaged speakers on a deeply personal level, in part because of its power to define group experience and ideas. Less predictably, the material spoke directly to the nonsouthern participants; it encouraged them to establish a personal connection to southern autobiographical writing. One infers in their responses a perception of southern autobiography as something approaching an ethnic literature. Robert Atwan acknowledged a lack of southern lineage, as though such a pedigree were, or might be considered, a necessary credential to speak on southern personal narrative. He offered, as a substitute, "Some of my best friends are southerners." Howarth, although asserting "nominal southern roots," confesses in his essay, "Whenever I go south, my feet feel welcome, but my head keeps looking around for the deportation notice." To examine the South is, at least indirectly, to explore America and the American, nationality and sectional consciousness being dual aspects of the same thing. The subject, speakers, and audience fostered or even implied a dialogue between the North and the South, each used to define and measure and vivify the other. This collection blends not only strong voices but also a variety of literary and critical approaches. James Olney focuses on Wright's narrative and Eudora Welty's *One Writer's Beginnings* to raise questions concerning the existence of a southern autobiographical tradition. The question of tradition also occupies George Core, who looks at a series of major writers who did not publish autobiographies. Robert Atwan reviews the three published editions of Mark Twain's autobiography to trace Twain's changing autobiographical intentions and, further, his very conception of autobiography. Elizabeth Fox-Genovese, who examines work by black and white southern women, enters a major theoretical debate concerning the status of the self. Marilyn Chandler, in her exploration of Ellen Glasgow's *The Woman Within*, submits a case study of the therapeutic functions of personal narrative. Sally Wolff compares Welty's *One Writer's Beginnings* and *The Optimist's Daughter* to ask questions concerning the relation of autobiography and fiction.

George Garrett and I turn aside from the critical essay and offer personal narratives. Garrett sketches "uncles and others" and investigates changes in American attitudes, values, and the meaning of family. I recount how it took New Jersey to teach me I was a southerner. By combining critical essay with personal narrative, the collection illustrates its own insights. It opens an implicit conversation between critic and autobiographer.

James Olney has elsewhere described the critic of autobiography as "a vicarious or a closet autobiographer."[7] In the essays by Cox and Pat Hoy and, to some degree, those by Howarth and Roy Reed, the critic and the autobiographer become one and the same. All four writers integrate personal essay with discussion of other autobiographers or the problems of autobiography. Cox treats Frederick Douglass's *Narrative* and William Alexander Percy's *Lanterns on the Levee* and places himself between these poles of southern experience. Hoy, in an essay-search for his father and himself, finds in southern autobiographical materials a new myth of community to replace an older myth espoused by the Nashville Agrarians. Howarth begins with personal narrative but moves on to locate in Douglass's *Narrative* and Edgar Allan Poe's *Pym* the roots of a southern autobiographical tradition, which, in an especially wide-ranging essay, Howarth follows down to the present. Reed chronicles, through their autobiographies, the evolution of the racial attitudes of the three most prominent southern journalists of the civil rights era, concluding with a suggestive note on his own experience and outlook. These critic-autobiographers converse with themselves as well as with other writers and invite, on several levels, the readings of us all.

Located Lives confronts writers on the writers' home ground. The contributors see a strong, coherent tradition of autobiography by southern black writers—at least a tradition that began in the South, though it now includes writers not, in any geographical sense, of the South. That tradition predates the American Revolution, alters over time, but remains continuous down to the present. Howarth and Cox explore Douglass's *Narrative*, which, as Cox puts it, provides "the most complete fulfillment of the rigid convention of the slave narrative." The slave narrative is formative for black autobiography. Olney focuses on Richard Wright's *Black Boy*, the "central text" in a line that extends from Douglass's *Narrative* to Ralph Ellison's *Invisible Man* and other, more recent books. These and other writings share a triad of overlapping themes: literacy, identity, and freedom—"lived thematic experiences," in Olney's telling phrase.

There is less agreement concerning a tradition of autobiography by southern whites. However, one recognizes first the contrast (pointed out by Atwan in an astute discussion of Mark Twain) with the pattern set forward by Franklin. Twain's autobiography—drifting, circling, full of a thousand accidents of time and place—denied by its very form Franklin's linear model of the self-made man. Twain looks to the past and sees only a desolate future or worse. He offers, rather than celebration, a scathing critique of the late-nineteenth-century industrial order and its ethos. The self-made man is detached from the circumstances of time and place, which exist mainly to be overcome. He is detached most powerfully from family. Women generally occupy diminished roles. "There were no women in Franklin's world of the self-invented self— only the wife as helpmeet in the most practical sense and as a practical object for excess sexual energy," Cox elsewhere observes. "There were no women at all in Thoreau. Although there was a feminine principle in Whitman he hermaphroditically absorbed it as he absorbed Kanada and Missouri and Montana."[8] Twain, on the other hand, is deeply "circumstanced" (to borrow Howells's word) in time, place, and family. Both his family of origin and his wife and children are refrains of the autobiography. Atwan notes that Twain even allows his daughter at one point to take over the writing of the narrative. Not even the autobiography is fully self-made.

Twain's autobiography is much too idiosyncratic to serve as a prototype of southern narrative. But most southern writers have shared with Twain an ambivalent relation to the first classic of American autobiography. It is an ambivalence based on different understandings. No one more loudly trumpets the success myth and ideal of the self-made man than a Colonel Sanders or a Sam Walton. Yet the ideals resonate a bit oddly through much of southern history. Even Colonel Sanders, titled, white-suited, and goateed, placed himself in an aristocratic tradition that directly contradicted the idea of the self-made man.

This points to the central problem of southern autobiography—a tension between American ideas and an overlapping, sometimes reinforcing, but often conflicting set of southern values and loyalties. "Southern" implies its opposite. "Southern" would be meaningless without the larger, embracing category, "American," upon which "southern" depends. For southern autobiographers, also, "self" has been contingent on the idea of America and the massive, immutable (however fiercely resisted) fact of being an American. Yet it has been equally contingent on being southern. Speaking of southerners generally, Thornton Wilder writes that they were "cut off, or resolutely cut themselves off, from the advancing tide of the country's modes of consciousness. Place, environment, relations, repetitions are the breath of their being."[9] For most southern autobiographers, Wilder's observation holds. Place is fundamental. Identity profoundly implicates, and is implicated by, family, community, and history, as illustrated by representative narratives from William Alexander Percy's *Lanterns on the Levee* to Melton A. McLaurin's *Separate Pasts: Growing Up White in the Segregated South.* The generalization applies to autobiographies by southern women, black and white, as Fox-Genovese argues. The contingency of "self" upon time and place is the very point of Harry Crews's apt title, *A Childhood: The Biography of a Place.* Locating their lives between the poles of southern place and American idea, southern autobiographers have spoken tellingly of each. Place comments upon idea and idea upon place.

In a famous passage, W. E. B. Du Bois describes a state of double consciousness: "An American, a Negro; two souls, two thoughts, two unreconciled strivings; two warring ideals in one dark body."[10] Cox both notes and illustrates a less tortured but corresponding sense of doubleness as southerner and American. The idea of dual identity, more than anything else, constitutes a central theme uniting autobiographies by black and white writers. This "twoness" runs throughout southern autobiographers' treatment of place: a love of the natural environment and a critical distancing from social institutions, an affectionate rendering of individuals, such as that of McLaurin's grandfather, and the stringent rejection of their narrowness and prejudice. It appears most poignantly among autobiographers who leave the South, perhaps bitter but inescapably nostalgic and (Willie Morris's title, *North toward Home*, notwithstanding) disabled from feeling at home wherever they go. "On some cold, lonely Sunday morning on Manhattan Island," Morris tells readers, he hears church bells and feels "guilt and the remorseless pull of my precocious piety."[11] The concluding section of the autobiography demonstrates that Morris feels no less strongly the remorseless pull of the community he had unavoidably, he remains convinced, forever left behind.

Writing of black autobiography, Robert Stepto has identified a "call and response" pattern: one narrative speaks to the next, and both speak to readers who share in a common experience.[12] Southern white autobiographies, as Hoy and Cox clearly exemplify, have a parallel call and response, each work speaking to the next and all speaking to readers who find in the narratives something of themselves and the meaning of their experience. The writers' divided consciousness gives southern autobiography its broadest significance. "We are fortunate as American writers in that with our variety of racial and national traditions, idioms and manners, we are yet one," Ralph Ellison tells readers of *Shadow and Act*. "On its profoundest level American experience is of a whole."[13] The double consciousness of the writers ensures that southern narratives speak to the lives of both northerners and southerners—Americans all, and united in the pleasures they discover in autobiography. Yet there is no easiness for the writers. Southern autobiographers remain inviolable in their isolation within the larger community; divided, pulled between two homes, they continue in tension, speaking of dualities, always at issue with themselves, and in conversation with other southern autobiographers.

Notes

1. Robert F. Sayre, "The Proper Study: Autobiographies in American Studies," in *The American Autobiography: A Collection of Critical Essays*, ed. Albert E. Stone (Englewood Cliffs, N.J.: Prentice-Hall, 1981), 11.
2. James M. Cox, "Autobiography and America," in *Recovering Literature's Lost Ground: Essays in American Autobiography* (Baton Rouge: Louisiana State University Press, 1989), 12.
3. William Dean Howells, "Autobiography, a New Form of Literature," *Harper's Monthly* 107 (October 1909), 798.
4. James Olney, "Autobiography and the Cultural Moment," in *Autobiography: Essays Theoretical and Critical*, ed. Olney (Princeton, N.J.: Princeton University Press, 1980), 14.
5. Robert F. Sayre, "Autobiography and the Making of America," in *Autobiography: Essays Theoretical and Critical*, ed. James Olney (Princeton, N.J.: Princeton University Press, 1980), 157.
6. William L. Andrews, "In Search of a Common Identity: The Self and the South in Four Mississippi Autobiographies," *Southern Review* 24 (Winter 1988): 28–46.
7. Olney, "Autobiography and the Cultural Moment," 26.
8. Cox, "Autobiography and America," 29.
9. Thornton Wilder, quoted in C. Vann Woodward, "The Search for Southern Identity," in *The Burden of Southern History* (New York: Vintage Books, 1960), 23–24.
10. W. E. B. Du Bois, *The Souls of Black Folk* (1953; reprint Millwood, N.Y.: Kraus-Thomson, 1973), 3.
11. Willie Morris, *North toward Home* (Boston: Houghton Mifflin, 1967), 55.
12. Robert B. Stepto, *From behind the Veil: A Study of Afro-American Narrative* (Urbana: University of Illinois Press, 1979).
13. Ralph Ellison, "Brave Words for a Startling Occasion," in *Shadow and Act* (New York: Random House, 1953), 106.

The Interpretation of
Southern Autobiography

Writing Upside Down

Voice and Place
in Southern Autobiography

WILLIAM HOWARTH

I was not leaving the South to forget the South, but so that some day I might understand it, might come to know what its rigors had done to me, to its children. I fled so that the numbness of my defensive living might thaw out and let me feel the pain—years later and far away—of what living in the South had meant.

Richard Wright, *Black Boy*

Whenever I go south, my feet feel welcome but my head keeps looking around for the deportation notice. I am an outsider there, with strong if not defiant Yankee roots. I grew up in Springfield, Illinois, Abraham Lincoln's hometown, and my first trip down south was in 1957 to Washington, D.C., with a high school history class. On the grounds of the Capitol we spied a pair of water fountains marked "White" and "Colored." History came home to us that day, for we had known segregation mainly in its muted, covert forms. Our town lay smack on the Mason-Dixon line, and over the years its population divided about evenly between settlers from the North and South. My grandfather reflected this schism, having passed in one generation from

Mississippi to Illinois. To the end of his days he was a fierce Republican who also loved biscuits and gravy. From him I learned that one need not live in the South to tell its stories, or be there to be from there.

I reinforced these nominal southern ties with four years of graduate study at the University of Virginia in the early 1960s. I went there hoping to have long talks with Mr. Faulkner, but he sensibly deceased just before my arrival. He never saw how drastically the South soon changed, as schools integrated and poll taxes fell after a Texan came to the White House. Living amid magnolias and dogwood, I stubbornly focused on Thoreau's New England, but several fine teachers also opened me to the intricacies of southern life and autobiography. Since then I have always associated the two, as both the genre and the region have struggled to gain broader cultural recognition.

That struggle is ironic, in view of the wealth of distinguished southern poetry, fiction, drama, and essays that have spilled forth since the Civil War and evolved into mainstream American writing. At Princeton I lecture to several hundred freshmen on "Major American Writers," nearly half of whom are southern: Edgar Allan Poe, Mark Twain, Kate Chopin, William Faulkner, Alice Walker—and I could add the marginal associations of Willa Cather, Virginia-born, or Stephen Crane, who set *The Red Badge of Courage* in Virginia. Among American literature surveys, this southern dominance is probably typical. Asked to defend it, I would turn to Walker Percy: "Why has the South produced so many good writers? Because we got beat."

If failure and success are both impostors, failure still tells the better story. One of America's best and most enduring stories is of the beaten South, dragged from a place of high fortune down into ruination and stagnancy. That tale repeats the central legends of Western culture, the expulsion from paradise and the collapse of dynastic families. In that light southern history reads as both allegory and autobiography, for it describes how nations and persons pass through complex cycles of inversion, seeing their lives pitched upside down.

People speak of going *up* north and *down* south, without reflecting much on those locutions. They probably derive from printed maps, with their up, down, and sideways dimensions. Vertical and horizontal lines dominate maps, flattening the spherical earth into a tidy grid of meridians and degrees of latitude. To a geographer, the compass measures motion: east and west lie on the line of axial rotation, while north and south are *left* or *right* of that line. But maps with text assume an up-down orientation, which also fosters a vertical scale of values. Hence ascendancy lies in the North—and the South fell because of its unfortunate geographical inferiority.

The notion seems absurd until we begin to relate southern history to its geography. Not everyone agrees on just what and where "the South" is. In *The Nine Nations of North America* (1981), Joel Garreau writes that the South is more of an emotion than a region. Even the physical area is a matter of dispute, defined by experts as consisting of between nine and seventeen states, not all of which fly the Stars and Bars or whistle "Dixie." The South is and always has been more than a soft, susurrant dialect or a reverence for Jefferson Davis. More Confederate sympathizers lived in Illinois than the Ozarks, but today that part of Missouri-Arkansas calls itself southern.

Emotions about the South seem to focus on a sense of place, one that southerners love and hate with equal fervor. At the end of Faulkner's *Absalom, Absalom!* (1936), a final conversation occurs between two Harvard students, Quentin from Mississippi and Shreve from Alberta, who have reconstructed a large chunk of the southern past, real and imagined. Shreve says: " 'Now I want you to tell me just one thing more. Why do you hate the South?' 'I dont hate it,' Quentin said, quickly, at once, immediately; 'I dont hate it,' he said. *I dont hate it* he thought, panting in the cold air, the iron New England dark; *I dont. I dont! I dont hate it! I dont hate it!* " In that feverish denial we hear exactly how divided Quentin is, and the heat of his passion, rising in cold northern air, suggests how much a southerner must identify his home through separation, disavowal, and contradiction.

The land itself never welcomed settlers, for the South consists of a low sandy coast, rising to piedmont uplands and then to the Appalachian Mountains. With few deep harbors or navigable rivers, the region was difficult to penetrate or explore. Settlement came slowly, and farming was hard: the coast was swampy, the uplands densely forested, the mountains rough and thinly soiled. Appalachia is the South's stony heart, a maze of hogback ridges and smoky hollows where few roads have ever entered.

The three regions grew up as worlds apart, not strongly tied by routes of commerce—unlike the North, where population spread rapidly across the flat, fertile prairies or gathered around rapidly expanding cities. The South's only major asset was its warm, moist climate, which supported a growing season of more than two hundred frost-free days. Thus wherever families could drain swamps or clear forest, they plowed fields and planted rice, tobacco, or cotton. Cotton was the big cash crop but required intensive labor, since the plants ripen over long intervals. To make profits, farmers had to establish huge plantations and work them with a cheap labor source, imported African slaves.

Nothing in the land itself dictated these events; it just responded to human pressures—and the rest of the story followed. Around the plantations developed a strong vertical class system, a few white rulers dominating a vast black peasantry. The South grew rich but also stagnant, for its culture was stable and traditional, slow to accept innovation and generally hostile to ethnic or religious diversity. Fewer newspapers, theaters, and schools developed in the South, in sharp contrast to the lively variety of northern states.

That was the antebellum South; it lost billions in capital after emancipation and military occupation, then steadily declined in wealth and power for the next seventy years. The image of a stagnant, depressed South in the 1920s and 1930s is familiar to readers of Faulkner or Erskine Caldwell, and that image of weathered shacks and red dirt roads has dominated many later writers. Today new voices such as Bobbie Ann Mason and Bruce Hornsby are depicting a New South, which began to rebound after World War II and accelerated in the 1960s following the much-dreaded federal mandates that gave education, public access, and voting rights to black citizens. Some historians have compared this recovery to the postwar transformation of Germany and Japan, which leads us to imagine how South Africa might prosper by rejecting its racist past.

Today the southern economy has evolved from agriculture into a booming, diverse mix of industry and services. Cotton has gone west, migrating from Texas to California; for every one dollar of southern income now generated by farms, eight dollars come from factories. And this manufacturing does not concentrate in large cities, as it does in the North, but spreads among many towns of fewer than ten thousand people. In the last decade ten million new jobs have been created, producing large population increases, especially among blacks who are returning from the northern cities of New York, Chicago, and Detroit, where they fled in the 1940s.

The New South is no longer news, yet most southern writers are still not telling its story. Usually, success has many authors and failure none; but the South has inverted that wisdom. Little in its history has prepared the region to enjoy success; its collective memory seems to fear prosperity as the portent of yet another fall. A conservative heritage also prefers to repeat old stories and deny change, even after it has undeniably come. Never mind our boomtowns of Atlanta and Charlotte, the voices intone, let us regard the slump in offshore oil, the shuttered banks in Texas, the public disgrace of our television evangelists.

This tendency to invert fortunes, to cast them upside down and deny improvement, is especially characteristic of southern intellectuals. That spirit led John Crowe Ransom in the 1930s to deny that "material production" was important for his region, despite a century of desperate poverty and illiteracy in the Tennessee Valley. A more recent version of that argument was offered by John Egerton in *The Americanization of Dixie* (1974), an eloquent attack on the spread of Yankee culture in the form of McDonald's golden arches rising along southern highways. But Egerton's subtitle, *The Southernization of America*, reminds us that plenty of Colonel Sanderses, Holiday Inns, and 7-11 stores, all southern franchises, now line northern roads. The real issue is whether or not the South, now grown more urban and affluent, less overtly racist, will accept that new identity without seeing it as "Yankee." Northern states, after all, have never been immune to poverty and racism. Times may have changed, but southerners are still living in the same country.

This history may explain why southern writers have so often turned to autobiography, a genre in which personal and regional fortunes persistently intertwine. Writing a life story, whether it be fictional or factual, delivers to the writer a particularly sharp sense of place and of the voice needed to love/hate it. At the head of this tradition stand two pre–Civil War works that reflect the social, cultural, and racial dichotomies of early southern life: Edgar Allan Poe, *Narrative of A. Gordon Pym* (1838), and Frederick Douglass, *Narrative of the Life of Frederick Douglass* (1845).

As opposite as Poe and Douglass may seem, in many ways they mirrored each other. Both were orphans, raised by adoptive parents and masters; both were largely self-educated; both went north as adults to find freedom; both became strong critics of the societies they found there. Poe especially disliked the transcendentalist idealism of Boston, which he mocked in an early satirical sketch, "How to Write a Black-woods Article." In it an editor tells a writer how to imitate "the tone transcendental. . . . Eschew, in this case, big words; get them as small as possible, and write them upside down."

Writing upside down describes the situations of both Poe and Doug-lass, two southern writers far from home, out of place like Faulkner's Quentin. In that distance they learn to explore alienation and find a voice in ironic deception, which they mainly direct toward complacent readers. Their narratives are subversive, seeking to contradict and in-vert prevailing norms, including the very conventions of writing itself— which cannot be inverted if readers are to understand it. Printers may learn to read transposed type, but for most of us texts are like maps, fixed in the vertical and horizontal planes of up-down, left-right, the lines marching along with a brisk authority.

The simple, linear form of text often masks its complex sense, which spawns divergent readings. In the North, Douglass writes, white people often believe that slave songs are happy: "It is impossible to conceive of a greater mistake. Slaves sing most when they are most unhappy. The songs of the slave represent the sorrows of his heart; and he is relieved by them, only as an aching heart is relieved by tears. At least, such is my experience. I have often sung to drown my sorrow, but seldom to express my happiness." If northerners mishear those songs, they are just as likely to misread a black writer. Although Douglass surely wants to be understood, he does not have a simple message to convey. His writing rises from several conflicts, for he is a man of mixed blood, black and white, a southerner gone north, a freeman still identified on his title page as "An American Slave."

Poe shares this vision of the divided psyche, which his fiction projects through repeated images of twins and doubles, as in the fraternal twins Roderick and Madeline Usher or the identical twin that haunts William Wilson. For Douglass the double is himself, once a slave and now an author of a book, as the title page states, "Written by Himself." Every scene he remembers forces him to play both witness and participant, as when he recounts and suffers over the brutal whipping of his aunt. Thus he remains bonded to his former bondage, shaken by anger and guilt, and—like Faulkner's Quentin—unable to escape the past by writing a definite closure to his story.

In both narratives the autobiographers struggle with problems of form, trying to make their books seem less planned than they actually are. For his nineteenth-century readers, Douglass needed to tell a "true" story about slavery. Yet truth is problematic in many slave narratives, since the authors often were illiterate and had to dictate to scribes who wrote in standard English. Accuracy and veracity were of little value to slaves, who frequently lied to protect themselves, "puttin on" their masters to win favors or avoid punishment. As Harriet Jacobs notes in her *Incidents in the Life of a Slave Girl* (1861), "Slaves, being surrounded by mysteries, deceptions, and dangers, early learn to be suspicious and watchful, and prematurely cautious and cunning." Most cunning of all was their appropriation of the Bible, their gaining literacy and spirituality from the very text used by masters to justify slavery.

For Douglass, the problem of truth requires him to honor but also invert such conventions. We can glimpse his difficulties in the preface contributed by William Lloyd Garrison, a prominent abolitionist who insists that the *Narrative* is essentially true and factual, with nothing overstated, "nothing drawn from the imagination." Garrison apparently hears no condescension in that phrase, no hyperbole in his claims for truth. He wants only to justify the book to its white readers, many of them already strong for antislavery. Of course, the *Narrative* is imaginative, for it does not simply report events but reshapes them into stirring memories, at times narrated in a trancelike present tense. Throughout, Douglass controls his story, imagining his grandmother (who may be dead) living out her last days in a woodland hut, locating the turning point of his life in defiance of a white master, protecting his fellow slaves by suppressing the exact route of his escape.

Whether free or enslaved, autobiographers give but partial accounts of their lives. Douglass could never speak in his natural voice, for it would have revealed his bitter racial anger. Any unbridled diatribes against whites would have alienated his readers, those well-meaning Christians who opposed slavery but shared the faith of many plantation masters: "For of all slaveholders I have ever met," Douglass writes, "religious slaveholders are the worst." Concern about a backlash among the faithful prompted him to add an appendix that avows, "I love a pure, peaceable, and impartial Christianity of Christ," and the preface by Garrison, which trumpets that slavery is "the foe of God and man."

Poe's *Narrative of A. Gordon Pym* echoes this twining of truth and artifice, with a similar hostility directed at complacent readers. He also mocks the illusory nature of text by mixing fiction and fact as the *Narrative* alternates between scenes of original fantasy and dry, informative passages copied from encyclopedias. This method has a purpose, as the narrator notes while explaining how to store grain in a ship's hold: "Great attention must be paid, not only to the bulk taken in, but to the nature of the bulk, and whether there be a full or only a partial cargo." A similar distribution of narrative goods serves to balance Poe's story, which operates through a nearly binary code of opposing images: land/ sea, dark/light, black/white. He also toys with the first-person conventions of autobiography, dividing his tale between an author named Pym and an editor named Poe, who in 1838 are referring to events that occurred in 1828.

Together they construct a plot that deconstructs autobiography, employing logical paradoxes to drive a cliff-hanger serial. The book consists of eight episodes of terror, each centering on a perilous disaster from which Pym is rescued in order to survive and face his next trial. This recursive sequence mocks the progress of a journey, reducing it to repetitive cycles of alternation, even as Pym passes southward from Nantucket toward the unknown waters of Antarctica. Pym's trip magnifies and reverses Poe's move in 1838 from Richmond to New York, for Pym advances into an upside-down world, where fantastic creatures dwell and the seasons are inverted: "*March 5. . . .* The Polar winter appeared to be coming on—but coming without its terrors."

At the end Pym encounters a final paradox, a giant cataract that threatens to destroy his boat: "But there arose in our pathway a shrouded human figure, very far larger in its proportions than any dweller among men. And the hue of the skin of the figure was of the perfect whiteness of snow." Pym's text suddenly ends there, followed by a note from Poe saying the story is unfinished because its last chapters were "irrecoverably lost through the accident by which [Pym] perished himself." What happened, and when, are left to our speculation.

The story's narrative premise holds that Pym did not die in 1828, since he has lived to tell this tale in 1838. Perhaps the white figure saved him, thus fulfilling the plot pattern of rescue and survival. If so, then Pym's accidental death must have interrupted his later act of *telling* the story, just as the white figure once more loomed up from the sea. That was a moment of salvation in 1828, allowing Pym to begin his tale, but in 1838 it becomes a portent of the ending, to life and story, that is about to transpire. For this autobiographer, white—Melville's "colorless, all-color" of hope and despair—comes to signify both what writing is and will never be. White is the unwritten and unprinted, the blank page standing before and after all composition, the empty space reminding us that every page has its inverse side.

Permutations of this sort have inspired John Irwin, in *Doubling and Incest/Repetition and Revenge* (1977) and *American Hieroglyphics* (1980), to develop a theory, largely built around Poe and Faulkner, that the writer's corpus is "an inscribed shadow self, a hieroglyphic double." Throughout Pym's story the narrative calls attention to its shadowy nature by reminding us of written texts and the difficulties of reading them. The plot hinges on acts of interpretation, of breaking down code and learning to decipher the world's mysterious signs. This idea, often traced to its roots in Puritan typology, has also appealed to southern writers, who lived in a world full of divisive contradiction. When Frederick Douglass learned to read, he found that this power split him into a body and a mind, half-slave and half-free.

For text liberates but also captures, binding lives to the narrow dimensions of print—up, down, sideways. Poe mocks these linear properties by building an arbitrary plot, making up events on a trial-and-error basis. Yet the random adventures of his hero make suggestive repetitions. Often Pym is lost and wandering through dark, cavernous mazes, where words elude him. In the hold of a ship he cannot read a written message; beneath a tropical island the caves seem to take on alphabetic shapes—and all that language is buried, lost in an underground tangle of conflicting sense. Such a tale must end abruptly, as though unfinished. Douglass had the same problem, writing two supplements to his life story, augmenting but never ending its text —or crossing the barrier between what black folks sang and white folks heard.

Poe and Douglass stand at the headwaters of southern autobiography, and beyond them writers seem to divide upon the emphasis of voice or place. Until recent years the division was mainly racial, since blacks held a lowly social "place" and rarely possessed their own land. Lacking material goods, they created a richly oral culture, searching through song, slang, and speech to find an empowering voice, what Zora Neale Hurston calls "a Negro way of saying" in her autobiography, *Dust Tracks on a Road* (1942). This emphasis tended to influence black autobiographers to favor ideology over art but also, in a classic instance of southern inversion, to prefer story to sermon even while disputing that natural inclination.

Political issues often forced these writers into awkward self-denials of artifice. Harriet Jacobs insists that her *Incidents in the Life of a Slave Girl* is no fiction, yet the story unfolds with novelistic suspense and addresses female readers by focusing on scenes of sexual harassment, most of it verbal. She escapes this captivity for another, hiding from her white master for seven years in the windowless attic of a shed, living day and night in silent darkness: "But I was not comfortless. I heard the voices of my children. There was joy and there was sadness in the sound. It made my tears flow. How I longed to speak to them!" The attic is not a place but a nowhere, the negative space of captivity, and only voices will one day end its suffocating oppression.

A parallel case is Booker T. Washington, whose *Up from Slavery* (1901) is less a life story than a collection of speeches threaded together with personal narrative. Washington wrote his book in the spare moments of a busy career, catching them in hotels or railway stations. His memories are verbal rather than visual, with many good moments of dialogue but only perfunctory descriptions of faces or scenes. Even Tuskegee Institute remains a vague, shadowy location, less realized than that moment in Atlanta when he declares to a cheering convention his policy of racial coexistence: "In all things that are purely social we can be as separate as the fingers, yet one as the hand in all things essential to mutual progress." While that idea later discredited Washington to many blacks, it summarizes accurately the life of a powerful, expedient orator who would go, as one of his chapter titles declares, "Two Thousand Miles for a Five-Minute Speech."

For later black autobiographers, many of them novelists, the challenge was to balance political statement against the subtle requirements of narrative craft. In *Black Boy* (1937), Richard Wright summons up scenes that create a powerful illusion of verity, polished by his years of writing strong plot and vivid talk. Biographers have confirmed that many of the book's details are imaginary, yet its thematic claims endure. At the end of his life Wright admits that he is a self-deceiver, caught in the surrounding lie of racism: "The pressure of southern living kept me from being the kind of person that I might have been. I had been what my family—conforming to the dictates of the whites above them

—had exacted of me, and what the whites had said that I must be." Like Huck Finn, Richard faces the challenge of finding truth in a world that demands lies of its survivors.

This conflicted response, part confessional and part jeremiad, dominates Ralph Ellison's *Invisible Man* (1952), a novel that casts in autobiographical form the history of black Americans between 1920 and 1950, and such works of the civil rights era as James Baldwin, *The Fire Next Time* (1963), and *The Autobiography of Malcolm X* (1964). Songs, sermons, and speeches chorus throughout these texts, and Malcolm X's book is entirely oral, consisting of dictation edited by Alex Haley. A reporter and novelist, Haley preserved Malcolm's jazzy idiom and shaped two years of rambling interviews into a coherent monologue with strong, well-knit chapters. Black critics praised Haley's effort but soon thereafter condemned William Styron's *Confessions of Nat Turner* (1967) for its blackface impersonation of a rebellious slave's thoughts and voice.

Two more recent works suggest that the traditional orality in black narrative may be expanding its racial horizons. Both Ernest J. Gaines, *The Autobiography of Miss Jane Pittman* (1971), and Theodore Rosengarten, *All God's Dangers: The Life of Nate Shaw* (1974), use the conventions of oral history to tell life stories. As her ostensible "editor," Gaines does not transcribe the fictional Miss Jane verbatim: "What I have tried to do here was not to write everything, but in essence everything that was said. I have tried my best to retain Miss Jane's language. Her selection of words; the rhythm of her speech." Rosengarten wrote the history of an acutal man, an illiterate but gifted narrator: "I learned how to listen and not to resist his method of withholding facts for the sake of suspense. Everything came out in time, everything." But not everything saw print. Rosengarten selected, combined, omitted, and arranged stories, changed names to protect privacy, and in the end half regretted his work: "There is something lost and something gained in the transformation of these oral stories to written literature. Their publication marks the end of a long process of creation and re-creation and removes them from the orbit of the storyteller."

In autobiographies written by southern whites after the Civil War, the emphasis is less on language and more on recording physical space, the scenic dimensions of a changed regional world. A prime example is Mark Twain, whose books ascribe the formative influences in his life to places: Hannibal, Virginia City, San Francisco, but most of all the Mississippi, where he came of age by learning to read a river. *Life on the Mississippi* (1896) recounts this education through his friendship with river pilots, those shadow selves of the writer he became. Twain remembers the pilots as men with an exquisite sense of place, meaning both social rank and working environment. Their journeys on the broad, ever-flowing river inspired them to tell long and sinuous narratives laced with glorious profanity. These unfettered masters of the vernacular became his heroes; unlike most genteel writers of the period, who were "manacled servants of the public."

In writing about the pilots, Twain discovers that they were his literary mentors. He recalls that a pilot first advised him to buy a notebook and write down everything he learned, memorizing the river: "You have to know it just like A B C." This language was not oral but spatial, requiring him to read the river upside down—watching its surface current to envision the invisible bars, snags, and channels that lay below. Through careful study he made this fluid, changing place take shape in his head and notebook. Recalling that process later gives Twain a natural analogy for writing: "The face of the water, in time, became a wonderful book—a book that was a dead language to the uneducated passenger, but which told its mind to me without reserve, delivering its most cherished secrets as if it uttered them with a voice. And it was not a book to be read once and thrown aside, for it had a new story to tell every day." For Twain the river had no dull pages, only italics and exclamations of its own; and his metaphor insists on linking the physical, scenic dimensions of both river and printed text. Like Rosengarten many years later, Twain realized that in recording this experience he stole something vital from it: "All the grace, the beauty, the poetry, had gone out of the majestic river!"

Twain's autobiography explains why *Adventures of Huckleberry Finn* (1885) flows smoothly with the river but stumbles when Huck leaves that place of natural progress. The same fault affects his later *Autobiography* (1907), a miscellany of narrative, clippings, and conversation that lacks any unifying form. From the river Twain derived his principles of motion, tempo, surface, and depth; it moved ceaselessly toward fresh places that he had never to invent, only to view as scenes. His happiest moments in *Life on the Mississippi* are being alone with the river and

describing its face, as a mirror of his own mind: "First, there is the eloquence of silence; for a deep hush broods everywhere. Next, there is
the haunting sense of loneliness, isolation, remoteness from the worry
and bustle of the world."

These river reveries stand in sharp contrast to other passages that
describe the difficulties of writing: correcting errors and modifying
claims, enduring the drudgery of scribbling for an income. Indolence
or fraud always beckon, as in the case of Sir Walter Scott, whom Twain
holds "in a great measure responsible" for the Civil War. Twain attacks
Scott largely for the sins of his language, that flowery eloquence that so
infected southern writing. In contrast, Twain celebrates the southern
vernacular as talk connected to a place, flowing like the smooth current
of a river: "I was a-askin Tom whah you was a-settin at." When southern
writers throw off the moldy standard of Scott and embrace their own
speech, Twain predicts, they will produce a great literature.

That prophecy would seem to anticipate the career of William Faulkner, whose fourteen Yoknapatawpha novels form a saga that imag-
ines southern history as unfolding in one place, a northern Mississippi
county that he mapped and inscribed "William Faulkner, Sole Owner
& Proprietor." This vast domain is autobiographical, since much of
it either arises from Faulkner's home in Oxford or projects the first-
person stories of his narrators, as with the three Compson brothers in
The Sound and the Fury (1929), all of them scarred by their family's
loss of place, both estate and social status. Later southern novels such
as Robert Penn Warren's *All the King's Men* (1946) and James Agee's
A Death in the Family (1967), entwine their characters' lives with similarly intense memories of place, from the heat and light of Baton Rouge
to the luminous memories of Knoxville on summer evenings.

So the stream of southern autobiography has flowed, divided between the bitter, denunciatory tradition of voice and the affectionate,
nostalgic tradition of place. Will it remain so as stories begin to rise
from the New South? Perhaps the most hopeful title in modern southern writing is that of Flannery O'Connors's story, "Everything That
Rises Must Converge." Until recently, few southern women writers—
O'Connor, Carson McCullers, Katherine Anne Porter—turned to autobiography, perhaps in deference to the southern tradition that privi-
leges women only through fictive masks, the flirting coquetry of a

Scarlett O'Hara. Asked why southerners write so often about freaks, Flannery O'Connor responded, "Maybe because we can still recognize them."

Yet changes have clearly emerged in recent years: Lillian Hellman's *Scoundrel Time* (1976), though challenged as a vindictive, inaccurate book about the House Un-American Activities Committee's inquiries, does come to acknowledge her own political naïveté and paranoia. By the end she has turned redemptive—if not to her enemies, then at least to her southern past. Forced to sell her New York farm, she replies with rebel defiance: "I am angry that corrupt and unjust men made me sell the only place that was ever right for me, but that doesn't have much to do with anything anymore, because there have been other places and they do fine."

Another powerful rising force lies with southern black women writers, who have chronicled a history of doubled oppression, racial and sexual. The work of Maya Angelou and Alice Walker allows those caged birds to sing, and not just songs of sorrow. Through narration, Walker becomes the admitted medium for her characters, those once-mute ghosts from the past. The people of *The Color Purple* (1981) told her to leave New York, then San Francisco, and settle in the country of northern California, a place that resembled both Georgia and Africa: "Seeing the sheep, the cattle, and the goats, smelling the apples and the hay, one of my characters, Celie, began, haltingly, to speak." Such narratives are beginning once more to link voice and place, the elements that make Walker's essay collection, *In Search of Our Mothers' Gardens* (1983), function as the autobiography of one artist who went looking for herself —and found a good deal in Georgia.

The South, we can now say, is no longer "down" there, but everywhere. The night in 1910 when Quentin Compson tried so hard not to hate the South, Eudora Welty was but one year old in Jackson, Mississippi. Seventy-three years later she came to Quentin's university to deliver a series of autobiographical lectures, later published as *One Writer's Beginnings* (1983). At the end she quotes from her novel, *The Optimist's Daughter*, a passage that offers a triumphant hymn to convergence. A young couple take the train from Chicago, heading south to get married. At sunrise they pass the confluence of the Ohio and Mississippi rivers:

They were looking down from a great elevation and all they saw was
at the point of coming together, the bare trees marching in from the
horizon, the rivers moving into one, and as he touched her arm she
looked up with him and saw the long, ragged, pencil-faint line of birds
within the crystal of the zenith, flying in a V of their own, following the
same course down. All they could see was sky, water, birds, light, and
confluence. It was the whole morning world.

And they themselves were a part of the confluence. Their own joint
act of faith had brought them here at the very moment and matched its
concurrence, and proceeded as it proceeded. Direction itself was made
beautiful, momentous. They were riding as one with it, right up front.
It's our turn! she'd thought exultantly. And we're going to live forever.

Of course they will die, but this buoyant idealism that speaks through
the earth cannot itself die. The confluence of waters marries North
and South for a moment as well, caught up in the couple's journey
that carries them out of past memories and toward their future desires.
Closing her own life story with this passage, Eudora Welty bids to make
the stream of voice and place converge once more, telling not the story
of a South that fell and hopes to rise again, but of a South that will
endure forever.

Works Consulted

Southern Geography, History, and Literature

Birdsall, Stephen S., and John W. Florin. *Regional Landscapes of the United
    States and Canada.* New York: John Wiley and Sons, 1978.
Chapman, Abraham, ed. *Black Voices: An Anthology of Afro-American Litera-
    ture.* New York: New American Library, 1968.
Egerton, John. *The Americanization of Dixie: The Southernization of America.*
    New York: Harper's Magazine Press, 1974.
Freehling, William W. *Prelude to Civil War.* New York: Harper and Row,
    1968.
Garreau, Joel. *The Nine Nations of North America.* Boston: Houghton Mifflin,
    1981.
Irwin, John. *American Hieroglyphics: The Symbol of the Egyptian Hiero-
    glyphics in the American Renaissance.* New Haven: Yale University Press,
    1980.

————. *Doubling and Incest/Repetition and Revenge*. Baltimore: Johns Hopkins University Press, 1975.

Osofsky, Gilbert, ed. *Puttin' On Ole Massa: The Slave Narratives of Henry Bibb, William Wells Brown, and Solomon Northup*. New York: Harper Torchbooks, 1969.

Winokur, Jon. *Writers on Writing*. Philadelphia: Running Press, 1986.

Young, Thomas Daniel, Floyd C. Watkins, and Richmond Croom Beatty. *The Literature of the South*. Glenview, Ill.: Scott, Foresman, and Company, 1968.

Southern Writers

Agee, James. *A Death in the Family*. New York: Grosset and Dunlap, 1967.

Angelou, Maya. *I Know Why the Caged Bird Sings*. New York: Random House, 1969.

Baldwin, James. *The Fire Next Time*. New York: Dial Press, 1963.

Douglass, Frederick. *Narrative of the Life of Frederick Douglass, an American Slave: Written by Himself*. New York: New American Library, 1968.

Ellison, Ralph. *Invisible Man*. New York: Random House, 1952.

Faulkner, William. *Absalom, Absalom!* New York: Random House, 1936.

————. *The Sound and the Fury*. New York: Random House, 1929.

Gaines, Ernest J. *The Autobiography of Miss Jane Pittman*. New York: Dial Press, 1971.

Hellman, Lillian. *Scoundrel Time*. New York: Little, Brown, 1976.

Hornsby, Bruce. *Scenes from the Southside*. New York: RCA Records, 1988.

Hurston, Zora Neale. *Dust Tracks on a Road: An Autobiography* ed. Robert E. Hemenway, 2d ed. Urbana: University of Illinois Press, 1984.

Jacobs, Harriet. *Incidents in the Life of a Slave Girl*. Ed. L. Maria Child (Boston, 1861).

Malcolm X. *The Autobiography of Malcolm X*. With the assistance of Alex Haley. New York: Grove Press, 1965.

Mason, Bobbie Ann. *In Country*. New York: Harper and Row, 1985.

O'Connor, Flannery. *Everything That Rises Must Converge*. New York: Farrar, Straus, and Giroux, 1965.

Poe, Edgar Allan. *Selected Prose, Poetry, and "Eureka."* New York: Holt, Rinehart, and Winston, 1950.

Rosengarten, Theodore. *All God's Dangers: The Life of Nate Shaw*. New York: Knopf, 1974.

Styron, William. *The Confessions of Nat Turner*. New York: Random House, 1967.

Twain, Mark. *The Autobiography of Mark Twain.* Edited by Charles Neider. New York: Washington Square Press, 1961.

————. *Life on the Mississippi.* New York: Harper, 1896.

Walker, Alice. *In Search of Our Mother's Gardens.* New York: Harcourt Brace Jovanovich, 1983.

Warren, Robert Penn. *All the King's Men.* New York: Harcourt, Brace, and World, 1946.

Washington, Booker T. *Up From Slavery.* New York: Dell, 1965.

Welty, Eudora. *One Writer's Beginnings.* Cambridge: Harvard University Press, 1984.

Wright, Richard. *Black Boy.* New York: Harper and Brothers, 1945.

Between Individualism and Community

Autobiographies of Southern Women

ELIZABETH FOX-GENOVESE

I ndividualism figures as the very stuff of autobiography, at least
in its most characteristic modern guise, for autobiography takes
as its subject the chronicle of the self understood as essentially different from all other selves. I am not claiming that I am better or worse
than any other man, only that I am different from all others, insisted
Jean-Jacques Rousseau, arguably the first modern autobiographer, in
his powerfully influential *Confessions*. The modern bourgeois culture
that spawned autobiography as an endlessly fascinating genre took individualism as given. Contrarily, community figured preeminently as a
form of nostalgia. As Raymond Williams has argued, bourgeois culture, beginning with romanticism, has regularly juxtaposed notions of
community, especially pastoral harmony, to the capitalist market that
constituted its mainspring. In Williams's view, the vision of the country
as a retreat from the competition and strife of the city amounted to a
myth that was engendered by and depended upon the dynamism of the
city, which it only superficially opposed. Community and individualism could, in most instances, be substituted for Williams's country and

city, with community's being understood as the nostalgia that trailed the central commitment to individualism.[1]

Conservatives have attempted to endow the myth of community with some semblance of reality, although frequently with chilling political implications. The conservative sociologist Ferdinand Tönnies drew the line sharply when he explicitly juxtaposed *Gemeinschaft* to *Gesellschaft*, arguing that the former embodied all the affective principles that the latter, instrumental modern society, denied.[2] The southern conservative tradition, notably represented by Allen Tate and the Agrarians, followed a similar spirit in arguing that the South embodied the last true community in the Western world precisely because it continued to combat the corrosive tendencies of individualism.[3] For these and other conservatives, the individual should, ideally, be understood as subordinate to and even constituted by the community to which he or she belonged. But they, like the bourgeois and radical thinkers they opposed, failed to provide a clear guide to the actual relations between individual and community in modern culture.

Contemporary studies of autobiography remain by and large silent on this problem. Modern autobiographies have so successfully privileged the self as the subject of its own history that its indebtedness to community remains largely unexamined. To be sure, autobiographers may nostalgically evoke the community—frequently rural or ethnic—of their youths, but rarely do they credit those communities with decisive roles in their adult identities. Almost invariably, autobiographers write as exiles from the worlds of their childhood. The language and experience that prompt them to write of that world derive from what they have done since they left it. Not infrequently, and very understandably, they emphasize what they believe made them unique, what permitted them to leave the world of their childhood behind. As a result, the self that figures in their pages emphasizes the unique qualities that endow it with interest for their potential readers.

Today, the most heated theoretical debates in the study of autobiography concern the status of the self that is the subject of autobiography —notably, whether it should be viewed as in some way absolute, or pretextual, or as essentially textual, a product of the act of writing. In principle, these debates could apply as well to female autobiographers as to male, unless one chooses to argue that the male self exists through writing whereas the female self is in some way essential, or pretextual—

or the reverse. Thus, short of accepting an essential difference between male and female autobiographers, it would seem that feminist criticism is condemned to address the nature of the (gendered) autobiographical self. Yet recent debates in feminist theory, which have underscored the problematic status of women's autobiography in general, have especially focused on the anxiety of women's self-representation within the confines of an androcentric culture. For women, it is generally agreed, the very autobiographical act remains inherently conflicted, for in writing autobiographies, women are, as Sidonie Smith has reminded us, caught in a "doubled subjectivity" as at once protagonists and narrators of their own stories.[4]

Nancy Miller has made the case with special force. Since, she argues, the dominant discourse has been resolutely male, women who attempt to represent themselves within that discourse confront the almost insurmountable difficulty of writing authoritatively within a discourse that casts them as object. To be sure, the condition obtains for all women's writing, but it becomes especially constraining in the case of autobiography—the case in which women attempt an unmediated representation of self. Susan Friedman, in contrast, argues that women autobiographers write differently, experience their selves differently, than men. For women, the self exists through merging with others rather than through differentiating itself from them, exists in relation to community rather than separate from it. But no more than others is Friedman referring to specific communities. She is referring to a psychological propensity presumably common to all women in all times and places. In this respect, feminist theory has remained closely tied to the assumptions and debates of male autobiographical theory by implicitly considering women primarily as individuals, albeit possibly different kinds of individuals.[5]

The problems of the female autobiographical self have been complicated by the intrusion of psychoanalytic, notably Lacanian, theory into poststructuralist theory, for psychoanalytic theory, in spite of or perhaps because of its unyielding androcentrism, has at least offered feminist critics a position from which to defend the essential difference between men and women as writing subjects. Lacanian theory has led Jane Gallop, among others, to argue that women who seek to represent their selves in writing confront a "patriarchal" language. Susan Friedman, following Nancy Chodorow, has attempted to turn the disadvantages of androcentric psychoanalytic theory to the advantage of female autobiographers. Both positions share the same weakness, namely, that women's writing in some way results directly from their biological condition as women. From this theoretical perspective, it makes little difference whether a woman is French or American, rich or poor, white or black: she writes out of her inescapable femaleness.[6]

The concern with fundamental difference grounded in biology has led very different kinds of feminist critics to treat women's biology as the material basis of female experience. This tactic has reinforced the tendency to focus either on women's autobiographical writing in general or on the writings of specific women autobiographers. Yet women, like men, belong to specific communities—nations, classes, races—that shape their relations as women to the dominant male culture. Women's autobiography, even more than women's writing in general, challenges us to understand the complexity of women's writing as simultaneously shaped by their specific experience as women among their people and by their specific access to dominant cultural discourses, which may or may not be those of their own people.

In practice, feminist critics have normally moved from considerations of the general category of female autobiography directly to the texts of specific women autobiographers without paying particular attention to identifiable groups of women autobiographers, although that pattern is beginning to shift. Essays have recently appeared on the autobiographies of Afro-American women, French women, Native American women, Quebecois women, lesbian women, and "privileged" British and American women. But even these essays have not especially attended to the specific communities to which these women belonged.[7] In other words, the discussions of individualism and community in women's autobiographies remain strangely abstracted from women's historical and social condition. The most sophisticated arguments address the women autobiographers' relations to the dominant male discourse of their culture but take little account of the historical and social dimensions of the women's experiences. Yet without explicit attention to women's social and historical locations within specific communities, we are in danger of claiming that the only significant aspect of women's autobiographies derives from their biology. As Nancy Miller has written, arguing that autobiography is as much a mode of reading as a mode of writing, "The historical truth of a woman writer's life lies in the reader's grasp of her intratext: the body of her writing and not the writing of her body."[8]

One of the most fruitful results of the debates about the nature of autobiography as a genre (if it can be at least provisionally accepted as one) has been the attempt to link the emergence of modern autobiography to the emergence of bourgeois individualism. This position, as developed, for example, by Philippe LeJeune and Georges Gusdorf, seeks to distinguish between self-representation in its various forms and autobiography in particular, holding that autobiography embodies a characteristic attitude toward the self that can be differentiated from previous attitudes toward it.[9] The position rests on the assumption that modern autobiography depends upon the emergence of a view of the self as an end in itself—a view of the self as the internal consciousness of that objective entity, the individual. Since the bourgeois individualism that promoted the emergence of autobiography continues to dominate theoretical discussions of autobiography, it is perhaps less clear than it should be that even the apparently ahistorical individual is also the product of a specific community or communities. In other words, all autobiographies result from the efforts of an individual to interpret his or her self in relation to community. Both the myth of the essential self and the myth of the textual self obscure the historical dimension of any self.

To argue for the historical contingency of both the male and the female self does not imply that men and women experienced historical conditions in the same way. Modern individualism did not open the same possibilities for women as it did for men. Indeed, it could reasonably be argued that modern male individualism relegated women to the supporting roles of mother, wife, and daughter. Yet because modern individualism claimed the status of a comprehensive ideology, it, however unintentionally, offered women a discourse through which they might also view themselves as individuals. The difficulty for women, upon which so many feminist critics have commented, has lain in writing of themselves as individuals under cultural or discursive conditions in which the models of individual excellence have been male and the models of female excellence have been circumscribed by specific gender roles. These conditions have strengthened the feminist temptation to consider all women, independent of nation, race, and class, through the prism of those roles, as if the roles were indeed as invariable as the universalist ideology of individualism sought to present them. Yet close attention to women autobiographers' self-representations does reveal differences.

The autobiographical writings of southern women, black as well as white, dramatically illustrate the advantages of considering women's autobiography in historical perspective, although I readily admit that in choosing southern women I am stacking the deck. Early-nineteenth-century southern women, black and white, differed from their bourgeois counterparts in the North and in western Europe in belonging to a modern slave society. That membership decisively marked their perceptions of themselves and, despite radical differences in their experiences, bound them to a common history. Even after the abolition of slavery and the defeat of the South, southern women remained uncommonly concerned with the history of their region as an aspect of their own identities. For many generations, no southern woman autobiographer wrote of her self without explicit reference to social and historical conditions. And even a woman as engaged with modernism and committed to the idea of the self as Ellen Glasgow allowed in her autobiography that, although she had resolved "to write of the universal, not of the provincial in human nature," she "knew my part of the South, and I had looked deep enough within and far enough without to learn something of human beings and their substance." She believed that she and other writers wrote better "when we write of places we know, and of a background with which we are familiar."[10]

Both black and white southern women autobiographers have struggled with the same problems of female self-representation through dominant male discourses. But they have done so under conditions in which race, class, and regional identification have played as important a role as gender in their self-representations. In the Old South, slavery effectively discouraged both white and black southern women from any form of public self-representation—white women because of the constraints of respectability, black women because of the constraints of being unlettered. White women, especially slaveholding women, did in fact write personal narratives; they simply did not publish them and normally did not even write them as autobiographies. Characteristically, white slaveholding women kept journals or diaries, which they wrote for the benefit of their children, especially their daughters, and in which they primarily attempted to take stock of their selves and their

souls. Occasionally, a slaveholding woman (for example, Eliza Clither-
all) would write an autobiography to summarize the events of her life
up to the moment of starting to keep a diary. Occasionally, a slaveholding woman (for example, Sarah Gayle) would include in her journal a
representation of herself as she envisioned herself as having been. Most
slaveholding women came closest to self-conscious self-representation
in their investigations of the state of their souls.[11]

Most slaveholding women's personal narratives differ from autobiographies in following the course of a life as it unfolded rather than in
interpreting the life as a whole from the vantage point of a particular
personal and historical moment. They nonetheless embody a concern
with self as the focus of the narrative, and a concern with bridging
the gap between private (female) experience and public (male) discourse. Slaveholding women regularly drew upon the texts of "high
culture" to express their own sentiments, beliefs, and aspirations. And
they frequently constructed self-representations grounded in an ideal
of personal honor informed by high standards of individual excellence.
But even when most concerned with their own status as individuals,
they understood the individual as grounded in ties of community—
ties of class and race, of kinship and culture. They thought of themselves as particular kinds of individuals—women, of course, but also
privileged, white southerners—whose individuality derived its meaning from membership in specific social groups. But their sense of their
relations to the communities cannot easily be understood simply as a
case of women's permeable ego boundaries, their general tendency to
merge with rather than to differentiate themselves from others. Rather,
their sense of those relations had more to do with a concept of delega-
tion, of themselves as distinct representatives of a community.

Significantly, the first autobiographical writing published by a southern woman was written by a former slave and was published in the
North. Harriet Jacobs's *Incidents in the Life of a Slave Girl*, notwithstanding its status as a slave narrative and notwithstanding Jacobs's use
of a fictional persona, Linda Brent, to mask her own identity, has strong
claims to being regarded as an autobiography. Written in the first person and explicitly from the perspective of a particular historical moment
—Brent's acquisition of freedom—*Incidents* begins with childhood and
represents the developing self-consciousness of a female self. Although
the account of an escape from slavery, *Incidents* adopts the idiom of

northern, white, middle-class domestic fiction, thus inscribing itself in a discourse foreign to the experience of its author and protagonist. The conventions of domestic fiction led Jacobs to emphasize the wrongs of slavery as primarily an assault upon female virtue and motherhood. In this spirit, she attempted to represent her self as seeking above all to conform to the roles deemed appropriate for the women of her intended audience. But despite her best efforts, *Incidents* above all represents the "unfeminine" tenacity, determination, and isolation of its protagonist. *Incidents* thus betrays a deep fissure between the cultural expectations of the dominant bourgeois discourse of womanhood and the identity, or self, of the former slave woman who brazenly insisted that her narrative was indeed "written by herself."

Jacobs's autobiography can, from one perspective, be read as an example of women's difficulty in representing the personal female self within the dominant discourse, but it cannot be read as only that. And it assuredly cannot be read as an example of women's propensity to represent the personal female self in relation to others. *Incidents* forcefully, if sometimes covertly, proclaims a fierce quest for independence and self-determination. The protagonist's refusal to subject her will to that of her master engages her in a lonely struggle in which she casts off all ties to secure her freedom. To establish herself for her readers as a person worthy of respect, she distanced herself from the condition of slavery, emphasizing the paleness of her skin and her father's instinctive feelings of freedom. The realities of southern slavery (and northern racism) powerfully inform Jacobs's narrative but not her self-representation. Her autobiography can only be understood as the product of specific historical conditions that would deny her any self-possession. But in struggling against those conditions, she claims a self more independent from the restrictions of gender than was possible for most women of her time. Jacobs's juxtaposition of her naked will against that of her master, like her tendency to repudiate the identity of a slave, comes closer than most female self-representations to an assertion of an essential self. Yet Jacobs, in the act of reaching for an essential self, searingly testifies to the historical condition she was determined to write herself out of.

After the war, when increasing numbers of elite southern women turned to publication, a significant group did in fact publish autobiographies or, perhaps more accurately, memoirs. The great majority of these authors focused on their early lives during slavery times, on the upheavals of the war years, and on the changed conditions of their lives after the war. Many insisted that they had always been hostile to slavery, thus providing evidence for those who would see slaveholding women as much the unwilling victims of the slaveholding regime as were their black slaves. Others were more candid in admitting the sense of loss that followed in the wake of defeat. But whatever position they adopted vis-à-vis the ancien regime, they all foregrounded the society to which they belonged and cast their personal stories as primarily representative of the experience of their region. Even those, such as Elizabeth Meriwether, who claimed to have always been opposed to slavery, emphasized the history of their region, thus underscoring the roots of self in community. Many southern women's personal narratives from the late nineteenth and early twentieth centuries may thus, at least in part, be classified as memoirs rather than as autobiographies in the strict sense.[12]

It would nonetheless be rash to dismiss entirely the element of autobiography—of self-representation—that motivated and informed southern women's accounts of their experiences of slavery, war, and recovery. In accounts that they explicitly wrote for publication, many southern women claimed the authority of the writing self. They may, in many instances, have veiled their intentions under disclaimers of any unfeminine or subversive intent. They may have insisted that they wrote in the interests not of self-display but of testifying to the experience of their community. But they did, disclaimers notwithstanding, assume the public mantle of witness. And in witnessing to the experience of their community, they insisted upon their right to speak in its name. Thus, even when they did not foreground the development of the female self, they did publicly represent it. They simply were more likely to emphasize the self as southern—whether typical or atypical—than as female.

Katharine DuPre Lumpkin, writing in 1946 as a white southern woman who had sharply repudiated many of the values of her region, cast her autobiography as an assessment of the historical legacy that had shaped her.[13] Eschewing a confessional mode, Lumpkin wrote little, if at all, of her personal feelings. Her autobiography begins not with her birth or her childhood but with her slaveholding great-grandfather, William Lumpkin. The title of her first chapter, "Of Bondage to Slavery," identifies her people's history as the fount of her own identity.

From the perspective of feminist criticism, it would be easy to argue that the anxiety of representing her self through a dominant male discourse had effectively silenced Lumpkin. But *The Making of a Southerner* contains no evidence of anxiety. Its very style testifies to a sure authorial presence, to her strong sense of herself as an individual. Much like Jacobs, if for different reasons, Lumpkin possessed a determined will. That will drove her north to define and consolidate her independent identity. Yet when years later she came to write her autobiography, she represented her self as above all the product of history.

Lumpkin begins "Of Bondage to Slavery" with an account of her great-grandfather, William Lumpkin, a man of many children, slaves, and acres, and progresses to her grandfather, who inherited his possessions and his authority. Deftly adopting the male slaveholder's perspective, she details the buildings and activities of his plantation, the members of his household, and the responsibilities that weighed upon his shoulders. Toward the end of the chapter, her perspective shifts. Grandfather, she notes, "did not have to bear his burden of management unaided. He was fortunate in having a slave who carried on his mighty shoulders a substantial share of the heavy load" (30). The penultimate section of the chapter depicts the responsibilities that devolved upon the slave, Jerry, emphasizing how heavily Grandfather Lumpkin depended upon him to influence and keep order among the other slaves. Jerry, the religious head of the slave community, reprimanded fellow slaves who were "neglectful of their duty toward the master." But he was also "their stay, whose mighty frame and steady spirit were the staff on which they leaned when trouble and sorrow overtook them—as it could overtake slaves" (34). Jerry buried the dead and baptized the living. "My grandparents," Lumpkin comments with devastating irony, "were not alone in seeing in Jerry's influence an exceedingly valuable possession" (34). But even Jerry had one weakness: he could not read.

Each Sunday Jerry would come up to the big house so that her grandmother could read him a chapter from the Bible. The reading completed, she would return the Bible, which she had given to him at his request, and he would depart. The same afternoon, he would rise before his slave congregation, open the Bible at the place Grandmother marked, and from his lips would pour "the entire chapter his mistress had read aloud to him in the morning. He would 'read' it word for word and from it take his text and preach his sermon" (35).

In the final section of this chapter, Lumpkin writes of her father's tenth birthday, his coming of age as "young master." On that day, his father called all the slaves together, telling them simply, " 'This is your young master' " (36). And then the slaves, who had known him since his infancy, came one by one to make their curtsies or bows. Young Will had known what to expect. "It had been the same for his father before him and his grandfather" (37). But he enjoyed his new status for only five years, the better part of which were dominated by the war. "Nevertheless until the very end he went on expecting to be even as his father had been" (44). Lumpkin concludes the chapter by observing that the way of life of the southern gentleman left a special stamp upon the men who lived it, "but more particularly in a special way it stamped their sons, who were reared to expect it and then saw it snatched away" (44).

In book 2, "Uprooted," Lumpkin writes of the trauma of war and defeat for the men of her family and other white southerners. Her childhood, like that of so many others, was shaped by tales of Negro " 'uppitiness,' 'sassiness,' molestation of whites" (86). They were told bitterly of Reconstruction, when true southerners were ruled by scalawags and carpetbaggers. "And to be ruled by Negroes! Ruled by black men! To have those born in the womb of slavery, those children of dark ignorance and lowest race, as they were spoken of, put in office over white men! The slave ruling over the master!" (87). For white southerners, there was no other side to the story, no possibility of seeing different views. There was only the disaster, injustice, and outrage that only white supremacy could counter.

Lumpkin, born into this world of defeat and uncertainty, lived in three different houses in the first three years of her life. Daughter of an uprooted slaveholder, she was reared on the dream that one day they would find a good plantation and begin to recover the old way of life. In the midst of uncertainty, her mother, like other southern mothers, did her best to keep up appearances, with "her silk dress that rustled, bonnet or hat touched with velvet ribbon, dainty black shoes, and black kid gloves" (106). But the moorings for the life they were defending had passed beyond recall. The places in which Lumpkin lived as a girl were each "just another house . . . only another house, as I thought of it then, from which we would inevitably move on" (108).

Lumpkin implicitly draws a sharp contrast between the impermanency of her family's residences, the uncertainty of their material situation, and the permanence and certainty of their beliefs. Between them, she suggests, both the uncertainty and the certainty established the core of her identity. "In the case of my particular generation, it seems that we first learned both behavior and belief at a time when those around us were peculiarly disturbed." She was (she informs us in book 3, "A Child Inherits a Lost Cause," more than halfway through her autobiography) "born in 'ninety-seven" (128). Her father's struggles on behalf of white supremacy nonetheless provided a constant center to her youth. As the children reached the "club-forming age," they "had a Ku Klux Klan" (136). In a debate at school, possible only because the class included one Yankee boy to take the opposing side, she defended white supremacy.

> Of course I told of our history and how the South had been saved by the courage of our fathers—we always told this. Probably I told of the Invisible Empire—we often did. Obviously, I recited all the arguments we had for Negro inferiority, and that this was why he must never be allowed to "rise out of his place." My peroration comes back to me in so many words, and how I advanced it with resounding fervor amidst a burst of applause from all the children in the room but my opponent: ". . . and the Bible says that they shall be hewers of wood and drawers of water forever!" (137)

Lumpkin deploys pronouns with virtuosity, variously using "he," "we," and "I" to represent the threads of her own identity. "He" represents her inherited identity, appropriately privileging the masculine cast of slaveholding values. "We" represents the identity of her generation as heirs to former slaveholding parents. "I" represents the emerging consciousness of self as capable of judging the inherited and collective aspects of her identity. After describing how she had absorbed the vocabulary of white supremacy and racism in her high chair, Lumpkin notes that she herself learned to speak it even before she understood what it meant. "Of course I did come to comprehend. When I did, it was a sharp awakening. This was mere chance" (130). One morning she heard the sounds of a ferocious beating, the victim of which, she knew, could not be one of the children, for even their corporal punishment was administered with some dignity. She edged carefully over to peer through the kitchen window and witnessed a severe thrashing that was being administered to "our little black cook": "I could see her writhing under the blows of a descending stick wielded by the white master of the house. I could see her face distorted with fear and agony and his with stern rage. I could see her twisting and turning as she tried to free herself from his grasp. I could hear her screams, as I was certain they could be heard for blocks" (132). The repeated use of "I" forcefully underscores the dawning of her independent consciousness, from the perspective of which her father becomes objectified as "the white master of the house." At the time of the beating, Lumpkin's independent consciousness remains a flicker that could be snuffed with the assurance that the cook had been beaten because she had been "impudent" to her mistress, had "answered her back." And, underscoring her younger self's retreat into the comfort of community values, Lumpkin notes, "It was not the custom for Southern white gentlemen to thrash their cooks, not by the early 1900's. But it was not heinous. We did not think so. It had once been right not so many years before" (132).

When Lumpkin was almost twelve, her family moved to a farm in a poor section of Richland County. "None of us called the place Father had selected 'plantation'" (151). Even she could understand that two hundred acres did not justify the term. However, poor by antebellum Lumpkin standards, the place was rich in comparison with those of their neighbors. The sense of the surrounding poverty led Lumpkin to think of the years on the farm as her "Sojourn in the Sand Hills." Her interactions with the local white children, who lived with a poverty she had associated only with blacks, led her to a new sense of her self. Her clothing was different; her lunches were different; and "there was the matter of manners" (158). The other children accused her of putting on airs, but, then, her knowledge and especially her sense of religion were different. In the end, these differences, which were those of class, resulted "in a sort of ignominious isolation from the people around us whom once I almost felt I had come to know" (173). They also resulted in that distance on one's community known as self-consciousness. Looking back on the experience, she nonetheless thought that something "was begun out there in the Sand Hills" (182). Something, which she had not entirely recognized at the time, "apparently had been taken away." That something was the glamour of the family history, of the old plantation that in her experience had been revealed as only a farm. Why, Lumpkin the autobiographer reflected, "would not the old picture be blurred by the insertion of this new one, in which Negro laborers came and went as strangers, among whom were no counterparts of the slave names so familiar in one's family annals" (182)?

The Sand Hills stay had also, she thought in retrospect, provoked the beginnings of her religious skepticism, which college accelerated. In the place of the God of wrath with whom she had been reared, college offered her a God of love who could be followed, in whose name one could work to transform the world. The message "went on soaking into my consciousness for a year without any peculiarly eruptive consequences. But then it came." And it came in the form of the Word made flesh, an idea she had accepted with no suspicion of what it might mean: "It had not remotely occurred to me what this might be thought to mean" (189). The Word made flesh meant that she, a southern white woman, would be spoken to on Christianity and the race problem by a southern black woman, whom she would be expected to call Miss Arthur.

Foreboding gripped Lumpkin and her friends: it was unthinkable. "*Jane* Arthur," perhaps, "*Miss* Arthur," never. "We had known and forgotten tens of thousands of Negro Marys and Janes. But never a '*Miss* Arthur.' How forget a '*Miss* Arthur'?" (189). But how could they refuse? They dared not. And, afterward, "I found the heavens had not fallen, nor the earth parted asunder to swallow us up in this unheard of transgression" (192–93). The event brought Lumpkin another flicker of consciousness as she listened to Miss Arthur. "If I should close my eyes, would I know whether she was white or Negro?" (192). Remembering the touch of exhilaration that accompanied the indefinable sense of discomfort that informed her memories of the event, Lumpkin evokes the biblical story of the man in the Book of Samuel who had defied the law by touching the sacred tabernacle of Jehovah. She had, by thinking that nothing essential distinguished Miss Arthur from a white woman, touched the "tabernacle of our sacred racial beliefs" (193). "I had reached out my hand for an instant and let my finger-tips brush it. I had done it, and nothing, not the slightest thing had happened" (193).

Lumpkin's fleeting vision of what she calls a new heaven preceded her complementary vision of a new earth in which she began to learn, concretely, that her inherited beliefs might not be accurate. Why, she queries in her final chapter, did she take this course? Could she not have better found the personal certainty that she sought in following in the ways of her forebears? "We may call it chance. We may speak of the mysterious chemistry of individuality" (238). Perhaps the very ideals of her childhood had shaped her course, enjoining her sternly to do her duty. Whatever the reason, once her eyes had been opened there was no turning back. Pressing forward, she learned that the South embodied in her family's sense of its history had been something more than that myth allowed—had included many whites who did not own slaves and many blacks who were not slaves. She learned that beyond her immediate community there was another South in which she could anchor her identity. "As it came about, it was this different South that in the end drew me towards my refashioning, even as my Old South receded ever farther into history" (239).

Writing of herself as a southerner, Lumpkin never explicitly emphasizes her gender. She sharply emphasizes the centrality of the master—of male dominance—in the Old South and even its persistence into the New South. But she does not cast her own struggle as one to escape male dominance in particular—or, rather, since everything she comes to oppose is represented by men, she does not cast her struggle for individuality in a female discourse. In a deep sense, she does not represent her identity as a woman as central to her efforts to come to terms with her past and to chart a new course. And even when she succeeds in charting that course, she brings it back to the South of which she feels herself a part.

Not all southern women autobiographers match Lumpkin's historical and sociological imagination. Nor, as many feminist critics have noted, do all women autobiographers match her determination to represent the development of her self. It is, in fact, tempting to argue that Lumpkin's explicit attention to the historical and sociological conditions of her self permits her to adopt the strong authorial position that she does. Like other women autobiographers, Lumpkin maintains a discreet silence on her sexuality; even more than many others, she eschews any hint of personal confession. *The Making of a Southerner*, like all autobiographies, including the most exhibitionist, contains its silences. But the silences do not weaken Lumpkin's representation of her self. And the evocation of history, for all its apparent impersonality, strengthens it by delineating the ties that bind any individual to her community.

Black southern women autobiographers have shared the history that Lumpkin emphasizes in her autobiography, however differently they experienced it. And, like their white counterparts, they have forged their representations of self in response to it. Zora Neale Hurston and Maya Angelou, in very different ways, followed Harriet Jacobs's lead in writing of southern childhoods from the perspective of the North and for a predominantly northern audience.[14] But in part because of a difference of generation, Hurston and Angelou followed different strategies in representing those southern roots. Hurston, writing in the 1940s and intent upon distancing her self from the fetters of the past, tended to transform southern black history into myth or folktale, thereby denying its consequences for her self. Angelou, writing at the end of the 1960s and benefiting from the militant struggle for civil rights, carefully detailed the community from which she sprang, openly acknowledging its roots in slavery. Hurston, seeking to establish her identity as a member of the republic of letters, denied the significance of all boundaries of race, gender, or class, as if in fear that they would compromise the worth of her self. Angelou accepted the boundaries, trusting that her ability to celebrate and simultaneously to transcend them would validate her self.[15]

In her life as in her work, Angelou represents the dawning of a new generation in which the female legacy and quality of a woman's self have been gaining new attention. In this sense, she properly belongs to the generations that have been developing the feminist theory through which we scrutinize previous women's writings. Lumpkin and Hurston were more reticent about their experiences and identities as women, but their reticence should not be taken as evidence of the fragility of their sense of self. To the contrary, both, as women, have insisted upon the strength and integrity of self. Lumpkin, in insisting more than once that chance may account for the specific way in which her self developed, is reaching for a language to explain the uniqueness of a self that is also a product of its community and history. Hurston, in drawing upon the mythic events and personal visions that shaped her unique self, is doing the same. Both have something in common with Ellen Glasgow, who begins her autobiography not with the South but with her own dawning consciousness.

> I see the firelight, but I do not know it is firelight. I hear singing, but I do not recognize my mother's voice, nor any voice, nor any singing. I feel myself moved to and fro, rocked in my mother's arms, only I do not know that I am myself, or that I am lulled to sleep with a murmur,

with a rhythm, a pause, a caress. All this I learn afterwards. All this is attached, long afterwards, to my earliest remembered sensation. (3)

Glasgow, focusing sharply on the "I" of self and consciousness, nonetheless underscores the relation between that self and community. Without community, the self of sensation would have no words through which to claim its identity. Her "I" cannot even know that it is her self without the help of those who subsequently give her words. In *The Woman Within*, Glasgow also writes of the specifics of her southern childhood, and although she recognizes the importance of history for her sense of self, she emphasizes the influence of the past less than does Lumpkin. But as a woman writer, Glasgow, like Hurston, reaches for a self that transcends the limiting claims of gender, race, and class.

Like other women autobiographers, southern women, black and white, have wrestled with the claims of individualism and community in their self-representations, but they have not normally seen those claims as incompatible. To be a woman has meant, for most, to be a woman among their people, within the specific communities that defined their womanhood. In the measure that southern women autobiographers have also reached for an essential self, they have viewed it as shedding gender together with other historical or material contingencies. The self of will—the will to resist oppression, the will to claim a place in the republic of letters—emerges from their representations as pure individual energy, talent, or chance. In this respect, they have insisted upon pushing the claims of individualism to their logical conclusion, where they meet the Christian vision of the soul. In contrast, most have understood the gendered self as above all historical—as the product of race, class, and region.

Notes

1. Raymond Williams, *The Country and the City* (New York: Harper and Row, 1973).
2. Ferdinand Tönnies, *Gemeinschaft und Gesellschaft: Grundbegriffe de Reinen Sociologie* (Leipzig, 1887).
3. Twelve Southerners, *I'll Take My Stand: The South and the Agrarian Tradition* (New York: Harper, 1930).
4. Sidonie Smith, *A Poetics of Women's Autobiography* (Bloomington: Indiana University Press, 1988), 17.

5. Nancy K. Miller, "Women's Autobiography in France: For a Dialectics of Identification," in *Women and Language in Literature and Society*, ed. Sally McConnell-Ginet, Ruth Borker, and Nelly Furman (New York: Praeger, 1980), pp. 258–73; Susan Stanford Friedman, "Women's Autobiographical Selves: Theory and Practice," in *The Private Self: Theory and Practice of Women's Autobiographical Writings*, ed. Shari Benstock (Chapel Hill: University of North Carolina Press, 1988), 34–62.

6. Jane Gallop, *The Daughter's Seduction: Feminism and Psychoanalysis* (Ithaca, N.Y.: Cornell University Press, 1982); Susan Friedman, "Women's Autobiographical Selves," in *The Private Self: Theory and Practice of Women's Autobiographical Writing*, ed. Shari Benstock (Chapel Hill: University of North Carolina Press, 1988), 34–62; Nancy Chodorow, *The Reproduction of Mothering* (Berkeley: University of California Press, 1976).

7. Elizabeth Fox-Genovese, "My Statue, My Self: Autobiographies of Afro-American Women," in *The Private Self: Theory and Practice of Women's Autobiographical Writings*, ed. Shari Benstock (Chapel Hill: University of North Carolina Press, 1988); Nancy K. Miller, "Writing Fictions: Women's Autobiography in France," in *Life/Lines: Theorizing Women's Autobiography*, ed. Bella Brodzki and Celeste Schenck (Ithaca, N.Y.: Cornell University Press, 1988); Carolyn G. Heilbrun, "Non-Autobiographies of 'Privileged' Women: England and America," in *ibid.*, 62–76; Helen Carr, "In Other Words: Native American Women's Autobiography," in *ibid.*, 131–53; Mary Jean Green, "Structures of Liberation: Female Experience and Autobiographical Form in Quebec," in *ibid.*, 189–99; Biddy Martin, "Lesbian Identity and Autobiographical Difference[s]," in *ibid.*, 77–103.

8. Nancy K. Miller, "Writing Fictions: Women's Autobiography in France," in *Life/Lines: Theorizing Women's Autobiography*, ed. Bella Brodzki and Celeste Schenck (Ithaca, N.Y.: Cornell University Press, 1988), 61.

9. Philippe Lejeune, *Le Pacte autobiographique* (Paris: Le Seuil, 1975); Georges Gusdorf, "Conditions and Limits of Autobiography," in *Autobiography: Essays Theoretical and Critical*, ed. James Olney (Princeton N.J.: Princeton University Press, 1980), pp. 24–48.

10. Ellen Glasgow, *The Woman Within* (New York: Harcourt, Brace and Company, 1954), 129–30. Page numbers for quotations from this work hereafter appear in the text.

11. For a general discussion of the self-representations of slaveholding women and specific references to their manuscript narratives, see Elizabeth Fox-Genovese, *Within the Plantation Household: Black and White Women of the Old South* (Chapel Hill: University of North Carolina Press, 1988).

12. Elizabeth Avery Meriwether, *Recollections of Ninety-two Years, 1824–1916* (Nashville: Tennessee Historical Commission, 1958).

13. Katharine DuPre Lumpkin, *The Making of a Southerner* (New York: Alfred

Knopf, 1946; reprint, Athens: University of Georgia Press, 1981). Page numbers for quotations from this work appear in the text.

14. Zora Neale Hurston, *Dust Tracks on a Road: An Autobiography*, ed. Robert E. Hemenway, 2d ed. (Urbana: University of Illinois Press, 1984); Maya Angelou, *I Know Why the Caged Bird Sings* (New York: Random House, 1969).

15. For a fuller development of these arguments, see Elizabeth Fox-Genovese, " 'What Are Those Blue Remembered Hills?': Discourse of Origins in Zora Neale Hurston and Maya Angelou," in *African-American Autobiography in the Twentieth Century*, ed. William Andrews and Nellie Y. McKay (Madison: University of Wisconsin Press, 1990). See also Nellie Y. McKay's fine discussion of Hurston's *Dust Tracks*, "Race, Gender, and Cultural Context in Zora Neale Hurston's *Dust Tracks on a Road*," in *Life/Lines: Theorizing Women's Autobiography*, ed. Bella Brodzki and Celeste Schenck (Ithaca, N.Y.: Cornell University Press, 1988), 175–88.

The Territory Behind

Mark Twain and His Autobiographies

ROBERT ATWAN

Most great writers acquire numerous biographers. It is Mark Twain's distinction to have acquired not only several biographers but a few autobiographers as well. When we speak of Mark Twain's autobiography, then, we need to specify whose version—for there is no definitive text, but there are three very different published editions.

The first of these grew directly out of biographical efforts. Twain had been toying with an autobiography for a long time, but he could never settle on a form or method. Some of his most successful early writings— *Innocents Abroad, Roughing It*, and the series of sketches, "Old Times on the Mississippi"—reflect the ways he used (or invented) personal experiences to create some of America's first enduring works of literary nonfiction. But these books were not directly intended or promoted as autobiography (though "travel" later served Twain as a dominant metaphor for how an autobiography should be written), and they did not force Twain into grappling with serious problems of autobiographical disclosure and method. Twain had also written or dictated several reminiscent pieces in the 1870s and 1880s, but not until 1897 did he begin

writing autobiography in earnest, diving headlong into his family history and Hannibal childhood. He soon put the work aside, however,
and turned to it only sporadically over the next several years.

In 1906, Twain agreed that Arthur Bigelow Paine, an experienced
editor and writer (he had recently published a biography of Thomas
Nast), could proceed with preparing Twain's official biography. But no
sooner had Twain—one of the most impatient of writers—begun to dictate responses to Paine's biographical questions than he suddenly found
the project impossible. Discouraged by the "idea of blocking out a consecutive series of events," Twain suggested that he simply "talk about
the thing that something suggests at the moment" and that Paine eventually mine this autobiographical material for the official biography.
Twain's dictations went on until his death in 1910.[1] In 1924, Paine pulled
together about one-half of this material, added some of Twain's earlier
reminiscences, and published in two bulky volumes *Mark Twain's Autobiography*.

The book was not a critical success. Reviewers found it fragmented,
cautious, incoherent, and self-indulgent. What apparently irritated reviewers most was Paine's adherence to Twain's request that the chapters
be "arranged in the order in which they were written, regardless of the
chronology of events." Twain's friend, the literary critic Brander Mat-
thews, complained that the book offered "no consecutive record of a
career." Even Paine seemed to apologize for the book's shortcomings.
In his introduction, he says that he thought Twain's plan was "the best
plan for his kind of autobiography, which was really not autobiography
at all, in the meaning generally conveyed by that term, but a series
of entertaining stories and opinions—dinner-table talks, in fact, such
as he had always delivered in his own home and elsewhere, and with
about the same latitude and elaboration."

Paine's successor to the Mark Twain Papers, Bernard DeVoto, agreed
with critics of the *Autobiography*. He was certainly not generous about
Paine's efforts: "If I should follow the plan of my predecessor, Mr.
Paine, which was to publish selections in the arrangement Mark Twain
originally gave them, interspersed as they were with trivialities, irrele-
vancies, newspaper clippings, and unimportant letters—disconnected
and without plan—then I should come out with something as shapeless
as the published portion, which had always seemed to me an annoying
book." For his own edition, DeVoto took only material that Paine had

omitted and, by "joining together things that belonged together," produced a series of autobiographical pieces arranged according to such themes and topics as "Theodore Roosevelt," "Hannibal Days," "In a Writer's Workshop," and "Various Literary People." Though DeVoto gave it the sensational title of *Mark Twain in Eruption*, the 1940 book is on the whole less emotionally expressive than Paine's edition, thanks to DeVoto's editorial efforts to eliminate Twain's "distressing" outbursts of "rage" and "vindictiveness" and his many "injurious" remarks about people both living and dead.

DeVoto also felt a need to protect his subject's literary reputation in the face of material that was so unlike conventional autobiography. Twain, he maintained, was fundamentally a novelist who could best express his autobiographical impulses in fiction alone (there is some truth to this); moreover, like Paine, he considered his subject to be less an accomplished autobiographer than an entertaining raconteur. DeVoto, too, asked that his book not be taken as autobiography. His disclaimer: "This book is presented not as autobiography but as a kind of table talk, as Mark Twain discoursing about men he knew, events that interested him, and occasionally himself. One of the most autobiographical of writers, he is least autobiographical when he seriously tries to be and does not carry his attempt to reveal himself very far or very deep."

As literary editors, Twain's autobiographers have been severe not only toward Twain but also toward each other. In 1959, when Charles Neider came out with *The Autobiography of Mark Twain*, he took both Paine and DeVoto to task in his introduction: "Paine either did not envision the possibility of a true autobiography or did not care to undertake to make one. The same can be said of DeVoto. Both said in their introductions that what they were presenting was not really autobiography but a kind of table-talk." Neider then adds ironically, "To both men I owe thanks because they gave me the opportunity to do the exciting job which remained to be done."

Was that the job of honoring Twain's literary wish and publishing the entire manuscript as intended? Hardly. Instead, Neider threw Paine and DeVoto—and Twain—out the window and introduced an entirely new edition based on his assumption of what an autobiography *should* be. For starters, it should be nothing less than chronological: "It must be said at once that now for the first time the material of the present volume is being presented as autobiography, and in the sequence which one would reasonably expect from autobiography." He makes his editorial program clearer in his attack of DeVoto's edition. DeVoto's "thematic order," he argues, "was an imposed one and could not accurately be called the tightest which can be given the Autobiography, the essence of whose internal order is time. The tightest order of any work is the order functional to it, inherent in it, the order which is in harmony with its subject."

Once again, Twain's autobiography was reinvented, this time in an edition that—for all its organizational convenience—totally distorted his literary intentions. Yet even after imposing his own order on the material and straightening out Twain's "odd methods of composition," Neider still confidently insists that the volume "correctly represents the creative slant of Mark Twain's mind." That creative slant, Neider implies, was simply at odds with the autobiograhical task: "His mind, rich in memory and nostalgia, kept seeking anecdotic forms of recollection, forms which did not easily suit the chronological organization of the classic autobiography." Like Twain's previous autobiographers, Neider believed that Twain was incapable of writing autobiography and needed all the help he could get.

What, then, are we referring to when we discuss Mark Twain's *Autobiography?* When Charles Neider, for example, claims that "Mark Twain's autobiography is a classic of American letters, to be ranked with the autobiographies of Benjamin Franklin and Henry Adams," what exactly is he talking about? Is he referring to the enormous unpublished manuscript in the Bancroft Library at Berkeley? Unlikely, since he has roundly dismissed Twain's misguided organization. Is he referring to the Paine or DeVoto editions? Not at all, since he feels that each is a very unsatisfactory book. Or is he claiming—and this seems the most likely possibility—that it is his own re-creation of Twain's autobiography that is really the classic?

It seems clear that if Twain's book deserves to be called a "classic" of American autobiography (and I am not sure it can be since it does not actually exist), it is because of—and not despite—the literary risks it takes with conventional form and method. Removing those risks, no matter how outrageous or self-indulgent they sometimes seem, by tidying up the chronology or eliminating "trivialities" is like preparing an edition of *Huckleberry Finn* and correcting the bad grammar. Jay Martin's assessment of Twain's autobiography, there-fore, seems far more on target than either DeVoto's or Neider's: "Even more than [Henry] Adams's, Twain's book marks a new stage in the autobiographical form." According to Martin in *Harvests of Change*, Twain's preoccupation with mental processes and his deliberate rejec-tion of conventional narrative sequence make his book not so much a failed autobiographical effort but an important precursor of modern self-consciousness.

For Twain, mental processes and narrative sequence were intimately linked. As an autobiographer he never seemed interested in taking a de-tached view of himself, in looking at his own career from the perspective of a historian or, for that matter, a biographer. (Twain's autobiography reminds us that the act of autobiography is usually at odds with the literal meaning of the genre: it can never be simply a biography of the self written by the self.) Twain thought that an autobiography should re-flect the mental processes of recollection; it was not merely the orderly product of those recollections. As he proceeded with his autobiography —and as his life almost literally became absorbed *in* it—he discovered his compositional challenge: to write about the past without ever losing sight of the fact that the act of writing always occurs in the present. He thus insisted on the primacy of composition, arranging the "story" of his life in the order in which it was composed rather than in the order in which it happened.

Neider notes Twain's decision with astonishment: "Mark Twain had requested him [Paine] to publish the Autobiography not in chronologi-cal order but in the sequence in which it was written and dictated. What an extraordinary idea! As though the stream of composition time were in some mysterious way more revealing than that of autobiographical time!" But what is "autobiographical time"? The consecutive, linear ac-count of a career? Is there some time scheme intrinsic to autobiographi-cal writing, to which autobiographers must systematically adhere? In his surprise, however, Neider raises the essential point about Twain's book: yes, Twain *did* find the stream of composition time to be in some mysterious way more revealing than that of autobiographical time— whatever that might mean. What Alain Robbe-Grillet says of the novel is even more true of autobiography: "Why seek to reconstruct the time of clocks in a narrative which is concerned only with human time? Is it not wiser to think of our own memory, which is *never* chronological?"

One of the dominant themes of Twain's autobiography (I am referring here only to the Paine edition, which, though terribly flawed, is the only available text that renders the spirit of Twain's enterprise) is the problem of autobiography itself. Unlike his editors, Twain was never sure how an autobiography should proceed. He often brought his compositional difficulties and insights into the open by discussing them as he went along. We can see from his many remarks on method, however, that the one thing he did feel certain about, almost from the start, was that his narrative should not proceed sequentially but—to use one of his favorite terms—should "drift."[2] What apparently distressed him about successive narrative—or a division of his life into convenient autobiographical periods—was the utter lack of surprise such a sequential ordering would entail, a lack of surprise not only for the reader but also, and more importantly, for the writer. The conventional autobiographer, the kind who follows Neider's principles of the genre, always knows where his story is going. But Twain wanted to travel without a map of his life, without a definite sense of direction. While living in Florence in 1904, he felt that he "hit upon the right way to do an Autobiography: Start it at no particular time of your life; wander at your free will all over your life; talk only about the thing which interests you for the moment; drop it the moment its interest threatens to pale, and turn your talk upon the new and more interesting thing that has intruded itself into your mind meantime."

As Twain worked his way into the autobiography, he realized that his free-associative narrative process was best handled *orally*. In a burst of enthusiasm he wrote to William Dean Howells in 1904 about the ease and pleasure of dictation. The best thing about it was its authenticity: "There are little slips here & there, little inexactnesses, & many desertions of a thought before the end of it has been reached, but these are not blemishes, they are merits, their removal would take away the naturalness of the flow & banish the very thing—the nameless something—which differentiates real narrative from artificial narrative & makes the one so vastly better than the other."[3]

Twain's rejection of written linear narrative in favor of a discursive oral narrative also suggests an important cultural dimension of his autobiography—its southern tradition. In its oral qualities, the book bears a family resemblance to such "authentic" nonliterary narratives as those of Daniel Boone and Davy Crockett.[4] But Twain was working within southern traditions on an even deeper level. His autobiography implicitly challenges the still dominant model of American autobiography, Benjamin Franklin's. By rejecting a linear autobiographical narrative, Twain also emphatically rejects Franklin's model of the self-made man, the paradigm of the classic American success story. To tell Franklin's kind of story, the writer must see each new experience as accruing logically and profitably from previous experiences, as though one's personal life were a capital investment (P. T. Barnum's autobiography and, more recently, Lee Iacocca's offer fine examples of the way a certain type of American mind "learns from experience"). Though in many ways himself one of America's most striking examples of the self-made man, Twain was clearly uncomfortable with a self-iconography that depended upon the orderly and cumulative progression of experience.

For the most part, the southern autobiographical tradition has opposed Franklin's paradigm of the self-made man. The southern writer, and even the contemporary southern writer—as Alex Harris's recent collection, *A World Unsuspected: Portraits of Southern Childhood*, gives ample evidence—cannot easily imagine a life separable from family, kin, and region. "My country is the Mississippi Delta, the river country," begins William Alexander Percy's *Lanterns on the Levee*. In this autobiographical tradition, there is less stress upon the individual —no one is truly "self-made"—and a greater emphasis on the individual's sense of belonging to a place, its people, and its way of life. Much of Twain's autobiography is as immersed in his Hannibal past as it is in his immediate family life. His daily domestic contact with his wife and daughters, some of it immensely troubled, makes up a large portion of the book. Twain even turns a few chapters of the autobiography over to his daughter Susy by introducing numerous passages from the biography she had begun of her father when she was fourteen.

Along with Twain's rejection of the American rags-to-riches story— and the *success*ive narrative mode that makes such stories possible— went an equally strong rejection of nineteenth-century views of progress. Twain had long been skeptical of the American success story, a tale told mainly by northerners and impressively ridiculed in *A Connecticut Yankee in King Arthur's Court*. As C. Vann Woodward argues in *The Burden of Southern History*, the South had enormous difficulties in subscribing to the American gospel of success and "the national faith in unlimited progress." Though he seems to have been no great favorite of the southern Agrarian writers, Twain in his later work and in his own fashion nevertheless fought as hard a battle against the modern myth of progress as did Donald Davidson, John Gould Fletcher, or Lyle H. Lanier. No optimist, Twain could not share in his age's evolutionary view of history as a force continually changing toward the better. In fact, he probably held devolutionary views. In the autobiography, he re- calls with interest the curious ideas of a Scotchman named Macfarlane, a self-educated worker he met in a Cincinnati boardinghouse in 1856. Twain was especially fascinated by Macfarlane's imaginative anticipa- tion of Darwin's *Descent of Man*. But, as Twain recalls, Macfarlane saw a different evolutionary scheme: "Development was progressive upon an ascending scale toward ultimate perfection until *man* was reached; and that then the progressive scheme broke pitifully down and went to wreck and ruin!"

Twain's antiprogressive sense of history kept him responsive to what Allen Tate refers to as the southerner's characteristic "backward glance," a peculiar state of mind that resulted in a "literature conscious of the past in the present." Twain's insistence on a compositional rather than a chronological time scheme for the autobiography not only shows his resistance to the modern trope of psychological "development" (a re- sistance that many readers of *Huckleberry Finn* find morally disturb- ing) but also opens the way to a blending—and often a clash—of past and present as recollection gives way to immediate thoughts and those thoughts in turn carry with them past associations. It is these collisions of past and present that Twain had in mind as early as 1880, when he ad- vised his brother Orion about the proper way to write an autobiography: "Keep in mind what I told you—when you recollect something which belonged in an earlier chapter, do not go back, but jam it in *where you are*. Discursiveness does not hurt an autobiography in the least." Twain himself heeded this advice; the autobiography is filled with an improvisational "jamming" of his remembrance of things past into his reflections of the moment. Besides revealing Twain's own historical con- sciousness, this procedure clearly resembles the performative style of southern storytelling and oral history.

As Twain saw his autobiography turning more and more into oral nar- rative, he began to identify the act of writing as the enemy of autobiography. It is, he says, and he was among the first to use the word pejoratively, too "literary":

> Within the last eight or ten years I have made several attempts to do the autobiography in one way or another with a pen, but the result was not satisfactory; it was too literary. With the pen in one's hand, narrative is a difficult art; narrative should flow as flows the brook down through the hills and the leafy woodlands, its course changed by every boulder it comes across and by every grass-clad gravelly spur that projects into its path; its surface broken, but its course not stayed by rocks and gravel on the bottom in the shoal places; a brook that never goes straight for a minute, but *goes*, and goes briskly, sometimes ungrammatically, and sometimes fetching a horseshoe three-quarters of a mile around, and at the end of the circuit flowing within a yard of the path it traversed an hour before; but always *going*, and always following at least one law, always loyal to that law, the law of *narrative*, which *has no law*. Nothing to do but make the trip; the how of it is not important, so that the trip is made.

In 1904, Twain wrote Howells that he had written "a good many chapters" of the autobiography but expected that upon reexamining them he would "throw them away & do them over again with my mouth."

Twain's experiments in dictation led directly to a new compositional insight: his narrative would combine diary and autobiography. "In this way," Twain believed, "you have the vivid thing of the present to make a contrast with memories of like things in the past, and these contrasts have a charm which is all their own." Twain did not mean by diary, however, a conventional written account of a day's events; he meant whatever was immediately on his mind at the start of dictation. To capture this immediacy, Twain, anticipating Dos Passos, began to introduce newspaper clippings into the autobiography. These were usually incidents that fascinated him because of their political stupidity, military brutality, or human folly. These, he felt, kept his work from deteriorating into mere *history*, and "history," he claimed, "can carry on no successful competition with *news*, in the matter of sharp interest." He was not speaking here only of a conflict between history and journalism, but—in a manner that suggests Robert Lowell's poetic enjambments of diary, news, and history in *Notebook 1967–1968*—he was also clearly thinking of his own compositional challenge: how to keep the history of his life immersed in the present. Twain himself saw these scraps of news as a daring experiment in form, and they frequently led him to reflect directly on his peculiar autobiographical methods.

Twain realized that throughout the dictations he was constantly mixing news and history. He was quite serious about his "discovery." He says at one point: "I intend that this autobiography shall become a model for all future autobiographies . . . and I also intend that it shall be read and admired a good many centuries because of its form and method —a form and method whereby the past and the present are constantly brought face to face, resulting in contrasts which newly fire up the interest all along like contact of flint with steel." Here we have at least one reason why Twain's "stream of composition time" is more revealing than that of Neider's "autobiographical time." By juxtaposing a recollected past with present interests, Twain's composition time allowed for something new to emerge—a surprising thought, an unexpected contrast that revealed the dynamics of his consciousness. In replacing Twain's time scheme with his own, Neider essentially eliminated the self-exploratory dimension of Twain's autobiography.

Self-exploratory, *not* self-revelatory. Twain rarely discloses private details of his life (though he does recount several ominous dreams), and he apparently had little sense of autobiography's therapeutic value, a value William James was then examining in *Varieties of Religious Experience*. As Jay Martin aptly puts it, "Twain was primarily concerned with his method—the exploration of himself as an artist—not with the mere revelation of himself as man or the detailing characteristic of literary memoirs." Though Twain insisted scatalogically to Howells that the "remorseless truth *is* there, between the lines, where the author-cat is raking dust upon it which hides from the disinterested spectator neither it nor its smell," we still seem a long way off from sniffing it out.

At times Twain thought his autobiography would have to wait one hundred years—until 2006—before it could be published. And it may take that long—or longer. But lest we expect too much from that final authoritative edition, we should recall James Cox's warning: "More and more," he says in *Mark Twain: The Fate of Humor*, "we shall come to ask the inevitable Editor of the Mark Twain Papers to give us the *Autobiography* exactly as it was dictated—a 'true' edition. Yet whoever knows Mark Twain's achievement as a writer will have to have the sense of humor to see that when the true edition appears it may be no more authoritative than the earlier 'editions.'" But even if Cox is correct—and we may all be sorely disappointed—we will at least have the *Autobiography* to judge for ourselves. And Twain will at last have the autobiography he intended.[5]

It strikes me as a wonderful coincidence of literary history that Twain seriously began his autobiography in Vienna in the same years that Freud was hard at work on *The Interpretation of Dreams*. In fact, in an 1898 letter to his friend Wilhelm Fliess, Freud tells of taking an evening off and treating himself "to listening to our old friend Mark Twain in person, which was a sheer delight." (There is no evidence that Freud and Twain ever met; by "old friend" Freud presumably meant "old favorite.") Many years later, when he was writing *Civilization and Its Discontents*, Freud recalled the humorous lecture he heard that night, seeing it as an illustration of how external frustrations enhance "the power of conscience in the super-ego."[6] Twain knew nothing of words such as "super-ego," but he did share a few of Freud's preoccupations—namely, conscience, repentance, guilt, and dread. But though Twain occasionally comes near to examining these internal conflicts in his autobiography, we miss the depths of self-disclosure that a less evasive writer might have reached.

In that first great burst of autobiographical energy in Vienna, Twain wrote glowingly and with loving detail of his Hannibal boyhood. Yet, as DeVoto points out, there was another side to that childhood: "When he invoked Hannibal he found there not only the idyll of boyhood but anxiety, violence, supernatural horror, and an uncrystallized but enveloping dread." DeVoto suggests that self-therapy did play a part in Twain's intentions: "I think that the impulse to write his autobiography was in part an impulse to examine and understand that dread. And I think that the impulse was arrested short of genuine self-revelation because the dread was so central in him that he could approach it only symbolically, by way of fiction."

Twain, however, did succeed at least once in following an autobiographical impulse that drew him deeply into dread, violence, and horror—his own version of *Civilization and Its Discontents*. It was in a book he called at first "Huck Finn's Autobiography," and that novel's opening chapters may represent the finest model of autobiography our literature has to offer.

Notes

1. Twain selected parts of this dictation and published it in twenty-five install-
ments in the *North American Review* between 1906 and 1907. This text
thus comprises a fourth source of autobiographical material.
2. The metaphor of "drift" is closely explored by Thomas Cooley in chap. 3
of *Educated Lives: The Rise of Modern Autobiography in America* (Colum-
bus: Ohio State University Press, 1976). In his examination of autobiography as process, *Design and Truth in Autobiography* (London: Routledge
and Kegan Paul 1960), Roy Pascal notes the importance of travel metaphors. Warren Chernaik has recently compared Twain's "wandering" narrative method to Henry Adams's more organized procedure: see "The Ever-
Receding Dream: Henry Adams and Mark Twain as Autobiographers" in
First Person Singular: Studies in American Autobiography, ed. A. Robert
Lee (London: Vision Press, 1988).
3. This enthusiasm for dictation lasted several years and carried Twain through
an enormous bulk of autobiographical discourse. A year before he died,
Twain wrote Howells a long letter outlining the "irremovable drawbacks" of
dictation, chief of which was the stenographer, whose presence seemed like
a "lecture-audience" and whose personality invariably skewed the direction of the monologue. Twain then proposed to himself a new "scheme" for
achieving autobiographical "frankness & freedom": he would write candid
letters to close friends and never mail them.
4. Arnold Krupat partly covers this dimension of Twain's work in "American Autobiography: The Western Tradition," *Georgia Review* 35 (Summer
1981): 307–17.
5. To be completely honest to Twain's literary intentions, the unenvied editors
of the authoritative autobiography—once they had established as accurately
as possible what those intentions truly were—would need to arrange in
"compositional" order: Twain's earliest attempts to write his life story; all
of the Paine dictations (a quarter of which apparently still remain unpublished and parts of which the Twain estate refused to allow previous editors
to use in their editions); relevant texts from the *North American Review;*
any newly discovered material; and perhaps a number of pieces (such as
"Is Shakespeare Dead?") that Twain incorporated into the manuscript but
eventually pulled out for separate publication. Though such an edition will
most likely be published one day by the University of California Press as
part of their *Works of Mark Twain* project, it is doubtful that this gigantic
autobiographical "work still in progress" would ever appeal to the general
reader.

6. Freud refers to Twain's "The First Melon I Ever Stole." As Freud describes it, this story corresponds to two of Twain's humorous lectures, "The Watermelon" and "On Being Morally Perfect," both of which can be found in Charles Neider's collection of Twain's speeches, *Plymouth Rock and the Pilgrims* (New York: Harper & Row, 1984).

Lives Fugitive and Unwritten

GEORGE CORE

Our question is simple and straightforward: why has autobiography so little appealed to the Vanderbilt Fugitives—and indeed to most major southern writers until the recent past? For some readers the question may seem supererogatory—not worth asking and answering. It's too late now to turn back: come along for the ride if you will, and if the roller coaster breaks down, perhaps you can get your money back.

When we survey southern literature from its beginnings until the past decade or so, we find precious little in the way of autobiography, which is to say little that falls under the heading of even reminiscence or memoir; and there is nothing to speak of so far as diaries and journals are concerned. Colonel William Byrd is an exception, of course; but one argues that his writing is more nearly English than American so far as its modes are concerned. And even Byrd's principal works are a good distance from autobiography.

If, on the other hand, we consider, even in a desultory way, the writing of New England, particularly of the great flowering of its literature in the nineteenth century, we will be immediately struck by the importance of various documents in which the distance between the self of the writer and the finished piece of work is very slight—Hawthorne's notebooks, Emerson's journals and Thoreau's journals, and even, in a special way, the poems of Emily Dickinson, all but seven of which remained unpublished in her lifetime. The diary and the journal are essential modes in the making of New England writing from Samuel Sewall onward. And in many respects the confessional mode of poetry that grew out of New England in the work of Robert Lowell, Anne Sexton, and others is a natural—or, if you will, unnatural—development of these forms of autobiography.

One of the oddest and most apposite ironies of the diaries of Arthur Inman, whom Lewis P. Simpson has called the last casualty of the Civil War, is that Inman, although a southerner, was educated at Harvard and spent most of his life in Back Bay Boston writing these odd documents, which his editor, Daniel Aaron, has called both private and public confession.[1]

V. S. Pritchett, to whom I will repair again in this essay, calls the "born diarists" "the snails of life." He explains: "They are secretive and enclosed in their shells, and their whispering contributes either to history or . . . case history." In contrast, "the pure autobiographer is concerned with shaping a past from the standpoint of a present that may be totally unlike it." It is a considerable leap from diary and letter to autobiography, as Pritchett warns us; and the worst autobiographies are often drowning in details culled from diaries and letters—what Pritchett dismisses as the "Boston memoir."[2] He makes this remark almost twenty years before the Inman diaries were published—a mere one million words selected from the original seventeen million that Inman wrote before ending his life, and his diary.

Although the diary is the most private of the various modes thus far mentioned, it is often written with an audience in mind; and Arthur Inman actually left detailed instructions for his putative editor. Even the diarist who invents his own code or shorthand, such as Samuel Pepys and William Byrd, does not by any means foreclose the possibility of publication and hence exposure of himself to the world.

I have indulged in this survey to secure my general point that most southern writers, especially those persons whom we think of as major writers, have been little interested in autobiographical writing from the diary and the journal to memoir and to autobiography itself. On the other hand, the mode has afforded a natural outlet to New England writers from Cotton Mather to Samuel Sewall and Sarah Kemble Knight to Benjamin Franklin, who wrote the first important autobiography in America. Autobiography in this country reaches its fullest flower in the waning of the New England renaissance, with the appearance of *The Education of Henry Adams*, one of our nation's great books.

Since the Vanderbilt Fugitives deliberately turned away from much of southern writing, we might argue, perversely or otherwise, that there was no compelling reason for any of them to avoid autobiography. But I would think that autobiography as a mode is as foreign to their natural bents or temperaments as it was to their southern forefathers.

The southerner, at least until the recent past, has been more inclined than New Englanders and others to maintain the distinctions between public and private, regardless of the mode of discourse; and that is particularly true of writing.

The southerner naturally is a conversationalist and storyteller, and in telling stories in conversation, he dissipates the urges that the New Englander bottles up in diaries, journals, autobiographies.

In an essay entitled "Vermont Silences," Noel Perrin tells an illustrative story about New England conversation, especially in the country. For twenty years Alfred and Eben met at the post office at 9:00 A.M. and spoke, then each would go his way—one to the west, one to the east.

"One morning during the twenty-first year, however, Eben came stumping out of the post office and, ignoring his usual route, started briskly south. . . . Alfred stared after him for a second, and then called, 'Eben, where on earth ye going.'

"Eben whirled around," Mr. Perrin continues. "'None of your goddamned business,' he snapped. Then he added, visibly softening. 'And I wouldn't tell ye that much if ye wan't an old friend.'"[3]

Educated and citified New Englanders indulge themselves in conversation, needless to say; but the quality of that conversation is usually substantially—and substantively—different from southern conversation. Allen Tate puts this very well in "A Southern Mode of the Imagination":

> The Southerner always talks to somebody else, and this somebody else, after varying intervals, is given his turn; but the conversation is always among rhetoricians; that is to say, the typical Southern conversation is not going anywhere; it is not about anything. *It is about people who are talking,* even if they never refer to themselves, which they usually don't, since conversation is only an expression of manners, the purpose of which is to make everybody happy. This may be the reason why Northerners and other uninitiated persons find the alternating, or con-

trapuntal, conversation of Southerners fatiguing. Educated Northerners like their conversation to be about ideas.[4]

Tate uses this cultural distinction to secure his point that "the Southerner has never been a dialectician" (p. 583) and that southern literature is far more rhetorical than dialectical, just as southern manners and mores are. Tate goes on to say how important manners—conventions —are to southern life and how essential conversation is to the essence of that life. He sees the rhetorical mode as leading to myth, and the mythical mode is as far removed from the self and autobiography as any literary impulse and form that we might adduce. The great southern writers of this century were working toward myth and carried within themselves "the fundamental dialectic" of their culture and civilization —"the inner strains, stresses, tensions, the shocked self-consciousness of a highly differentiated and complex society," as he puts it (p. 589). So Faulkner, Warren, Ransom, Caroline Gordon, Katherine Anne Porter, and others, including Tate himself, were writing out of this collective "shocked self-consciousness" of a society far more than they were exploring the limits of the individual self—that is, the individual self of the writer. (I would be quick to admit that such writers of the piedmont South as James Agee and Thomas Wolfe wrote far more directly out of an agonized individual consciousness of the self—and hence wrote far more autobiographical work than did Faulkner and the Fugitive-Agrarians and the various writers, such as Miss Porter, Miss Gordon, and, later, Flannery O'Connor, who were closely associated with them. It is this difference—the relation of the self—that separates Faulkner and the Fugitive-Agrarians most strongly from Wolfe and Agee.)

Wolfe, it may be recalled, "got along well with the Agrarians personally," as David Donald reports in his biography; but "he received some hard critical blows" (p. 361) from them—but not, as Donald suggests, because they were annoyed he had not become an Agrarian.[5] Warren, who liked Wolfe personally, expressed deep reservations about Wolfe's first two novels while praising his raw talent as enormous. Warren's criticism is aimed squarely at the autobiographical elements in *Look Homeward, Angel* and *Of Time and the River*. He finds that the novels are too lyrical, too much devoted to detail and description and other devices of reporting, too much "depend on the direct intrusion of the novelist's personal sensibility," which is confused with Eugene Gant's character and sensibility. "At the center" of the novel *Of Time and the*

River Warren finds "this chaos that steams and bubbles in rhetoric and apocalyptic apostrophe, sometimes grand and sometimes febrile and empty." He describes this chaotic center as a "maelstrom." And he concludes his examination by saying that "probably all of these defects, or most of them, are inherent in fiction which derives so innocently from the autobiographical impulse." He has already observed that "the transference of the matter from the actuality of life to the actuality of art cannot be accomplished . . . easily." What Wolfe's failures spring from is his "attempt to exploit directly and naively the personal experience and the self-defined personality in art." Warren ends his powerful indictment by observing that "Shakespeare merely wrote *Hamlet;* he was *not* Hamlet."[6] Only T. S. Stribling, another contemporary southern novelist of that time, ever suffered Warren's criticism more severely than Wolfe.

Warren, in passing, compares Wolfe with Melville in that both men attempted to write prose epics. "Melville," he observes, "had a powerful fable, a myth of human destiny, which saved his work from the centrifugal impulses of his genius, and which gave it structure and climax," but Wolfe could not "compensate for the lack of a fable . . . by all his rhetorical insistence."[7] We remember Tate's distinction between the author exploring the self and becoming self-consciously aware of the myth that underlies his society and exploring it through his writing. Wolfe could find neither the appropriate form nor fable for his sprawling novels, and the autobiographical impulse tended to undermine them all.

Warren, needless to say, is objecting to autobiography admixed with fiction.[8] He is by no means objecting to autobiography per se as a mode, but it must be said that autobiography little engaged any of the Fugitives and Agrarians, who seldom wrote about it, even in letters. Faulkner had even less interest in writing it than they did, as his famous epitaph, intended as autobiography and biography—"He made the books and he died"—makes plain.[9]

The Fugitives and the Agrarians began with biography—Warren with *John Brown: The Making of a Martyr,* Andrew Lytle with *Bedford Forrest and His Critter Company,* John Donald Wade with his life of A. B. Longstreet, Allen Tate with his biography of Stonewall Jackson. The principal members of these two groups—John Crowe Ransom, Tate, Warren, Donald Davidson, and Lytle—are men of letters chiefly devoted to writing poetry and fiction, especially poetry, and secondarily concerned with the making of criticism. But they have also written in many other modes—Warren almost anything you can think of—except autobiography. The closest that Warren comes to autobiography, aside from some of his poems, is a long moving profile and reminiscence about his father published early in 1987 in the *Southern Review*—"Portrait of a Father." This portrait tells us very little about Robert Penn Warren but much about his father and a good deal about other members of the family.[10]

Andrew Lytle's last book that is not a collection is a family history or chronicle entitled *A Wake for the Living*, but it, too, is removed from autobiography. Mr. Lytle has said to me in conversation that the author uses his experience in his writing, of course, but that he doesn't know himself well enough to write his autobiography. "Only God knows you well enough for that," he says.

This brings us naturally enough to Allen Tate, Lytle's friend and colleague for many years. Tate, late in his life, began an autobiography in a vague way—what, if completed, would have probably been more nearly a memoir or series of reminiscences than a full-fledged autobiography. By that time in his life—his sixties—Tate had accumulated an impressive record of unfinished projects, particularly books. It began with his famous biography of Robert E. Lee, which he finally abandoned after long struggles and for which he had to repay the advance to the publisher. Tate encountered, in extreme form, what Warren said of Lee: "A man who's smooth as an egg. Turn him around, this primordial perfection: you see, he has no story. . . . You know he had some chaotic something inside . . . , but you can't get at it. . . . You have to improvise a story for him. You don't know his story. It's only the guy who's angular, incomplete, and struggling who has a story. If a person comes out too well, there's not much story."[11]

Allen Tate subsequently conceived and abandoned a critical history of southern literature; a critical biography of Edgar Allan Poe, a man much closer to him in temperament and spirit and values than Lee; what would have been his second novel; a cycle of poems, of which only a few poems, including "The Swimmers," were written and published; and, finally, his memoirs, which appear only in small part in *Memoirs and Opinions*.

Aside from the fact that Tate abandoned almost as many books that he intended to write as women to whom he intended to be faithful but was not, how does this mundane fact signify in the present context?

Tate, alone of the Fugitives and Agrarians, actually planned to write an autobiography or memoir, and the pieces of it that we have are among his most impressive writing. That is especially true of "A Lost Traveller's Dream." In that essay he says: "Autobiography would demand more of myself than I know; it is easier to know other people than oneself because one may observe them; for one can but observe oneself, like André Gide, gazing daily into a looking-glass, a way to self-knowledge from which I should recoil."[12] In conversation Tate remarked to Monroe Spears that he did not know why he behaved as he did during the crises of his life and that he found it easier to explain such turning points in the lives of others than in his own life.

In the preface to *Memoirs and Opinions*, which Tate intended to be entitled *Memories and Opinions*, not *Memoirs*, he writes: "Unlike Ernest Hemingway in *A Moveable Feast*, I couldn't bring myself to tell what was wrong with my friends—even mere acquaintances—without trying to tell what was wrong with myself." He continues: "I am not sure, even now, what was, or is, wrong with me, and I was unwilling to give the reader the chance to make up his own mind on this slippery matter."[13] Tate is here being honest and straightforward, so far as I know him—his work as a writer, his character and probity as a man. He is protecting himself—his privacy—and that of his various friends and acquaintances, including the privacy of his three wives.

So on the personal side there is the matter of privacy: Tate, like Lytle and Warren and Ransom and other Fugitives and Agrarians, sharply distinguishes between matters public and matters private. On the artistic or literary side we have this statement: "I fell back on authority: I couldn't let myself indulge in the terrible fluidity of self-revelation."[14] Tate here is being deliberately ambiguous—or playing both sides of the street. But, in any event, as a severe classicist in matters of art, he would have naturally shied away from the terrible fluidity of autobiography—what he would have considered romantic—and fluid—self-revelation. (He might have seen autobiography proper as falling on the thorns of life and bleeding all over the page.)

In general, although most of the Fugitives and Agrarians lived lives that would have survived the closest scrutiny, Tate's life was another matter entirely, as I have already intimated; and as he has suggested, it would not have survived his own scrutiny. Even so, there is no doubt that he could have written a brilliant memoir, had he chosen to write about the public aspects of life and to hew to the line suggested by that term or mode, *memoir*—that is, to stress the events and people of public and historic importance in his life. That he did not continue with his memoirs is unfortunate.

Tate, unlike Ransom, Warren, Davidson, Lytle, and other of his colleagues, probably would have agreed with B. L. Reid's axiom that "every literate person who lives a notable life ought to write a memoir."[15] In *First Acts* (1988), Reid himself has done as much—but only for his first thirty years, up until the time he began teaching. As I say that, the example of Eudora Welty springs to mind: she, in writing her brilliant memoir, carefully cut it off as her public and mature life began, so that *One Writer's Beginnings* is more nearly an account of her parents and grandparents than it is of herself. In this context we are also reminded of Andrew Lytle's family chronicle, *A Wake for the Living*.

Few of the major writers associated with the southern literary renascence have had much to hide. Katherine Anne Porter was offended when George Hendrick and others discovered the facts about her early life, which she had carefully changed and remade, giving herself a distinguished family that ended in genteel poverty rather than the family to which she actually belonged—which was perilously close to poor white trash. Her actual life, as we know since the publication of Joan Givner's biography of Miss Porter, is much more memorable and admirable than the life that she had invented for herself. Perhaps she realized that toward the end of her ninety years, for she assigned Mrs. Givner to the job of writing her life and helped in some ways.[16]

If Katherine Anne Porter, born Callie Russell Porter, put as much energy into reinventing herself and remaking her family history as she did into writing her fiction (which, especially in the Miranda stories collected in *The Old Order*, often parallels her invented life), the same is by no means true of the Fugitives and the Agrarians, nor indeed of Faulkner or any other modern southern author of my acquaintance.

But we are going to learn little about their lives firsthand except from letters, conversations, and the memories of others; and none of them, it would now appear, will have lived to read his biography. In other words, private considerations—modesty, reticence, concern for the feelings of other persons—will prevail over the desire for fame, fretfulness about one's posthumous reputation in the literary marketplace, financial matters, and so forth. The private world that Robert Penn Warren re-creates in writing the portrait of his father—a world in which voices were dropped and conversations were changed when children came into the presence of their elders, a world in which emotions were masked in times of crisis—has powerfully affected the modern southern writer's attitudes about revealing his own life or willingly allowing others to reveal it.

I find myself with contradictory judgments and feelings about these matters, which is to say that although I would like to have autobiographies of various southern writers—especially Tate, Warren, Caroline Gordon, Cleanth Brooks, and Andrew Lytle—at the same time I admire them for their good manners, their reticence, their principled defense of their privacy and that of their families and friends; and there is a part of me that applauds them for refusing to write detailed autobiography and for being slow to authorize biography. To think that Faulkner or Ransom or Warren or Katherine Anne Porter or Eudora Welty would write autobiography in the real sense of the term is to misunderstand their natures as human beings and as writers so thoroughly as to be daft. I still find it funny that Mr. Ransom told Thomas Daniel Young there wasn't enough material of interest in Ransom's life for Young to make it into a biography. I salute Robert Penn Warren for writing about nearly everything under the sun but himself and for being all but intransigent when it came to authorizing his biography. My attitude about Miss Porter is considerably more complicated, but I think I fully understand why she did not write an autobiography and why she waited until the eleventh hour to authorize that her biography be written. And I sympathize with her despite her lying and her histrionics, for Miss Porter would have had even more trouble with writing her autobiography or memoirs than Allen Tate did—far more. The prospect of a biography must have been chilling to her in many respects.

Most of the writers whom I have discussed—from John Crowe Ransom, born in 1888, and Katherine Anne Porter, born in 1890, to the generation of Lytle, Warren, Brooks, and Eudora Welty, born in the first decade of this century—hold what may now be considered old-fashioned and quaint views about privacy. Most of them have guarded their families and their private lives, usually with great firmness but equal politeness; Faulkner's rudeness often came when his privacy was intruded upon.

This tradition of reticence and guardedness about private matters is loosening considerably. Soon southern writers may be as intemperate about allowing their private lives to be violated as are writers throughout the rest of the country. And in an era when the Supreme Court had ruled that public people give up many of their rights to privacy, we are all the more inclined to agree with B. L. Reid when he observes that "when a man makes himself a public man . . . , he abandons the privilege of privacy that has been his option." Mr. Reid adds: "Nobody requires a man to lead an interesting life in the world's eye; but my heartless biographer's feeling is that once he has done so he becomes a property of history and so of biography."[17] And so we are brought back to the matter of autobiography: should you have lived such a life, then you may well have the duty to write about it, as Reid suggests. This is a question that will become increasingly urgent to the good writers of the future. Younger southern writers are already writing reminiscences and autobiographies: consider Mary Lee Settle, George Garrett, Richard Marius, Reynolds Price.

We are reasonably safe in making the generalization that the more minor the southern writer—and the less committed he is to the profession of letters—the more inclined he has been in the past to write autobiography. That is the case with Colonel David Crockett. That is true of the writers whom James M. Cox is considering—William Alexander Percy and Frederick Douglass; it is true of such writers in our time as Willie Morris. This is not—and I want to stress this point— either to depreciate or to deprecate the writer or the autobiography. I like autobiographies; I probably am more inclined to read autobiographies than biographies; I am eager to have more good autobiographies written and published. I would predict, with all the confidence of Mark Twain's Christian holding four aces in a high-stakes poker game, that more autobiographies, many of them good, are going to emerge from the South in the near future.

In the Age of the Essay and the Age of the Self, autobiography will become increasingly important in the South. As I consider this matter I find myself surprised that the autobiographical impulse in the South has not already emerged more strongly. It probably hasn't owing to the powerful continuing influence of good poetry and fiction written by Ransom, Tate, Faulkner, Warren, Welty, and the others from the late 1920s until the recent past. The natural instinct of younger writers is to continue writing poetry and fiction; autobiography will probably have to wait until the late years of the younger generations of writers, and it will probably come naturally, in due course, to generations born after 1930.

What has been occurring in the South—more slowly than elsewhere in the United States but with increasing sureness—is that traditional attitudes toward privacy are giving way to a greater openness within and without the family, within and without one's circle of friends, within and without the community. I will pass over the sociological and cultural reasons for this change in attitude, an attitude now spilling over into the writer's perspective about his or her world so far as that world impinges upon the writer's material. I will observe in passing that as our social conventions shrink, our literary modes and techniques seem to expand.

While I have perhaps overemphasized the matter of privacy, I have scanted the relation of the modern writer—especially the modern southern writer—to his world. Allen Tate, in speaking of the shift in southern writing from rhetoric to dialectic, with the result that the dialectical conflict takes place within the fictive characters and ensues in what Tate calls "internal dialogue, a conflict within the self," stresses the way that the southern writer used this dialectic to explore "the Southern legend . . . of defeat and heroic frustration."[18] Elsewhere, in his essay on *Sanctuary*, he explores some of the ramifications of southern myth, which he says "informed the sensibility and thought . . . of the defeated South." He sees this myth as true and as affecting "the common life" of southern society between 1865 and 1940, "so that the myth is reality."[19] The myth remained available to southern writers until well after World War II but is probably now irrecoverable as a source for fiction and poetry.

The southern writer today—that is, since the late 1950s—is confronted with a world that is less stable and definable and far more fragmentary than the world that Faulkner, Tate and the other Fugitive-Agrarians, and various other southern writers explored in fiction and poetry.

What has occurred is that the ratio between the self—what Lionel

Trilling calls the opposing self—and society at large has changed for the southern writer; and he or she no longer can draw upon the almost infinite possibilities of southern legend—what Tate calls "the Greco-Trojan myth (Northerners as the upstart Greeks, Southerners as the older, more civilized Trojans)." [20] With such a fecund field of legend and myth to draw upon, it is no wonder that the writers of the high southern renascence were more interested in that subject than in the self. With such a vast and engaging subject before them, southern writers were naturally so drawn to it that they never got around to chronicling their own lives, as my wife has suggested to me.

The case is far different now, and the politics of our culture are far more confused. We live in a society that has no underlying common myth, and so as time goes on each writer is probably going to be more inclined to set sails on the seas of the self. In Trilling's formulation, it is going to be more and more difficult to "hold in balance the reality of self and the reality of circumstance." [21] And so the self will beckon, and we will have more memorable autobiographies and fewer memorable fictions.

How can those of us who are living notable lives prepare ourselves for such a time and for such a voyage? I answer this question by quoting V. S. Pritchett once more:

> On the face of it, to write one's autobiography is the easiest and most grateful task in the world. No search for anti-hero or hero: he is you. No search for material, it is all there: your own life. No imagination is necessary; the question of structure . . . is automatically solved by sticking to chronology, year after year. The first person singular seems to be the perfect camera-eye. . . .
>
> So you set out. You write 20 pages and suddenly you stop. Why is it you are bewildered? Why do you have the sensation of being in a rowing boat in the middle of the ocean and having lost your oars? Who is this, "I," you wonder, which of my many selves is writing? [22]

"One is less and less sure of who one is," as Pritchett says in *Midnight Oil*, particularly if he is the empty husk of the artist. "The professional writer who spends his time becoming other people and places, real or imaginary, finds he has written his life away and has become almost nothing." [23]

So writing your autobiography won't be as easy as Pritchett seems to be telling us at the outset. I leave you the job.

Notes

1. Lewis P. Simpson, "The Last Casualty of the Civil War," *Sewanee Review* 95 (Winter 1987): 149–62.
2. V. S. Pritchett, "Writing an Autobiography," in *Autobiography: A Reader for Writers*, ed. Robert Lyons (New York: Oxford University Press, 1977), 397–403.
3. Noel Perrin, "Vermont Silences," in *Second Person Rural* (Boston: Godine, 1980), 78–83.
4. Allen Tate, "A Southern Mode of the Imagination," in *Essays of Four Decades* (Chicago: Swallow, 1968), 584.
5. David Herbert Donald, *Look Homeward: A Life of Thomas Wolfe* (Boston: Little, Brown, 1987), 361.
6. Robert Penn Warren, "A Note on the Hamlet of Thomas Wolfe," in *Selected Essays* (New York: Random House, 1958), 170–83 passim.
7. Ibid., 182.
8. See Robert Penn Warren, "Poetry Is a Kind of Unconscious Autobiography," *New York Times Book Review*, May 12, 1985, 9–10. In a letter to me Mr. Warren wrote that the reason autobiography has been scanted in the South "may be that the world around or in memory seems too interesting."
9. Malcolm Cowley, *The Faulkner-Cowley File* (New York: Viking, 1966), 126.
10. *Portrait of a Father* (together with "Mortmain") has been published as a book by the University Press of Kentucky (1988).
11. *Robert Penn Warren Talking*, ed. Floyd C. Watkins and John C. Hiers (New York: Random House, 1980), 66.
12. Tate, *Memoirs and Opinions, 1926–1974* (Chicago: Swallow, 1975), 3.
13. Ibid., ix.
14. Ibid.
15. B. L. Reid, "Practical Biography," *Sewanee Review* 83 (Spring 1975): 362.
16. As I have written elsewhere, the shape of Porter's fictitious life is this: "The Young Woman from the Provinces (east Texas) decides to write herself out of poverty and ignorance, and along the way she reinvents herself, creating a family past that is not only romantic, engaging, and sentimental, but also usable for her purposes as the stuff of fiction." See "No Safe Harbor," *Hudson Review* 36 (Autumn 1983): 563.
17. Reid, "Practical Biography," 363.

18. Tate, "A Southern Mode of the Imagination," in *Essays of Four Decades*, 591, 592.
19. Tate, "Faulkner's *Sanctuary* and the Southern Myth," in *Memoirs and Opinions*, 151.
20. Tate, "Homage to William Faulkner," ibid., 85.
21. Lionel Trilling, *The Opposing Self* (New York: Viking, 1955), 41.
22. Pritchett, "Writing an Autobiography," ibid., 397.
23. Pritchett, *Midnight Oil* (New York: Random House, 1972), 4.

Autobiographical Traditions
Black and White

JAMES OLNEY

When Bill Berry recently suggested to me that I might write about a tradition of autobiography in southern literature (or at least a tradition of autobiographical writing: there is an important distinction to be drawn, I think, between the substantive "autobiography" and the adjective "autobiographical," to which I will return later), my first inclination was to deny that any such tradition exists or has existed and that hence there was no subject to be addressed. But on second thought I came to feel that this was not altogether accurate and was also not something that I really wanted to say, particularly in light of the fact that I have written more than one essay in which I argued for a very strong tradition of autobiography among southern writers—or at least a tradition that began with specifically southern writers and that then, without ever ceasing to be a tradition of southern writing, reached out to inform the work of writers not of the South in any literal, geographical sense. Perhaps it was this regional dislocation that caused my first reaction to be that no tradition of autobiography existed in southern literature. In any case, what I now feel to be a more correct and more complex answer to the question of whether such a tradition exists is this two-headed response: no, there is not a tradition of autobiography among white writers in the South; but, yes, there is a tradition of autobiography among black writers coming from the South. Now, with this as my thesis, what I would like to do is, first, to consider what constitutes a tradition of writing; second, to look closely at two exemplary instances of southern autobiography, Richard Wright's *Black Boy* and Eudora Welty's *One Writer's Beginnings;* and finally, to speculate on possible explanations for why *Black Boy* situates itself in a tradition that stretches back one hundred years into the past and forward forty-five years to the present—a tradition that moves and changes over time but that remains nevertheless one and continuous—while *One Writer's Beginnings*, as fine and as moving as in itself it is, does not take its place in any discernible, definable tradition of southern autobiography.

What does it mean to speak of a tradition? More specifically, what does it mean to speak of a literary tradition? Most specifically, what does it mean to speak of a literary tradition of autobiography? I shall avail myself of the time-honored crutch of a dictionary definition here, because *Webster's New Collegiate* seems to me awfully good on tradition, at least for my purposes: tradition is first, the handing down of information, beliefs, and customs by word of mouth or by example from one generation to another without written instructions; second, an inherited pattern of thought or action; and third, cultural continuity in social attitudes and institutions. As I am specifically considering a *literary* tradition—that is, a tradition that for the most part manifests itself in written form—I think I can safely disregard the phrase "without written instructions," and I might further say that the "inherited pattern of thought or action" of the second definition is inherited precisely in the form of written texts, in written accounts of a life, in the case of autobiography. Borrowing from Aristotle, could we not say that as Sophoclean drama is the imitation of an action, so autobiography is the symbolic, the written imitation of a life, and that the handing down of information, beliefs, and customs and the cultural continuity in social attitudes and institutions that constitute tradition are achieved exactly in and through this written imitation of a life? The individual autobiographies that corporately form a tradition are thus particular outcroppings or realizations of a whole people's beliefs and customs, and they provide for the cultural continuity in social attitudes and institutions that define this people. The give-and-take from one account of a life to another, or the call and response from text to text and from life to life ("call" and "response" are Robert Stepto's terms in *From behind the*

Veil), provides the dynamics of tradition making. And what I will argue is that this dynamic process, this ongoing shaping of a tradition by one call and response after another, is present in and crucially important to black autobiography from the South, while, conversely, it plays little or no part in autobiography by southern white writers.

There are so many reasons for choosing Richard Wright and Eudora Welty as my exemplary cases that the choice may seem overdetermined. There is first of all the quality of the books themselves: vastly different as the two books are, they seem to me, individually and in each case, as fine as any book we have from Wright or Welty. Then there is the circumstance, which makes it natural to pair the two books, that Wright and Welty were born within a year of one another (Wright in 1908, Welty in 1909) and lived their formative years in the same city— or relatively small town, as it was then (some twenty thousand people) —Jackson, Mississippi. And finally, either book could bear some such subtitle as *A Portrait of the Artist as a Young Man/Woman* or, in the Wordsworthian manner, *The Growth of a Poet's Mind,* altering the formula only to the extent of substituting "Fiction Writer" for "Poet." One could no doubt discover other ties or incidental similarities between the two books and the lives they recount, but the real truth is that *Black Boy* and *One Writer's Beginnings* are about as different as two books written in this century could be—which, of course, is another reason (and really the most important one), among all the overdetermining reasons, for bringing the two books together. It is this utter contrast that serves to make the points that I would make: that autobiography by black southern writers is altogether different from autobiography by white southern writers and that one of the crucial differences—perhaps *the* crucial difference—is the relationship of the individual talent of the autobiographer to a tradition of writing in this mode.

Moreover—to turn directly to *Black Boy*—it seems to me altogether reasonable to argue that no American book of this century is more important than Wright's autobiography. It is not a perfect book, but one of its greatnesses is precisely that it is *not* perfect; indeed, one of the greatnesses of autobiography itself, as a mode or as a genre, is that it is never perfect. Again, one thing (though not the only thing) that makes *Black Boy* so important is that it is solidly within a tradition of autobiography from the black community, is the central term, one might say, or the central text in a progression that extends from Frederick Douglass's great *Narrative* of exactly one hundred years earlier (1845) down through Wright and others to *Invisible Man, Go Tell It on the Mountain, The Autobiography of Malcolm X,* and *The Autobiography of Miss Jane Pittman.* That three of these last-mentioned titles are novels (*Invisible Man, Go Tell It on the Mountain,* and *The Autobiography of Miss Jane Pittman*) and the fourth a generic anomaly, since it should properly be *The Autobiography of Malcolm X* by Alex Haley, in no way tells against the point that I would make about a tradition of autobiography in the black writing community. On the contrary, this fact of generic continuity into and through Afro-American novels of the past three decades, a generic continuity capable also of creating and sustaining an anomalous authorial mix in the Haley/Malcolm X book, confirms rather than confutes the strength—one might say the inevitability—of the tradition of autobiography for black writers throughout the history of Afro-American literature. The same argument could be made equally well with *The Narrative of the Life of Frederick Douglass, an American Slave, Written by Himself* or with *The Autobiography of Miss Jane Pittman* or with any of the other books named and many more in addition, but the central position of Wright's book, midway, as it were, between Douglass's *Narrative* and Gaines's *Autobiography of Miss Jane Pittman,* makes it particularly effective in demonstrating the continuity of the tradition that informs all three of the books and several dozen more besides.

John Blassingame has argued, and I believe altogether correctly, that two distinct but intertwined traditions of Afro-American writing, one a tradition of history, the other a tradition of literature, began with the slave narrative. Think first of Douglass's *Narrative,* which I take to be fully representative of the entire body of slave narratives and of the thematic triad of literacy, identity, and freedom; think then of *Black Boy* and its virtual repetition of this three-in-one theme, and try simultaneously to recall the variations on the same three-part theme in Washington's *Up from Slavery* and Du Bois's *Souls of Black Folk* and *Dawn of Dusk;* and think, finally, of how literacy, identity, and freedom, as lived thematic experiences, play in *The Autobiography of Malcolm X,* and one will have some enhanced understanding of what a literary tradition is—a greater understanding, that is to say, of what the informing presence of a tradition of autobiography has meant for Afro-American writing. Going a step further, we should observe that these

autobiographies are as thematic as any novel—*Black Boy* is themati-
cally as intense and as controlled as *Native Son*—and that the themes
of Afro-American fiction and poetry are these same themes of literacy,
identity, and freedom, born ultimately out of the experiences of slavery
and out of narratives recounting that experience and escape from it.
This is a tradition simultaneously of history and of literature, and here,
as with autobiography in general, it is the dynamic, generative tension between history and literature that would have made the act and
the text of autobiography so unacceptable to the New Critic of the old
school but that makes the same act and text so fascinating to us today.

Throughout *Black Boy*, various individuals and groups—the principal of the school, employers, fellow employees, members of his own
family, and so on—attempt to impose numerous identities on the young
protagonist of this "record of childhood and youth," all of which he finds
false and all of which he resists furiously. It is as if he were involved in
a story that he could not understand, with a role to play that in no way
fitted his own character. "The white South said that it knew 'niggers,'
and I was what the white South called a 'nigger.' Well, the white South
had never known me—never known what I thought, what I felt. The
white South said that I had a 'place' in life. Well, I had never felt my
'place'; or, rather, my deepest instincts had always made me reject the
'place' to which the white South had assigned me." Naming him with
a name that was not his, "placing" him where he did not belong, the
white South was in effect telling a story, of itself and of him, that was
utterly alien to Richard Wright, and the project of *Black Boy* might be
said to be the wresting of that story from the white South and the telling of it as Wright knew it should be told—with the white South now a
character, however, and with Wright as the storyteller.

Nor is it only the white South that weaves tales that entangle the boy
in plots that he can neither understand nor adapt himself to. There are
the stories of their lives, which involve his life too, told by the young
Richard's Granny and Aunt Addie, by his Uncle Tom, indeed, by everyone around him; and the boy finds these stories constantly baffling—
he finds them, in a term Paul Ricoeur uses in *Time and Narrative*, "unfollowable." He tries to "read" the stories of others around him and to
interpret them, but he regularly fails in the attempt precisely because
they are stories told by others and not by himself. As Wright makes clear
in *Black Boy*, this need to interpret the essentially uninterpretable, to

follow the unfollowable, finally forced him to shape his own story, em-
plot it as he would, and tell it in his way. "The tension I had begun to
feel that morning," he says of one incomprehensible experience—a tension that required resolution in a story that could be followed—"would
lift itself into the passion of my life." The genius of *Black Boy* is that the
emplotting of the book, taken as a whole, is Richard Wright's doing,
and included within that encompassing act of emplotment are always
the incomprehensible, baffling, unfollowable plots or stories created by
others. *Black Boy* is thus the followable story of a string of unfollowable
stories.

Wright's determination that he *will* tell his story, and tell it in the
individual way that it demands to be told, is one feature (though not
the only one) that keeps his telling from becoming merely conventional
or formulaic. For all the observable similarities between *Black Boy* and
other books in a clearly discernible line of black autobiographical writing, Wright was fiercely individualistic both in his thought and in his
writing. Like Douglass before him, Wright fought furiously against any
attempt to impose an identity on him or any attempt to tell him what or
how he should write. And the difference-in-sameness where *Black Boy*
and the Afro-American autobiographic tradition are in question is to be
explained also in part by the fact that Wright was first and last a writer
—an imaginative writer, with nothing of the mechanical or formulaic
about him, for whom traditional forms were a great strength precisely
because they could be bent and shaped to his specific ends, in this case,
the specific end of telling his own followable, indeed compelling story.

The power of story is both a theme and a fact in *Black Boy*, and the
overwhelming need to tell one's story is surely the motive, one way
or another, of all autobiography. In the first volume of his *Autobiographies*, called *Reveries over Childhood and Youth*, W. B. Yeats tells
of the doings of people in the west of Ireland, and he goes on to say,
"All the well-known families had their grotesque or tragic or romantic legends, and I often said to myself how terrible it would be to go
away and die where nobody would know my story." That Wright's story
should be told and known is unquestionably the moving force behind
Black Boy; what sets it apart from the story told in Yeats's *Autobiographies*, or from the story told in *One Writer's Beginnings*, for that
matter, is that Wright's story is, *mutatis mutandis*, so very much like
the story of Frederick Douglass in the *Narrative* and also so very much

like the story of the protagonist of *Invisible Man*. *Black Boy*, in other words, while being stamped throughout with Wright's unique character as a writer, is also and at the same time at the very heart of a tradition of autobiography that extends from the beginning of Afro-American literature right down to the present time.

Meanwhile, across town, the same cannot be said of *One Writer's Beginnings*. Eudora Welty's book, while it is as much devoted to the making of stories as *Black Boy*, tells of *one* writer's beginnings, *this* writer's beginnings; it is not the generic tale of a white girl growing up in the South as, one might fairly say, Wright's book is the generic tale of a black boy growing up in the South. I use the word "generic" deliberately to suggest that the story that Wright tells is generic—it is the story, oft repeated, of a group of people—and to suggest also that in the end that story discovers a form for telling that makes it virtually a genre of autobiography unto itself. Whether the autobiography is largely fictional, as it is with *Invisible Man* and *The Autobiography of Miss Jane Pittman*, or whether it is largely nonfictional, as it is with *Black Boy* and *The Narrative of the Life of Frederick Douglass* and *The Autobiography of Malcolm X*, seems to make very little formal difference. I cannot, on the other hand, think of any other books from the South that I would put together with Eudora Welty's book and claim that, taken *ensemble*, they form a distinctive genre or a coherent tradition. *One Writer's Beginnings* is very much a book by Eudora Welty; it takes its place in the whole corpus of her work rather than taking its place, as does *Black Boy*, in a line of generically similar books by other writers.

Consider how *One Writer's Beginnings* begins.

> When I was young enough to still spend a long time buttoning my shoes in the morning, I'd listen toward the hall: Daddy upstairs was shaving in the bathroom and Mother downstairs was frying the bacon. They would begin whistling back and forth to each other up and down the stairwell. My father would whistle his phrase, my mother would try to whistle, then hum hers back. It was their duet. I drew my button-hook in and out and listened to it—I knew it was "The Merry Widow." The difference was, their song almost floated with laughter: how different from the record, which growled from the beginning, as if the Victrola were only slowly being wound up. They kept it running between them, up and down the stairs where I was now just about ready to run clattering down and show them my shoes.

Thinking of these two books together—*One Writer's Beginnings* and *Black Boy*—it strikes me that, dangerous as it is to dispute Tolstoy, we might have to reverse the famous dictum with which *Anna Karenina* begins: "All happy families resemble one another, but each unhappy family is unhappy in its own way." I would not want to deny the distinctiveness of the Wright family's unhappiness, but I do believe we would have to say that, at least as Eudora Welty presents it, her family was happy very much in its own way. And this is what her book is about: how, out of the unique set of legacies conferred on her by her mother and father and more distant ancestors, Eudora Welty came to be the fiction writer that she is.

Toward the end of her book, she says:

> It is our inward journey that leads us through time—forward or back, seldom in a straight line, most often spiraling. Each of us is moving, changing, with respect to others. As we discover, we remember; remembering, we discover; and most intensely do we experience this when our separate journeys converge. Our living experience at those meeting points is one of the charged dramatic fields of fiction.
>
> I'm prepared now to use the wonderful word *confluence*, which of itself exists as a reality and a symbol in one. It is the only kind of symbol that for me as a writer has any weight, testifying to the pattern, one of the chief patterns, of human experience.

It is the confluence in herself and in her memory of mother and father and many others that makes Welty the particular artist that she is. *One Writer's Beginnings* is a return in memory back to times in the past before the streams had flowed together, before the confluence had formed itself, to discover the individual and familial sources of her talent and her vision. "Of course," Welty concludes, "the greatest confluence of all is that which makes up the human memory—the individual human memory. My own is the treasure most dearly regarded by me, in my life and my work as a writer. Here, time, also, is subject to confluence. The memory is a living thing—it too is in transit. But during its moment, all that is remembered joins, and lives—the old and the young, the past and the present, the living and the dead."

Opposite this passage in my copy of *One Writer's Beginnings* I have scribbled "cf. St. Augustine on memory," as, in a similar way earlier in the book when Welty is describing very early sensory experience that played its part in her becoming a fiction writer, I have jotted down "cf. first pages of Joyce's *Portrait of the Artist.*" By contrast, at various places in my copy of *Black Boy* I find notations such as these: "cf. Douglass," "cf. *Invisible Man,*" "cf. *Nobody Knows My Name.*" What this suggests to me is that in reading *One Writer's Beginnings* one is not reminded particularly of other writing from the South, whereas in reading *Black Boy* one thinks constantly of other books by black writers who, whether actually from the South or not, draw on a tradition that in its origins was profoundly southern.

At the outset of this paper, I remarked that there is a distinction to be drawn between a tradition of autobiography and a tradition of autobiographical writing and to which I promised to return later. I want to fulfill that promise now by looking first at the adjectival form of our subject. There is a great deal of autobiographical fiction by southern writers—Faulkner might be cited as a prime example—and I imagine it may be possible to trace a tradition of autobiographical fiction from the South. White writers from the South seem for the most part unwilling to write autobiography without veiling it or presenting it as fiction. Let me hasten to say that this is not unique to southern writers: Dickens is the classic case, and one has only to mention the names of Virginia Woolf, Marcel Proust, and James Joyce to see how widespread the practice of autobiographical fiction has been in this century. Nothing surprising here. But think, by contrast, of what happens so often in Afro-American writing, where what we have is not autobiographical fiction but fictional autobiography: *The Autobiography of an Ex–Colored Man, The Autobiography of Miss Jane Pittman, Invisible Man, Their Eyes Were Watching God,* and, in variant ways, *The Color Purple* and *Go Tell It on the Mountain.* These books, these fictional autobiographies, are in addition to all the straight autobiographies produced in such profusion by black writers: three by Frederick Douglass, two or three by Booker T. Washington and two or three by W. E. B. Du Bois (two or three in either case depending on how you define autobiography), two by Langston Hughes, three or four (is it?) by Maya Angelou, and so on down to the flood of autobiographies that came out of the civil rights movement of the sixties and seventies. Autobiography, straight and fictional, has been the heart and soul of Afro-American literature from the beginning to the present time; no similar claim could be made about the literature of the white South.

Why should this be so? I will briefly sketch two or three possible ex-

planations and hope that discussion will either confirm them or will produce others that are more likely than those I think of. Wole Soyinka, the
Nobel laureate from Nigeria, when asked why autobiography seemed
to be so prominent in African literature, responded that he thought
it might be because the African writer, unlike the European or white
American writer, lived at different times in his life in two radically different sociopolitical worlds, the traditional world of the home in which
he grew up and the colonial world that he had to learn to cope with
upon growing up. "When the colonial or ex-colonial writer wants to
express or to really record this divide in his experience," Soyinka said,
"he makes it more frankly autobiographical because he is trying to
recapture something which is so totally different." Soyinka's analysis
reminds me of nothing so much as this passage early in Du Bois's *Souls
of Black Folk:*

> The Negro is a sort of seventh son, born with a veil, and gifted with
> second-sight in this American world,—a world which yields him no true
> self-consciousness, but only lets him see himself through the revelation
> of the other world. It is a peculiar sensation, this double-consciousness,
> this sense of always looking at one's self through the eyes of others, of
> measuring one's soul by the tape of a world that looks on in amused
> contempt and pity. One ever feels his twoness,—an American, a Negro;
> two souls, two thoughts, two unreconciled strivings; two warring ideals
> in one dark body.

I think it may well be just this "twoness," this "double-consciousness,"
that accounts, at least in part, for the frequency with which Afro-
American writers have had recourse to autobiography. What is it to
be both an American and a Negro, to be possessed of two souls, two
thoughts, two unreconciled strivings? "What's it like? Let me tell you.
Let me tell you my story," has been the response of almost innumer-
able people in that state of double-consciousness and twoness. "It's a
complex fate being an American," Henry James declared; how much
more complex to be, in Du Bois's phrase, "an American, a Negro"—
to say nothing of the horrendous complexity of being, in the violent
paradox of Douglass's title, "an American slave." I should remark that
the tradition of autobiography that I have been at some pains to trace
here is quite consciously a dual tradition: Douglass, Washington, Du
Bois, Wright, Ellison, Malcolm X, Ernest Gaines, besides writing autobiography within a black tradition, write also within a general American

tradition of autobiography descending from the Declaration of Inde-pendence—they write within it by way of challenging the tradition.

Another reason the tradition of autobiography has been such a coher-ent one among black writers, I believe, is that it has been most often an act of testifying, of bearing witness. Testifying in this sense is not something done individually but is the revelation of a whole group ex-perience; or perhaps we should say that in the individual experience is to be read the entire group experience. Douglass testified individu-ally, communally, historically, and with great rhetorical power to what slavery was; Wright testified, not on behalf of himself alone but on be-half of "black boy" or "black boys," to what it was like living the ethics of Jim Crow. This sort of testifying is an attempt to fix an historical reality, and as the reality was remarkably consistent, so the testimonial response from decade to decade and generation to generation displays much the same consistency.

I want to introduce here an idea that is rather off to the side of my sub-ject but that I find fascinating to contemplate all the same. I have seen it suggested that "the captivity narrative [is] the prototype for Ameri-can autobiography by women and minorities." Now, I do not mean to say that this is the way in which Eudora Welty and Richard Wright, or white autobiography and black autobiography from the South, can be brought together, for in the sense intended I do not think that Eudora Welty writes in *One Writer's Beginnings* specifically as a woman. She writes instead as a *writer*. Hence this formulation does not really in-clude Welty, but I wonder if it might not be that women who write consciously and intentionally as women, black writers who write con-sciously and intentionally as members of a minority (and very few do not), would be included as adopting a kind of paradigmatic form that would make their individual autobiographies sound very much alike, thus establishing a generic tale and a tradition of autobiography. This is only speculation, however, and it is as such that I offer it.

I want to conclude by returning to the question of the southern-ness—or otherwise—of southern autobiography. Robert Penn Warren, whose credentials as a southern writer, I take it, are pretty well impec-cable, has said, in some meditations on the nature of autobiography, that "poetry is a kind of unconscious autobiography," and, therefore, Warren implies, since he has produced a good deal of poetry, he has no reason to write an autobiography. "For what is a poem," he asks, "but a hazardous attempt at self-understanding? It is the deepest part of auto-biography." Though Warren himself may be southern, however, there is nothing particularly southern about this claim, and it does nothing to establish a tradition of specifically southern autobiography. On the other hand, the pattern of bondage, flight, and freedom that a graduate student of mine finds in virtually all black autobiography bears witness to something specifically southern in the history of our nation, and, for better or worse, it is the South's to claim as its bittersweet own.

Eudora Welty's Autobiographical Duet

The Optimist's Daughter *and* One Writer's Beginnings

SALLY WOLFF

> The events of our lives happen in a sequence in time, but in their significance to ourselves they find their own order, a time table not necessarily—perhaps not possibly—chronological. The time as we know it subjectively is often the chronology that stories and novels follow: it is the continuous thread of revelation.
>
> *One Writer's Beginnings*

Eudora Welty's most recent works, *The Optimist's Daughter* and *One Writer's Beginnings*, hold a significant place among twentieth-century autobiographical writings. Unlike each other in form —the former, a novel; the latter, a set of lectures presented at Harvard and collected in one volume—these works reveal complex correspondences between Eudora Welty's art and her life. Together, they epitomize both the distinctions and the likenesses between factual and fictional autobiography and the writer's experience in creating each form.

The autobiographical nature of Eudora Welty's art is difficult to discern fully, partly because the writer is an extremely private person who believes that knowing the life is not essential for understanding the fiction. Like William Faulkner, who wished to be remembered by the words "He made the books and he died," Welty maintains that successful fiction conveys the writer's feelings apart from any biographical context.[1] Welty's statements about her autobiographical work are ambiguous. On the one hand, she insists on a clear distinction between fiction and fact, upholding the artist's prerogative to transform fact into fiction: "Of course, any character you write has bits and pieces of somebody: but they are really conceptions of the imagination, which are invented to carry out what I want to do in the story. Of course, I endow them with things I have observed, dreamed or understood, but no one represents a real person" (*Conversations*, 213–14). On the other hand, she acknowledges that a writer creates out of personal experiences and feelings. Even though the subject may vary, she says, fiction is the history of a writer's "life's experiences in feeling."[2] Her own imagination, she says, "takes its strength and guides its direction from what I see and hear and learn and feel and remember of my living world."[3] Welty makes a crucial distinction: she writes out of "emotional experience, which is not necessarily out of factual experience" (*Conversations*, 253).

But scholars have long recognized the degree to which Welty locates and defines the characters and setting in her fiction from the sources of people and places in her life. Place, she says, has a "more lasting identity than we have and we unswervingly attach ourselves to identity" (*Eye of the Story*, 119). Much of the material for her stories, she admits, derives partly from "a lifelong listening to talk on my own block where I grew up as a child" (*Conversations*, 255). Her fictional settings and characters have some direct parallels to places and people in the Mississippi, and particularly the Jackson, of her childhood: Peggy Prenshaw has cited, for instance, the little store, Laura McRaven's Jackson home in *Delta Wedding*, Josie's home and parents in "The Winds," the Fondren sisters' beauty shop, which provided the model for "The Petrified Man," the Fats Waller concert that Welty attended in Jackson's old city auditorium, the summer camp at Moon Lake, the blackberry lady, and the watermelon man. Other Mississippi places in her works show that, like Faulkner, Welty has drawn upon the native soil of her Mississippi childhood for her artistic resource.[4]

In her latest works—her novel, *The Optimist's Daughter*, and her autobiographical essays, *One Writer's Beginnings*—Welty draws more substantially than in any of her previous work upon autobiographical materials from her family history and her own emotional experience. Though differing in form, these two works chronicle events and, to an even larger extent, emotional experiences from the writer's past. The distinction between the genre of fiction and that of autobiography blurs in these two books: the novel is highly autobiographical, with only slight alteration of facts and situations, and is so close to her personally, Welty herself has stated, as to be painful (*Conversations*, 116); the essays are storylike, with narrative voice, scene delineation, character development, and the sense of revelation that readers have come to expect from Welty's fiction. The common unifying agent for the highly autobiographical novel and essays is Welty's imagination, illustrating well Paul Eakins's view that "autobiography in our time is increasingly understood as both an act of memory and an act of the imagination."[5]

These two autobiographical pieces reflect one another, illuminating meanings and aims from work to work. They suggest how closely related to each other Welty's techniques of writing fiction and autobiography can be. In *The Optimist's Daughter*, Welty takes for her main subject self-confrontation and self-comprehension. The book, as one scholar has put it, is Welty's "most profound look into the nature of mortality";[6] the protagonist faces grief, unburdens herself of it, and reaches a deepened perception of self. In an interview Welty has likened the quest for self-comprehension that her character Laurel makes to the author's own self-inquiry. Writing the novel after the death of her mother, Welty responded in an interview, was "very painful; but also it helped me to understand. . . . I believe in really trying to comprehend something. Comprehension is more important to me than healing" (*Conversations*, 116). On one level the novel is a partly fictionalized account of the author's own desire for understanding and consolation.

The artistic achievement of *One Writer's Beginnings* builds upon the intricate relationship Welty forms among fact, fiction, and autobiography. A portrait of the artist as a young woman, this book recollects Welty's "beginnings"—as a child and as a writer. This self-portrait emphasizes the pleasure of her childhood in a loving family and recounts how early influences shaped her dawning artistic sensibility. But as with any autobiographical writing, this account is partial and selective. By her own statement, she chose certain facts and omitted others: "The things that didn't magnetize I threw out."[7] What emerges is a personal myth of her family and childhood that is rendered virtually perfect: aside from the descriptions of the deaths of her parents and their parents, the book admits little information that is troublesome or unflattering to the character of the family it reveals. Such conscious structuring of one's life—even if only its beginnings—is inevitable for the autobiographer, since memory and the writing process are both inherently selective. Welty embodies Somerset Maugham's view that no writer tells the whole truth about himself.

The Optimist's Daughter and *One Writer's Beginnings*, taken together, reveal Welty more fully as autobiographer than either one separately can. The novel shows the artist fictionalizing highly significant and painful aspects of her emotional life that she seeks to externalize through writing; the essays reveal the factual basis for many scenes and events from the novel as well as their impact upon the author's emotional and artistic growth. Reflection and imagination form the basis for both works, and yet, as Terrence Rafferty has pointed out, "The moment it becomes part of a novel, reflection changes its essence."[8] Together, these books offer a rich accounting of the emotional, physical, and psychological forces that have shaped the life of this artist. Welty describes the act of writing the autobiographical essay as self-revealing and enlightening (Devlin and Prenshaw, "Conversation," 452). In both these books, the fictional autobiography and the more factual one, Welty discovers what she elsewhere describes as the "moral power" of art—finding the inner truths that reveal us to ourselves.[9]

Place has always been essential for locating and defining the self in Welty's fiction. This holds true for her autobiographical writings as well. In an interview she describes the simplicity, security, and ease of childhood in Jackson, Mississippi, a place that has always fed the stream of her creativity.

> When I was growing up, it had much more of an identity than now because it was smaller. And it was so small that one knew everybody practically. Also, it was a very free and easy life. Children could go out by themselves in the afternoon and play in the park, go to the picture show, and move about the city on their bicycles and everything, just

as if it were their own front yard. . . . The town was easier, no, easier to get a sense of place. All of which is gone now, of course, because Jackson is a city. (*Conversations,* 170)

Welty fictionalizes a similar view of the effects of modern city life in the setting of *The Optimist's Daughter.* She laments, perhaps, the time when place could have a more lasting identity for us to attach to. Different from Jackson in significant ways, Mount Salus in the novel nevertheless recalls the Jackson of Welty's youth. In the "new part" of the cemetery in which her father will be buried, Laurel, the protagonist, senses the loss of value and tradition that have accompanied the growth of the city. The degeneration of setting is symbolic of a lost world of her past. Her mother's grave is adorned with a beautiful, blossoming camellia bush in the old part of the cemetery which Laurel passes. The camellia represents the old ways of cherishing and the continuity of love, renewable with each season of blooming: "Laurel's eye travelled among the urns that marked the graves of the McKelvas and saw the favorite camellia of her father's, the old-fashioned *Chandlerii Elegans,* that he had planted on her mother's grave—now big as a pony, saddled with unplucked blooms living and dead, standing on a fading carpet of its own flowers."[10] Symbolic of continuity, like memory, the camellia unites the living and the dead. Welty echoes this image later in the novel in the perennial blooms of Becky's prized climbing rose: "Memory returned like spring, Laurel thought. Memory had the character of spring. In some cases, it was the old wood that did the blooming" (*Optimist's Daughter,* 136).

The new part of the cemetery contrasts starkly with the old one. The new section is located "on the very shore of the new interstate highway" with enough traffic and noise to rattle the earth and wake the resting dead. The graves here are marked with "indestructible plastic Christmas poinsettias" (108). Unlike the graceful "carpet" of flowers beneath the perpetually flourishing camellia, the grass underfoot here is "the odorless pistachio green of [the undertaker] Mr. Pitts' portable grass," which responds only to the vibrations from the new highway. The lights and noise from the traffic accentuate the feeling of doom in this waste landscape, sharpening the grief Laurel feels as her father is buried. She cannot hear the minister for the traffic noise: "She might not even have heard the high school band. Sounds from the highway rolled in upon

her with the rise and fall of eternal ocean waves. They were as deafen-
ing as grief. Windshields flashed into her eyes like lights through tears"
(110–11).

The West Virginia setting of both *The Optimist's Daughter* and *One
Writer's Beginnings* figures centrally in Welty's memories of her childhood. "I did draw on some of the childhood and early married experience of my own mother," Welty states of the novel. "That was literal
memory, up on the mountain and the sounds and sights up there";
"all that part about West Virginia was true" (*Conversations*, 116, 175,
334). In an unpublished account of Welty's West Virginia background,
Floyd C. Watkins has noted the preponderance of realistic detail of
place and event in this section of the novel. The mountain environment, the Elk River in Clay, West Virginia, the bell that rang to call
the boat across Eagle Bend in the Elk River, the bridge across the river
at Clay, and, in general, the river, hills, height, and wildness of the
landscape derive from the actual sites surrounding Welty's mother's
mountain home and her memories of childhood experiences there.[11]
"Certain virtues," Watkins writes, are "attributable to the West Virginia
heights": strong will, strength, and independence—the characteristics
Welty gives to her characters in the novel.[12]

In *One Writer's Beginnings* Welty further explains the effect of mountain life upon her own sensibilities:

> It took the mountain top, it seems to me now, to give me the sensation
> of independence. It was as if I'd discovered something I'd never tasted
> before in my short life. Or rediscovered it—for I associated it with the
> taste of the water that came out of the well. . . . The coldness, the
> far, unseen, unheard springs of what was in my mouth now, the iron
> strength of its flavor that drew my cheeks in, its fern-laced smell, all
> said mountain mountain mountain as I swallowed. Every swallow was
> making me a part of being here, sealing me in place. (57)

Old family stories provide a source for plot in *The Optimist's Daughter* and for narrative structure in *One Writer's Beginnings*. The real
and fictionalized accounts of the death of Welty's grandfather corre-
late exactly with one another (except for names). Watkins has reprinted
the newspaper account of the death of Welty's grandfather from the
Clay County *Star*, March 30, 1899: "Mr. E. R. Andrews, attorney-at-
law, died at the John [*sic*] Hopkins Hospital, Baltimore, Md., Saturday,

March 25th, 1899, at 2 p.m. Mr. Andrews started to Baltimore Sunday, March 13th, going in a skiff as far as Charleston; on account of slides on the track, the trains not running. His daughter, Miss Chessie, accompanied him" ("Journey to Baltimore," 437). In the novel, Welty fictionalizes the same journey to the Baltimore hospital and to death:

> Becky had gone with her father, who was suffering pain, on a raft propelled by a neighbor, down the river at night when it was filled with ice, to reach a railroad, to wave a lantern at a snow train that would stop and take them on, to reach a hospital. . . . In the city of Baltimore, when at last they reached the hospital, the little girl entrusted the doctor with what he had told her: "Papa said, 'If you let them tie me down, I'll die.'" (143)

In *One Writer's Beginnings*, Welty renders the story again, indicating the poignance of this family story and its significance in Welty's imagination: "Mother had to return by herself from Baltimore, her father's body in a coffin on the same train. He had died on the operating table in Johns Hopkins of a ruptured appendix, at 37 years of age. The last lucid remark he made to my mother was 'If you let them tie me down, I'll die'" (51).

Other like passages in *The Optimist's Daughter* and *One Writer's Beginnings* reveal their important thematic and technical similarities. Passages echo and reflect one another from book to book, suggesting the imaginative interplay between fact and fiction. In *The Optimist's Daughter*, the act of reading takes on a highly symbolic significance that corresponds closely with its significance in the essays. Reading symbolizes the security of childhood and parental love and, later, when roles reverse, when the child reads to the parent, the loyalty, responsibility, and gratitude the child pays in return.

In the novel and the autobiography, reading and then the loss of vision represent symbolically the human connections with love and even life itself. In a recent interview Welty explains her original wish to focus the title of the novel on vision by calling it *Poor Eyes*. She explains the difficulty of translating literal truth into fiction.

> I used certain things I had been familiar with. My mother had eye trouble, but she didn't have a detached retina. I did know someone who had a detached retina, though. You do this when you write any character. I nursed my mother through cataract surgery, and some of

the details I used for the judge. She had sandbags, for instance, and she couldn't move her head. It's not literal, though. If it were it would be a damn difficult task to write the literal truth. It was hard to do in *One Writer's Beginnings*, to give an account of family illness. I don't think I could have done that in a novel.[13]

Welty takes the fact of her mother's poor eyesight and fictionalizes it into the judge's requiring surgery for a detached retina or what he calls "dislocated vision" (23).

As *The Optimist's Daughter* unfolds, reading and listening evoke memories of the protected happiness of childhood. These themes echo strongly in *One Writer's Beginnings*. Welty, who describes herself as "a writer who came from a sheltered life," depicts her early sense of security in her parents reading to one another.

> In the lateness of the night, their two voices reading to each other where she could hear them, never letting silence divide or interrupt them, combined into one unceasing voice and wrapped her around as she listened, as still as if she were asleep. She was sent to sleep under a velvety cloak of words, richly patterned and stitched with gold, straight out of a fairy tale, while they went reading on into her dreams. (*Optimist's Daughter*, 57–58)

Later, the daughter finds herself the protector rather than the protected. At the bedside of her sightless father, she seeks to halt what Faulkner calls the "dark, harsh flowing of time," sweeping those she loves to destruction. As Laurel's father moves closer to death, he responds less and less to her reading voice, in correlation with his diminishing will to live. She begins by reading him the *Picayune* during his breakfast. Remembering that he had "loved being read to once," she brings him paperbacks and his favorite detective novels. "He listened without much comment. She went back to one of the old ones they'd both admired, and he listened with greater quiet. Pity stabbed her. . . . She could not help him" (280).

The reading and listening between father and child have a sustaining power: "I'm not asleep," said her father. "Please don't stop reading" (33). Finally, though, the judge succumbs to a darkness of the spirit and becomes "too completely silent." Despite the wonderful connective, even restorative powers of reading, Laurel cannot protect her father from death, and she must relinquish him.

Likewise, reading and listening symbolize the mystery of human connection and comfort in *One Writer's Beginnings*. Welty learns early
that "any room in the house . . . was there to read in, or be read to"
(5). She describes scenes with her mother: "She'd read to me in the
big bedroom in the mornings, when we were in her rocker together,
which ticked in rhythm as we rocked, as though we had a cricket accompanying the story. She'd read to me in the diningroom on winter
afternoons in front of the coal fire, with our cuckoo clock ending the
story with 'Cuckoo,' and at night when I'd got in my own bed" (5).
This passage from *One Writer's Beginnings* suggests the same sense of
security and belonging that she fictionalizes in the novel: "They would
begin whistling back and forth to each other up and down the stairwell.
My father would whistle his phrase, my mother would try to whistle,
then hum hers back. It was their duet. . . . They kept it running between them, up and down the stairs when I was now just about ready
to run clattering down and show them my shoes" (1). Hearing the talk
between parents offers the young Welty a feeling of protectedness and
a sense of the mystery of the marriage union. Too young even to know
"what to listen for" in the private conversation between her parents,
the child nearby in the "protected dark of the bed" is "free to listen
to every word" between the young pair. This provides Welty with a
profound feeling of mystery and belonging: "I was present in the room
with the chief secret there was—the two of them, father and mother,
sitting there as one. I was conscious of this secret and of my fast-beating
heart in step together" (*One Writer's Beginnings*, 21).

The theme in *One Writer's Beginnings* of shelter, protection, over-
protection, and eventual independence underscores important aspects
of Laurel's character in *The Optimist's Daughter* as well as of Welty's
own self-evaluation and education. Welty explains the safeguarding influence of her parents: "Of course it's easy to see why they both over-
protected me, why my father, before I could wear a new pair of shoes
for the first time, made me wait while he took out his thin silver pocket
knife and with the point of the blade scored and polished soles all over,
carefully, in a diamond pattern, to prevent me from sliding on the polished floor when I ran" (*One Writer's Beginnings*, 20–21). The result of
overprotecting, however, is increased desire for her own independence.
Yet at the same time, she explains, she felt guilty for that freedom, "for

I loved those who protected me—and I wanted inevitably to protect them back" (22).

The tension is central for growth in *The Optimist's Daughter*, and in maturing Laurel learns a balanced perspective of the two. In her adult marital relationship Laurel sees that mature love is significantly different from the "protected" parental love. Marriage leads Laurel to take risks, emotional risks, which inevitably coax her out of the safety of her former self. Until she marries Phil, Laurel conceives of love as "shelter; her arms went out as a naïve offer of safety" (161). But eventually Phil teaches Laurel a new kind of love. She learns that love only as shelter "need not be so. Protection, like self-protection, fell away from her like all one garment." She now views her naïve conceptions of love as "some anachronism foolishly saved from childhood."

What Welty suggests in *One Writer's Beginnings* about her own willingness to risk relationships echoes this section of the novel:

> I have always been shy physically. This in part tended to keep me from rushing into things, including relationships, headlong. Not rushing headlong, though I may have wanted to, but beginning to write stories about people, I drew near slowly: noting and guessing, apprehending, hoping, drawing my eventual conclusions out of my own heart, I *did* venture closer to where I wanted to go. As time and my imagination led me on, I did plunge. (*One Writer's Beginnings*, 21–22)

In the novel and autobiographical essays, confrontation with grief initiates the harsh passage to maturity. With the death of her parents and her own widowhood, Welty's character Laurel begins her dark night of the soul and her quest for understanding. Welty acknowledges the closeness of fiction here to her own life: "I would say it was my own inquiring mind that corresponds to the girl's in the novel" (Interview, July 21, 1988). In a long, meditative chapter, Laurel faces the past with its attendant loss. This third section of the novel opens with the words "Laurel faced the library." "Faced" is the key word as she prepares for her final confrontation with her memories of her family—now all deceased. As the night wanes, Laurel journeys downward into herself to meet head-on her memories of the dead.

Welty brings the theme of judgment and self-scrutiny to fruition in Laurel's moments of self-confrontation. Symbolic of her imprisonment within her own grief is the bird trapped in the house. Laurel needs to find and name her grief in order to "unburden" it. As if she, rather than her father, were the judge now, Laurel presents evidence that could convict Fay, her father's petty second wife, of the blame of this death. In her thoughts, Laurel finds Fay guilty of "assailing a helpless man": "I saw Fay come out into the open. Why it would stand up in court! Laurel thought, as she heard the bird beating against the door, and felt the house itself shake in the rainy wind. Fay betrayed herself. . . . She had the proof, the damnable evidence ready for her mother" (157). Though Laurel judges and convicts Fay, it is Laurel who receives the punishment. Laurel can present this evidence to no one, and she must endure the torment herself. Seeing no relief for her burden, she asks, "What would I not do, perpetrate, she wondered, for consolation?" (157).

Understanding and some consolation do come in both *The Optimist's Daughter* and *One Writer's Beginnings*. But in order to receive them, Laurel, the character, and Welty, the author, endure painful memories of a beloved family. Laurel "back[s] into" her mother's darkened sewing room (157) in a desperate attempt to recapture the feeling of protection and shelter she knew there as a child. The room is dark and cold now, and she can only reminisce about the warmth of former days:

> It was cold in here, as if there had been no fire all winter; there was only a grate, and it was empty, of course. . . . But it had been warm here, warm then. Laurel remembered her father's lean back as he sat on his haunches and spread a newspaper over the mouth of the chimney after he'd built the fire, so that the blaze caught with a sudden roar. Firelight and warmth—that was what her memory gave her. (158)

In her novel and autobiography, Welty combines images—blindness and knowing, memory and sight—recalling Faulkner's line in *Light in August*, "Memory sees what knowing remembers." Through memory, both Welty and her character Laurel are able to review the lives of the family and better understand the relationships among them. Welty explains in an interview that Laurel "may be mistaken in some things, but the whole story is a growth of her understanding. . . . I was writing with a passionate conviction on the part of one who is telling it that she was trying to get at the truth" (*Conversations*, 236).

The image of sightlessness recurs here as memory becomes the "somnambulist." In the autobiography, Welty provides her own gloss for this word, which reminds her of Conrad Veidt making his way in the dark, "seeing with his fingers" (*One Writer's Beginnings*, 36). In both books, confrontation with death and despair eventually leads to self-revelation, a moment when hindsight and perception reveal truth: "It was a focusing and a bringing together and revelation—self-revelation —when everything cleared for her. She realized a great many complicated things at once about herself and her parents and about Fay, all together" (*Conversations*, 237).

Hindsight is the key to comprehension in both works. In an interview, Welty says "I seem to come to understanding belatedly" (Interview, July 21, 1988). In *One Writer's Beginnings*, Welty explains that "as we discover; we remember; remembering, we discover; and most intensely do we experience this when our separate journeys converge" (102). The human memory, Welty adds, is "the treasure most dearly regarded by me, in my life and my work as a writer. . . . The memory is a living thing—it too is in transit. But during its moment, all that is remembered joins, and lives—the old and the young, the past and the present, the living and the dead" (104). Through memory, the living can pay tribute to the dead, can give them their due. Through memory, Laurel, and the author who created her, can remain close to the lost world of the past yet simultaneously be freed from it.

Welty's final optimism in her novel and autobiography depends upon several revelations: the sheltered life gives way to a daring one; strength emerges to bear pain alone; and the future becomes valuable without relinquishing the past. Welty's description of character applies equally to her self-insight; she knows "that there is a world that remains out there, a world living and mysterious, and that she is of it" (*One Writer's Beginnings*, 101). Images in the final lines of *The Optimist's Daughter* suggest freedom and regeneration of the heart: "Memory lived not in initial possession but in the freed hands, pardoned and freed, and in the heart that can empty but fill again" (208). The theme of judgment resolves—Laurel's long trial ends—she is pardoned and freed. Her final verdict is release.

Restoration of a sense of order pervades the last moments of the novel. The final paragraph is reminiscent of that in Faulkner's *The Sound and the Fury*, when Benjy at last rides around the courthouse square in the proper direction. On her journey out of town, Laurel "flashed by the Courthouse, turned at the school" (208). Each landmark is in its ordered place. Like Welty's father, who always looked to the future, Laurel finally turns her face toward tomorrow.

Welty's autobiographical works have been born from her self-acknowledged need "to know," to comprehend, to clarify. Of *The Optimist's Daughter* she says, "I did not undertake it for any therapeutic reason, because I don't believe in that kind of thing. I believe in really trying to comprehend something" (*Conversations*, 116). James Olney has written that "the great virtue of autobiography is . . . to offer us understanding that is finally not of someone else but of ourselves."[14] Writing about her life has led Welty to this self-comprehension: "But it was not until I began to write . . . that I found the world out there revealing because (as with my father now) memory had become attached to seeing, love had added itself to discovery, and because I recognized in my own continuing to keep going, the need I carried inside myself to know—the apprehension, first, and then the passion, to connect myself to it" (*One Writer's Beginnings*, 76). This "belated understanding" that Welty has found has afforded her what Brian Finney calls the "opportunity to pursue the truth about himself from within the self" (23).[15]

> It seems to me, writing of my parents now in my seventies, that I see continuities in their lives that weren't visible to me when they were living. Even at the times that have left me their most vivid memories of them, there were connections between them that escaped me. Could it be that I can better see their lives—or any lives I know—today because I am a fiction writer? See them not as fiction, certainly—see them perhaps, as even greater mysteries than I knew. (*One Writer's Beginnings*, 90)

Just as Laurel finds release from her "imprisonment" at the end of *The Optimist's Daughter*, Welty's autobiographical experiences afford her the self-confrontation that ultimately frees her: "Through learning at my later date things I hadn't known or had escaped or possibly feared recognizing, about myself—I glimpse our whole family life as if it were freed of that clock time which spaces us apart so inhibitingly, divides young and old, keeps us living through the same experiences at separate distances" (*One Writer's Beginnings*, 102). "Becoming a writer," Michael Kreyling points out, is becoming "free but not lost."[16]

For Welty, autobiography, like memory, preserves the past, rendering it "impervious" to the diminishment of time. Georges Gusdorf claims that autobiography has two functions—"to draw the meaning" from the writer's life and yet to become "itself a meaning in the life" of the writer.[17] His idea applies to Welty's fictional and her factual autobiographies, which draw meaning from her life for herself and her audience. These works fulfill what Welty believes to be the purpose of art: "To reveal us to ourselves." Of the act of writing autobiography Welty says, "It was so much fun putting my life together, so much enlightenment." She adds, "I advise everybody to do it" (Devlin and Prenshaw, "Conversation," 452).

Notes

Full bibliographical information will be given in a note at a work's first mention; thereafter, reference to that work will be made in the text.

1. *Conversations with Eudora Welty*, ed. Peggy Whitman Prenshaw (Jackson: University Press of Mississippi, 1984), 253.
2. Eudora Welty, *The Eye of the Story: Selected Essays and Reviews* (New York: Random House, 1979), 142.
3. Eudora Welty, *One Writer's Beginnings* (Cambridge: Harvard University Press), 76.
4. Peggy Whitman Prenshaw, "Two Jackson Excursions," *Eudora Welty Newsletter* 2 (Winter 1978): 3–4.
5. Paul Eakins, *Fictions in Autobiography: Studies in the Art of Self-Invention* (Princeton, N.J.: Princeton University Press, 1985), 5.
6. Floyd C. Watkins, "The Journey to Baltimore in *The Optimist's Daughter*," *Mississippi Quarterly* 38 (Fall 1985): 435.
7. Albert Devlin and Peggy Whitman Prenshaw, "A Conversation with Eudora Welty," *Mississippi Quarterly* 39 (Fall 1986): 452.
8. Terrence Rafferty, "Articles of Faith," *New Yorker*, May 16, 1988, 113.
9. Eudora Welty, Speech at the Inaugural Symposium of Governor William Winter, January 21, 1980, Eudora Welty Collection, Mississippi Archives, Jackson, Miss.
10. Eudora Welty, *The Optimist's Daughter* (New York: Random House, 1969), 109.
11. Floyd C. Watkins, "Notes from the Trip to Welty Country," now on reserve in the Special Collections Department, Woodruff Library, Emory University, Atlanta, Ga.

12. Floyd C. Watkins, "Death and the Mountains in *The Optimist's Daughter*," *Essays in Literature* 15 (Spring 1988): 78.

13. Eudora Welty, Interview with Author, Jackson, Miss., July 21, 1988. To be published under title of "Some Talk About Autobiography" in the *Southern Review*.

14. James Olney, *Metaphors of Self: The Meaning of Autobiography* (Princeton, N.J.: Princeton University Press, 1972), x.

15. Brian Finney, "Factual Accounts of the Self," in *The Inner I: British Literary Autobiography of the Twentieth Century* (New York: Oxford University Press, 1985).

16. Michael Kreyling, "Subject and Object in *One Writer's Beginnings*," *Mississippi Quarterly* 39 (Fall 1986): 637.

17. George Gusdorf, "Conditions and Limits of Autobiography," in *Autobiography: Essays Theoretical and Critical*, ed. James Olney (Princeton, N.J.: Princeton University Press), 43.

Healing the Woman Within

Therapeutic Aspects of
Ellen Glasgow's Autobiography

MARILYN R. CHANDLER

I n the introduction to his autobiographical work, *Montauk*, Max
Frisch writes that the work was "a kind of therapy accompanying
the acceptance of my own life."[1] Frisch's explanation of his autobiographical impulse is typical of an overwhelming number of modern
autobiographers who have undertaken to record their life stories as a
form of self-therapy. Many writers regard the therapeutic dimension
of autobiographical writing as its justification. Anaïs Nin attributed her
whole writing career to a therapeutic initiative, calling her writing a
"necessary part of living," a habit acquired during a sickly adolescence
when writing became "a way of learning to live."[2] As Nin traced the
therapeutic core of her autobiographical impulse to the beginning of
her career, so Carl Jung discovered anew the healing properties of writing in the autobiography he began in old age—a work that he at first
resisted writing, but ultimately found to be indispensible to his own
well-being: "It has become a necessity for me to write down my early
memories. If I neglect to do so for a single day, unpleasant physical
symptoms immediately follow. As soon as I set to work they vanish and
my head feels perfectly clear."[3]

Ellen Glasgow's autobiography, *The Woman Within*, resembles these others as a therapeutic enterprise. Written at intervals over the last ten years of her life, a period of descent into "mortal illness," it chronicles a career but also, and perhaps more importantly for her, a lifelong struggle with debilitating physical illness and mental anguish. The narrative both relates and enacts an emergence from and triumph over conditions that had drained her energies, threatened her physical and mental health, and driven her to shut out most of the world that she believed incapable of understanding or helping her to bear her fate. After forty years of writing novels that indirectly addressed the profoundly personal issues that dominated her life and thought, she undertook to treat those issues directly and candidly and, laying aside her habitual masks of detachment and diplomacy, to commit her secrets to writing before she died. It was a way of setting the record straight. It was also a way of purging her soul of the sorrows that had festered there and healing the "wound in the soul" that lay beneath the smooth facade of technical mastery.[4]

The personal issues paramount in the autobiography cannot be understood, however, without reference to some of the ways in which they analogously reiterate cultural issues she defined as peculiarly southern. Again and again in Glasgow's work one finds evidence of a belief in the historical contingency of the self. Explicit analogies are drawn between the self and the South, both suffering from conditions of chronic ambivalence about identity, both suffering from the effects of exaggerated gender polarities, both caught between acceptance and denial of the terms of strict Calvinism and Victorianism, and both victims of misunderstanding by "outsiders." Being "inside" the South, like being inside her own body, affected this "woman within" as a species of ambiguous entrapment, and the insularity she describes as having characterized her intellectual and spiritual life is repeated in her portrayals of southern culture as a phenomenon unto itself, easily misunderstood from without. Like Edith Wharton, who identified with the insularities of her native New York even as she scathingly satirized them, Glasgow could claim on the one hand, "I am a Virginian in every drop of my blood and pulse of my heart," while on the other hand staging a revolt against the ladylike traditions represented by her mother, "a perfect flower of the Tidewater, in Virginia," and her father's local brand of Scottish Calvinism.[5]

The ambivalence she felt toward these indigenous styles of existence is reiterated in numerous aspects of her life. She was ambivalent toward marriage, which she generally depicted as an institution that promised a high romantic destiny but doomed women to exquisite suffering, and toward sexuality, cherishing heroic notions of romantic partnership that inevitably resulted in disillusionment. Her attitude toward religion was similarly two-sided; as her biographer, Marcelle Thiébaux, points out: "She intellectually renounced orthodox religion, yet she felt she was a believer in her heart."[6]

If one is willing to consider the notion of illness as metaphor, or at least as a symbolic response to and somatic record of certain kinds of psychic pressures, Glasgow's migraines, particularly, seem a logical response to the experience of living with chronic conflicting pressures. Her mind was a battleground, her sense of boundary between internal and external worlds acute, and her periodic social "secessions" dramatized and emphasized by the complete isolation the headaches enforced. The sense of the self as a battleground is a metaphor frequently employed by migraine victims attempting to describe the sensations generated by the total psychosomatic experience. In her passionate identification with the South and especially with Virginia (the name of one of her more autobiographical heroines in her 1913 novel, *Virginia*), Glasgow had available to her a ready source of metaphors of the self and a way of understanding bodily life that gave it a symbolic importance as an enactment of a communal fate. Her strategies for coping with physical illness serve, among other things, to illuminate her ways of coming to terms with living in a South she cherished in its uniqueness even as she vehemently resisted the appellation of "southern" or "regional" writer, wanting to be understood as a scholar of human nature. Both involve rather insistent intellectualization of experience, a habit of careful denial, and a certain refined defensiveness that expressed itself as a posture of dignity.

In a letter left with the manuscript of her autobiography, Glasgow wrote to her literary executors, "My memoirs may not be worth publishing. I do not know. It may be the part of wisdom to put the manuscript aside, in some safe place, to await the uncertain future. But do not destroy it. I was writing for my own release of mind and heart."[7] "Release" is a word whose meaning becomes clearer as one reads *The Woman*

Within; images of imprisonment abound in this story of a woman whose will to live contended for most of her seventy-two years with nervous disorders, migraine headaches, seriously low blood pressure, and an acute susceptibility to infection that made her a victim of a multitude of diseases. She suffered most of her adult life from a gradual hardening of the Eustachian tubes that resulted in deafness. Not only the encroaching deafness itself but also the self-imposed strain of concealing it in public plagued her constantly. Upon realizing, after visits to many specialists, that the condition was irreversible, she began to build a "wall of deceptive gaiety" around herself, deliberately cultivating "the ironic mood, the smiling pose, which I have held, without a break or a change, for almost forty years" (139). All of her most constant afflictions —nightmares, depressions, headaches, and deafness—are described in similar terms: as experiences of entrapment behind walls that close in pain and terror, from behind which there is no escape. The autobiography, by detailing these afflictions with uncharacteristic candor, seems to provide a long-awaited form of release from behind those constraining walls of irony and gaiety, which she ultimately realized were themselves impediments to healing.

Throughout the narrative the vocabulary of pain is consistent. The literal and the metaphorical merge in descriptions of inner conflicts translated into bodily suffering; intense emotional responses to the events of her life were consistently accompanied by physical pain. She describes frequent sensations of extreme pressure from within and without; searing and burning, especially of nerves and skin; pounding "into the ears" and in the head; shrinking and recoiling; creeping chills and blackness. Her body is a barrier and an enclosure, invaded and overtaken by noise and painful sensation, and her head a place filled with unbidden images and encroached upon by pressure and pain moving upward from the viscera along the spine. Much of this language matches classic descriptions of migraine, in which pain is variously recorded as hammering, throbbing, pressing, bursting, stretching, rending, and radiating and its progression through the body as an invading force.[6] The connections Glasgow traces between these physical symptoms and the social and psychological "pressures from without and within" that produced them reveal this autobiography to be not only an act of intricate self-diagnosis but also a therapeutic gesture—an antidote to sicknesses rooted in chronic tension, isolation, silencing, fear, and self-division.

The narrative opens with an account of a recurrent waking nightmare first experienced in infancy and that serves as a key to the character that unfolds in the succeeding chapters:

> Beyond the top windowpanes, in the midst of a red glow, I see a face without a body staring in at me, a vacant face, round, pallid, grotesque, malevolent. Terror—or was it merely sensation?—stabbed me into consciousness. Terror of the sinking sun? Or terror of the formless, the unknown, the mystery, terror of life, of the world, of nothing or everything? Convulsions seized me, a spasm of dumb agony. One minute, I was not: the next minute, I was. I felt. I was separate. I could be hurt. I had discovered myself. And I had discovered, too, the universe apart from myself.
>
> This is my earliest impression: a face without a body hanging there in the sunset, beyond the top windowpanes. All the rest comes in fragments. I scream; I struggle; but my screams and my struggles tell them nothing. I cannot, even now, divide the aftergrowth from the recollection. Only one thing remains, unaltered and vivid as fear: a bodiless apparition, distorted, unreal, yet more real to me than either myself or the world. (3–4)

This bodiless face reappears at intervals as a symbol of Glasgow's most basic sense of life: that the ground of awareness is suffering and inarticulate terror and that there is no guarantee of being heard or understood. For this child, to feel often meant to feel pain. To be heard was often to be misunderstood. Her mother and nurse, who on this occasion heard her cries, could not interpret them and were therefore powerless to relieve her agony. This is her first lesson in communication. In light of this original scene of terror and isolation, it is not surprising that she later says of her urge to write, "I was consumed with the longing to write and the will to be heard" (106). The dream vision prefigures a pattern of seeing the outer world from behind a barrier she is powerless to dissolve. She sees from a place within walls that is virtually inaccessible to another human being. "When I was very small," she writes, "much of my time was spent at the windows, where I could watch, a little wistfully, other and more robust children at play in the street" (7). And she recalls that during her headaches she was closed in a darkened room, listening to the sounds outside, "where other children, children without headaches, without nerves, without fears, children who neither dreamed dreams nor saw visions, were playing my favorite 'Fox in the Warner'" (50).

This chronic sense of exclusion led to a radical separation of inner and outer worlds, inner and outer voices. "Even in childhood," she writes, "my soul was a battleground for hostile forces of character, for obscure mental and emotional antagonisms" (16). This, too, matches a classic, though not thoroughly proven, characteristic of migraine victims: they are often people who struggle with chronic and profound ambivalence to the point of sensing themselves as split personalities. Thiébaux has observed that "much of what Glasgow wrote about herself stresses her divided spirit. . . . Fascinated by her own genealogy, for which she gathered voluminous notes, she thought of her personality as split from conception."[9] This last notion Glasgow explained quite specifically as an having inherited "a long conflict of types," her father a Scottish Calvinist and her mother "a perfect flower of the Tidewater, in Virginia."[10]

The sense of self as a locus of conflict played itself out in the pounding headaches that invaded and usurped her body, moving from viscera to brain like an alien force. One account of a headache suffered shortly after starting school—a place where her shyness and fear of self-exposure were particularly acute—conveys the experience vividly:

> A black chill was creeping up my spine and into my thoughts, a chill I learned afterwards to associate with my few school days and my bleak endeavor to acquire a systematic education. . . . [Later] I felt a chill crawling up my spine, like a beetle. Sickness, black and chill, attacked the pit of my stomach, and all the stamping feet and treble voices coming closer were stabbing down into my ears, into my throbbing head. It was the beginning of one of my nervous headaches, and a cold sweat broke out while I struggled not to disgrace myself by throwing up before my natural enemies. (47)

Glasgow's education thereafter was intermittent and asystematic. Her real learning took place in self-imposed solitude and even secrecy. "Always I have had to learn for myself, from within," she writes. The drive to read and write in fact became at times another form of possession, leading her to seclude herself for long hours in study from which she frequently emerged racked with pain. "I wrote always in secret," she recalls, "but I wrote ceaselessly in dim corners, under beds, or, in the blessed summer days, under the deep shrubbery and beneath low-hanging boughs. Until my first book was finished no one, except my mother, who suspected but did not speak of it, was aware that, below the animated surface, I was already immersed in some dark stream of identity, stronger and deeper and more relentless than the external movement of living" (41). At this point in her life, writing was a means both of self-identification and of escape from self—a source of control exercised in growing mastery of language and a way of escaping the stringent moral and social controls she internalized in a self-destructive manner.

These habits of secrecy and solitude, which ultimately proved enormously artistically fruitful, were grounded in fears of which she never quite broke free. Fear is an emotion often associated with the onset of the sort of headaches described above—a "pressure from within" that expressed itself as pain. On such occasions fear and pain become a vicious circle: the sensation of entrapment in a body that has become a hostile environment is itself frightening, and the claustrophobic feelings it generates heighten the tension that produces pain.

The vocabulary in which she describes her emotional life is full of sensational and hyperbolic terms: terror, torture, anguish, tragedy. She manages to avoid the melodrama such terms suggest by means of precise clinical descriptions that detail those emotions and their effects in a manner oddly and paradoxically detached from their subject. This stance of detachment was a habit of long standing that she maintained in public and on paper until in her autobiography she began to attempt to reunite the woman without and the woman within. The text of the autobiography betrays lingering ambivalence about giving up that protective distance. The narrative voice is uneven—at times fully and sympathetically engaged with the self being described, at other times clinical and impassive. What we can discern in that complex voice is a woman who recognizes her strengths as weaknesses. She was as disciplined and even stubborn as she was frail and nervous; her will was as strong as her constitution was weak. That very determination to self-conquest was both her greatest strength and the source of her afflictions; her inability to relax, to be open to the world, to receive compassion and let go of her defensive striving, created an inner environment of acute tension that both shaped and disciplined her fiction and produced in her body entrenched patterns of pain.

These pressures from within were exacerbated by equal and opposite pressures from without, mostly in the form of the demands of a stringently Calvinistic father and a social life from which she "recoiled" in acute shyness, "shrinking within herself" to escape the humiliations to which her deafness, she felt, exposed her, though the place into which she shrank was not always a haven. Recounting a period of particularly intense reading as well as continuing headaches, she describes her studies of philosophy as an attempt to adjust to "a world I had found hostile and even malign." "How could one live," she goes on, "without a meaning in life? Fortitude alone was not enough to support life" (89). Her urgent pursuit of truth in philosophy and science was an extension and manifestation of the conflicting pressures of the need to believe and the inability to believe in the severe God her father had taught his children to fear: the wrathful Jehovah of the Old Testament. "I hated the prayers and the hymns," she writes, "and the red images that colored their drab music, the fountains filled with blood, the sacrifice of the lamb" (72). In the months following her mother's death, when she was suffering from headaches for which doctors prescribed the infamous "rest cure," her father was subjecting her, as she put it, to a "minor religious persecution," which consisted of pleas, threats, and arguments aimed at curtailing her reading of Gibbon and Darwin and persuading her to return to church services. When she was surprised one day with one of the forbidden books, she writes, "there was at first rebuke, then moral suasion, and, after that, since milder methods had proved futile, righteous rage stormed about me" (92). These tactics, amounting in effect to psychological abuse, intensified her inner drive to find truth and cling to it. Glasgow expended her limited energies in this period searching for a certainty strong enough to sustain her in combat with the misguided moral certitudes of her father and the righteous orthodox around her. Plaintively she writes at the end of this chapter, "Search for Truth," "And all the time, if only they had suspected it, I needed God more than they needed Him, and, in my own rebellious way, I was trying to find Him" (93). It is no wonder that in the face of such conflicts she developed a permanent posture of irony toward most things that threatened to hurt her.

To Glasgow's mind the greatest of these threats was her worsening deafness. She writes with remarkable candor about the half century she spent resisting and denying and finally succumbing to its effects. She describes the humiliation it entailed as her greatest suffering during her young adult years; the numerous other sufferings she describes give some measure of the magnitude of this fear, as does her recollection of a scene of childhood humiliation: "My skin felt naked and scorched, as if a flame had blown over it" (37). In the chapter devoted to the progress of her deafness, "The Shadow of the Wall," she recalls Hamlin Garlin's puzzlement over her apparent unease in conversation. "What he did not discern," she writes, "was my agonizing tension because his voice was not clear enough for me to understand what he said," and she goes on to explain, "For my sensitive shyness, my fear of betraying an affliction was, in itself, an incurable malady" (137).

The author recounts her fruitless pilgrimages to specialists in search of a cure and comments upon the moment of finally conceding defeat: "Science had failed my body as ruinously as religion had failed my soul" (138). Thereafter she felt herself to be once again alone, thrown upon her own spiritual resources. The vast reserves of energy and creativity that produced her many novels and finally the autobiography came, by her account, from an irresistible and driving need. She describes her urge to write in terms that suggest that it was a compensation for the many parts of life she could not experience directly. She made her imprisonment "behind the wall" into an asset and came to believe that it gave her a privileged vantage point from which to contemplate human nature, though most often the nature she contemplated was, in fact, her own. Her belief that writing was her call and destiny was doubtless the stronger because into that belief she poured the conviction that might otherwise have been channeled toward religion or science. She knew, with increasing certainty, that she could write and had to write. It was, she believed, her destiny. The autobiography accomplishes a final act of self-assertion, justification, apology, and healing for the wounded spirit portrayed so vividly in its pages. Partly because of the isolation that deafness imposed, partly because of her other hypersensitivities, and partly because of her complex intellect, which rarely met a peer in genteel Victorian Richmond, Glasgow felt herself for most of her life to be quite alone among people who would not or could not read what she read, sympathize with what she thought, or help her in her lonely life of the mind. She described this solitude both as her natural and happiest state and, at other times, as wretched isolation.

Some of the isolation was real. Her mother died when she was an adolescent, and in young adulthood she witnessed the untimely deaths of her favorite brother and sister and of a man she passionately loved. In each of these four intimates, the only people in whom she felt sufficient trust to let her mask of "irony and gaiety" drop, she felt she had lost a rare and irretrievable confidant; intimacy did not come easily to her, and each loss deepened her sense of aloneness in the world. After their deaths she found the past intolerable and at the same time inescapable. Later and lesser relationships are treated as far less important or authentic. Her "real life" had already been lived. Those formative intimacies had given her a standard of measurement against which all other companionship was found wanting. Perhaps for that reason the anonymous audience of the aging autobiographer was the final confidant of choice—the final ear into which she could pour the sorrows of a lifetime and hope for understanding.

Glasgow often described her writing as a refuge. In it she found escape from a claustrophobic personal world to the realm of the impersonal and imagined, from isolation to a kind of safe intimacy, and from fear of censure to the presumed sympathy of an ideal reader. She educated herself as a writer with little instruction or encouragement beyond her own wide reading. In doing so she fought more than the chronic headaches and nervous fatigue; her scholarly and literary inclinations worried her family and physician, and they did their best in the early years of her self-styled career to dissuade her from serious effort. The subterfuge and at times simple rebellion required to resist her father's efforts to censor her reading and curtail her writing further burdened her limited resources of energy.

Her early novels feature young women artists or writers in the throes of conflicting allegiances to love and to work, driven to crisis and at some points sickness by the conflicting roles of female life. In several obvious ways these women are psychological self-portraits, created during Glasgow's own period of adjustment to New York life, with its bewildering and often threatening liberties. The men in these novels tend, as Thiébaux points out, to be heavy-handedly ideological, reflecting an aspect of herself that Glasgow clearly derived from male mentors and associated with masculinity.[11] By her third novel she established a pattern of viewing many social and psychological conflicts as gender-based. She betrayed on numerous occasions attitudes bordering on contempt for what she characterized as the female, though equally often she expressed a kind of wistful admiration of the idealized "Old Southern" notions of femininity, personified in a generation of women rapidly passing, and viewed herself as bridging a generational gap that had much to do with shifting gender identification.

In her later "Virginia novels," which depict the life of post–Civil War Virginia in long family sagas, Glasgow seems to have projected her personal conflicts onto a wide social canvas. Her claim to be a Virginian down to the last drop of her blood suggests how profoundly she identified with her region and people, as elsewhere she reveals the extent to which she thought in terms of social types and of herself as both atypical and prototypical. In these social-historical novels, the intra- and interfamilial conflicts among the characters act out in epic and dramatic fashion familiar personal themes: the tensions between the sexes, in which it seems inevitable that one gain ascendancy at the other's expense, the defeated party often sinking into sickness, death, or despair; conflicts between work and love; the disillusionments of marriage; the costs of survival. In this last may be seen the fundamental question underlying many of Glasgow's novels: what does it take to survive? The answer is not encouraging. Survivors are often joyless, having endured at the price of all optimism or idealism and having largely lost their capacity for human pleasure, though she often provides some redemptive moment at the end. Publication of these novels was a matter of enormous urgency with her; her hunger for recognition rivaled Gertrude Stein's notorious drive to self-advertisement. Her evangelical didacticism comes at some points to seem a thinly disguised outcry for a hearing.

Her autobiography was the only work that Glasgow did not avidly seek to publish. She enclosed it in an envelope and later a strongbox, with instructions to her executors to publish it if they saw fit. This reflects a characteristic hesitancy to reveal herself unmasked—a hesitation that had always ironically competed with strong introspective and expressive tendencies. She claims at one point, where her memories become difficult to confront, "it is more than difficult to write, literally, of those years. Yet no honest story of my life could be told without touching upon them, and the only reason for this memoir is the hope that it may shed some beam of light, however faint, into the troubled darkness of human psychology" (161). In fact, it is her own psychology that occupies her throughout, but she typically couches that preoccupation in terms of a quest for something more universal. Even in autobiography, focus upon the self is mitigated by a desire to depersonalize, a desire rooted perhaps in a feeling that such unmasking was a dangerous and questionable business. The "woman within" still needed protection and validation.

Glasgow's abiding interest in philosophy and later in psychology as systematic ways of describing and confronting the human condition provides an important context for reading the autobiography. What she seeks in these disciplines is always intimately and directly related to her own "wounds" and her own yearnings. The resistance to the auto-biographical that in one sense characterized her whole career belied a profound autobiographical urge, which can best be understood as a longing to break out from behind the wall that hid and intensified her pain and thus to reunite the woman within and the woman without and make herself whole. This is clearly the project underlying the autobiog-raphy, though it is accomplished by means of a curiously ambiguous narrative strategy that itself sets up polarities and tensions between the "inner" and "outer" perspectives.

The chapters of the autobiography alternate between intensely per-sonal accounts of episodes in her inner life (mostly a chronicle of the struggle against pain, grief, disillusionment, and despair) and oddly san-guine accounts of events (publication, travel, acquaintances, reading) —a polarity that graphically reflects her divided sense of herself. Each of these latter, however, leads her back to the interior and to a private past that she declares "inescapable." The term suggests concession to something she has in fact tried unsuccessfully to escape. The somewhat interrupted momentum that this alternation of focus effects is reminis-cent of a remark that Christa Wolf made about her own autobiography: that it is like "driving with one foot on the brake," is an entry into the past that one both dreads and longs for, knowing it will bring pain and knowing also that that pain will be the beginning of healing.

Another odd feature of Glasgow's narrative is the frequent elliptical closures. Three dots conclude many sections of the text, as though, after all, what needed saying could not quite be said. Moreover, she ends a number of chapters with the corrective "but I'm running too far ahead." She seems uncomfortably constrained by chronology, somewhat com-pulsively bound to the stringencies of sequential form yet equally im-pelled to break out of it and view her life from an atemporal, panoramic, philosophical perspective. She keeps herself from ever quite doing so, and the noticeable effort strikes the reader as a half-deliberate way of protecting herself from being overwhelmed—a strategy that mirrors the life strategies she records.

Glasgow had, overwhelmingly, a "tragic sense of life"; the word "tragic" comes up repeatedly in her descriptions of the lives and sensibilities of her closest family members. She describes her own sensibility as a child as "rendered morbid by physical pain" and heightened by repeated shocks of bereavement. She asks, when recounting the death of her most beloved sister, "Was I never to have a breathing space while I lived? Was my whole life to be smothered in tragedy?" (193). Her novels and ultimately her autobiography offered her such a breathing space—a release into action and realization of a strong, convinced, and convincing voice that could and did find sympathetic hearers. A book was literally a space she entered for final refuge; she describes the simultaneous works of her final novel and her autobiography as "the topmost block in my building."

Alfred Kazin once wrote of the autobiographical impulse, "We write to make a home for ourselves, on paper." Of no writer is this more true than of Ellen Glasgow. And the sorrows that were the material of narrative seem finally to have been purged, shaped, and transformed into a medium of strength and peace. On the final page of the autobiography, she reflects, "In the life of the mind, glad or sad, there will always be laughter, and the life of the mind alone, I have found, contains an antidote to experience" (296).

Notes

1. Max Frisch, *Montauk* (New York: Harcourt Brace Jovanovich, 1976), i.
2. Anaïs Nin, "The Personal Life Deeply Lived," in *The American Autobiography*, ed. Albert E. Stone (Englewood Cliffs, N.J.: Prentice-Hall, 1981), 161.
3. Carl Jung, *Memories, Dreams, and Reflections* (New York: Random House, 1963), vii–viii.
4. Ellen Glasgow, *The Woman Within* (New York: Harcourt Brace and World, 1954; New York: Hill and Wang, American Century Series, 1980); hereafter, references to this work are cited in the text.
5. "The Dynamic Past," *The Reviewer* (March 15, 1921), 73–80; *The Letters*

of Ellen Glasgow, ed. Blair Rouse (New York: Harcourt Brace and World, 1958), 329, letter of August 14, 1945 to Signe Toksvig.

6. Marcelle Thiébaux, *Ellen Glasgow* (New York: Frederick Ungar, 1982), 11.

7. Glasgow, preface, *The Woman Within,* v.

8. Oliver Sacks, *Migraine* (Berkeley: University of California Press, 1985), 14.

9. Thiébaux, *Ellen Glasgow,* 11.

10. *Letters,* 329.

11. Thiébaux, *Ellen Glasgow,* 32.

Autobiography in
Southern Journalism

ROY REED

The outcome of the civil rights movement in the South might well
have been different had the journalism of the South been different. A small group of white liberals in the region's leading newspapers
exercised large influence. They were the opinion molders whose columns, editorials, and bold reporting went against the conservative tide
and, to a great extent, prevailed. These journalists, working alongside
other men and women of similar convictions on both sides of the racial
divide, helped to bring the South through the greatest upheaval of our
time and into the American mainstream. Some would say that they also
helped to create the upheaval. I would not dispute that.

What kinds of men were these liberal journalists? (I use the word
"men" quite deliberately; virtually all the people at the top of southern journalism at that time were men.) What history motivated them?
Where did their loyalties lie?

To try to answer these questions, I have perused the autobiographical writings of several leading southern journalists of the mid-twentieth
century. I have narrowed the field to three whose work began before
World War II and extended into the civil rights era. All three were at
work before the movement began in the 1950s. One is still writing.

There was also a personal consideration in my selection. I was acquainted with all three. They were my first heroes in the newspaper business. One was my boss.

To restate the larger question: what is the relevance of autobiography from journalists? What difference does it make in the civil rights story or any other?

The answer lies in something beyond simple curiosity. There is a growing interest among Americans in the people who report and comment on the news that affects them and their country. A study a few years ago suggested that most of the top American journalists are well-to-do white men of liberal bias. I was suspicious of that finding. A more recent study has cast serious doubt on its conclusions. But aside from that, Americans have a legitimate interest in knowing who their messengers are. The same impulse makes us curious about those who bore the message during the turbulence of the 1950s and 1960s.

Autobiography does not appear in the writing of most of the southern journalists of that period. The tradition in modern American journalism is that of the anonymous reporter. Few people outside the newspaper business were ever aware that the reporting that won the *Arkansas Gazette* a Pulitzer Prize in 1957, when Central High School was desegregated, was mainly the work of two faceless young men, Ray Moseley and Jerry Dhonau. They were driven to the streets and back to the typewriter every day by a faceless city editor named Bill Shelton. Mr. Shelton retired from full-time work at the *Gazette* in 1988. Mr. Moseley is now a distinguished foreign correspondent for the *Chicago Tribune*. Mr. Dhonau is the editor of the editorial page of the *Gazette*. None of the three, to my knowledge, has ever inserted his personal biography onto the printed page. Except for their friends, few know anything about these men.

And yet even the anonymous reporter tells much of himself. He reveals his fears, yearnings, and ideals every day by what and how he reports and by what he chooses to ignore. In that sense, all of us in journalism engage in autobiography. But I am interested here in the more overt revelations of the three men whom I consider to be the most influential liberal journalists in the South during the fascinating time when I came of age. They are Ralph McGill, Hodding Carter, Jr., and Harry S. Ashmore.

Ralph McGill was known to millions, friends and enemies, through his front-page column in the *Atlanta Constitution*. He carried the title of publisher, but his real influence was in his writing. Day after day, he preached racial justice from the pulpit of page one of the *Constitution*. His enemies called him Rastus McGill. His friends called him a prophet. Mr. McGill died in 1969.

Hodding Carter, Jr., owned and edited the *Delta Democrat-Times* in Greenville, Mississippi. His young band of reporters covered all the news, and that in itself would have been enough to drive the Delta society to a frenzy; black people were not supposed to make news in those days. But it was Mr. Carter's acid editorials that enraged the conservative whites of Mississippi and the South and that made him into a national voice for that other, more tolerant South. Unlike Mr. McGill, who tended to turn the other cheek, Mr. Carter loved a fight. He died in 1972.

Harry S. Ashmore was a South Carolinian who made his name in Arkansas. He edited the proud, family-owned *Arkansas Gazette*, the oldest newspaper west of the Mississippi. When Governor Orval E. Faubus scotched the desegregation of Central High in 1957, Mr. Ashmore lashed back in the *Gazette*'s editorials. Some people credit his editorials, almost as much as Mr. Faubus's resistance, with prodding President Dwight D. Eisenhower into intervening to uphold the rule of law in what was probably the gravest constitutional crisis of the civil rights era. Mr. Ashmore is still alive and still at work.

What can we learn of these three journalists from their own words? Each wrote books, and those books are rich with autobiographical material. Typically, the personal notes and narratives are used to make a larger point in the context of the stories they are telling. From these anecdotal jottings, we learn the following.

Ralph McGill first saw a Negro when he was five or six years old. He spent his first years on a farm in eastern Tennessee. The farm was six hundred acres and had a big barn—significant details in the hill country. His family moved to Chattanooga when he was six. His father worked as a salesman. The McGills were never hungry, but money was not plentiful. Education was prized; the children were urged to read and study. The Civil War, the great divider of the nation, had also divided the boy's family. He grew up hearing tales of ancestors who had fought on both sides. That was common throughout the upland South, where slavery was not dominant. McGill's older relatives were mainly Republicans—Lincoln Republicans. Young McGill liked Lincoln and disliked Jefferson Davis. There was a coal-mine owner among his uncles, but one of his heroes was John L. Lewis, the stormy leader of the United Mine Workers union.

Hodding Carter, Jr., came from the landed class of southern Louisiana. A great-great-grandfather had moved to New Orleans from Kentucky, made a fortune, and invested in huge tracts of land in Tangipahoa Parish, north of the city. When Hodding was born in 1907, his father was one of the most substantial landowners in the area. There was no dichotomy in the Carter family on the subject of the War Between the States; they were all Confederates, and most were slave owners. One family story glorified the original Ku Klux Klan for saving southern culture from the Yankee Reconstruction. Mr. Carter recalled that he applauded wildly at the movie *Birth of a Nation*, a pro-Klan film, in 1916. The young journalist's first political fight was against Huey P. Long. Long won, and the Carters moved to Mississippi. He recalls never feeling like an outsider in the Delta because he and his family were taken in and sheltered and given credibility by the Percy family, the reigning aristocrats of that region.

Harry Ashmore's clan in South Carolina produced large numbers of shopkeepers and local politicians but no people of wealth. He is careful to point out the absence of aristocratic stock. They were Scotch-Irish. They had migrated twice in two centuries, first from lowland Scotland to Ulster, then on to the United States. The established and well-to-do of the clan had no reason to migrate. Only the have-nots were motivated to pick up and move on. His father was a moderately successful small businessman who was ruined by the Great Depression. His mother, like Thomas Wolfe's, took in boarders. Young Ashmore had a paper route. He grew up as a natural aspirant to the middle class. His people were hustlers, risers, optimists, given to strong opinion and strong drink. He heard the usual Confederate war stories as a boy and grew up with the customary racial opinions of the place and time: "My relatives considered white supremacy a fact of life." He also remembers being whipped by his mother for using the word "nigger" in front of a servant. On the central question: "I had been conditioned to accept inequality as the natural order, and I did not then equate it with injustice."

It is apparent that Carter, McGill, and Ashmore were products of their time, class, family, and religion as well as their common region.

Their common attitude toward race, which came together in one cause as the civil rights struggle began, stemmed from quite different backgrounds. There was no common moral distillery that inspirited their adult lives.

McGill and Carter, for example, show quite striking differences in their views of the Civil War and Reconstruction, as brought into their consciousnesses through the stories of their older kinfolk. Carter heard lurid tales of Reconstruction from a grandmother. She had sewed her husband's Ku Klux Klan robes. She once upbraided young Carter for presuming to derogate the Klan at a family dinner. For at least one modern observer, John T. Kneebone, the author of *Southern Liberal Journalists and the Issue of Race, 1920–1944,* Carter's family demonstrated the truth of some historians' observation that Jim Crow was seen at the time as a form of moderation—a way of keeping order. Kneebone asserts that the southern liberals of the 1920s and 1930s grew out of a tradition of believing in the rightness of segregation and in the inherent inferiority of the Negro. The corollary to this thinking, according to Kneebone, was a liberal belief in noblesse oblige, a notion that decent whites were obligated to take care of the Negroes and make them into good citizens, even though they were believed to be inferior in capacity.

It is easy to see the roots of such a belief in Mr. Carter's background. Noblesse oblige was certainly the prevailing rule among the "better" people of his time and place. What Kneebone's assertion leaves out is the possibility that Carter might have grown far beyond his upbringing. My personal belief, from close observation of the man and his Mississippi place, is that his later racial attitudes were governed by a combination of educated enlightenment (he studied at Colby College in Maine) and the paternalism that he learned as a boy. For all his enlightenment, Mr. Carter was never disloyal to his family and class. For example, his personal mentions of the Civil War in his writing made little reference to the reasons for the war. From the prejudice of my own hillbilly perspective, those reasons had to include the willfulness of the planters and the arrogance of the southern moneyed class. In his own time, Mr. Carter tended to ascribe the antiblack violence to the hatreds and jealousies of the white trash, although he was willing to credit the segregationist politicians with prodding those resentments into flames and to suggest with some regularity that those politicians were themselves trash.

Mr. McGill's background was southern but not at all like Mr. Carter's. Young McGill admired his ancestors on both sides of the Civil War, but he had no sympathy for the men who, in his view, had started it. His account of the beginning of the war in *The South and the Southerner* leaves no doubt as to its causes. Slavery, he said, was a dying institution until the cotton gin was invented. "Then had come the cry from the planters, 'Let us and our property alone.'" One consequence of McGill's upbringing was a deeply held egalitarianism. What sometimes looked like paternalism in Carter's editorials came across as simple respect for fellow human beings in McGill's columns.

Ashmore, a few years younger than the other two, occupied in terms of his background a middle position between Carter and McGill. There were plantations in his South Carolina family, but mainly there were petit bourgeois townspeople and upland farmers. He heard the Civil War stories, and he took for granted his family's view of the Negro. But his adult view of the Negro in history was a little broader than that of either of his colleagues. He wrote in *Hearts and Minds* of his growing recognition of the historical place of the blacks he grew up with. "They were my people—not in any proprietary sense left over from slavery, not in obeisance to some romantic notion of noblesse oblige, not in subliminal acknowledgment that our blood lines may very well have mingled, but in recognition of the inescapable entanglement of shared history and common experience. I still cannot imagine the South that gave me my identity without the pervasive black presence."

Some of the most revealing autobiography in the writings of Carter, McGill, and Ashmore is in their accounts of personal relationships with blacks. Each of the three has a story of a black male who was important to him in his youth.

Carter's black friend was Son McKnight, "companion, body servant and bodyguard." Son taught young Hodding how to box. Hodding taught young Son the basics of reading; the black boy never attended school. After they grew up, Carter became McKnight's protector, and the roles were reversed. The story has more than a hint of the old white paternalism; Mr. Carter acknowledges that. He also observes that such relationships would no longer be possible in the South, for better or worse.

Ashmore's experience was similar. His black boyhood friend was one Nathaniel, the child of a worker on an uncle's plantation near Greenville. They spent summers together wrestling, roaming the woods, seemingly equal in all things in spite of race. "On my side," Ashmore recalls, "the consciousness of racial difference vanished under this intimacy, but I doubt that it ever did on his, for he could not forget that when dark came on and we headed home he would pass on to one of the shacks across the road as I turned into the big house to wash up and join those who were his masters."

McGill's friendship was revealingly different. His first summer job during college was working for a roofing crew at the company for which his father was a salesman. Ralph was the only white member of the crew. His foreman was black. Charlie White, who was in his sixties, protected the tenderfoot college boy, but he also gave him orders. The tenderfoot toughened and survived the hot, exhausting work. As he earned the respect of his boss, he also earned the friendship. I think there may be more than a subtle difference between an Old South friendship of a black boy and a white boy and one shared by a white boy and an older black man, with the black man giving orders—a reversal of the usual cultural expectation. It is tempting to ascribe McGill's embracing of this friendship to the stern Calvinist Presbyterianism of his upbringing. It might also be ascribed to his being reared in the hills, where blacks were scarce and attitudes a little more relaxed. I am not sure that either would be correct, but the temptation is natural for me because of my background.

I wish to share a personal story, an autobiographical note of my own. I grew up in and around Hot Springs, Arkansas, a hill town with a rather small black minority. I remember a period when several other boys in my high school class began to act "southern." I don't know what brought it on. It might have been the popularity of an entertainment personality known as Senator Claghorn; it might have been Civil War history in a class. Whatever triggered it, these boys went through several weeks of singing "Dixie," carrying Confederate flags, talking with exaggerated drawls, and, of course, bad-mouthing Negroes.

I happened to know several Negroes. My father had a grocery store on the edge of town, and they were customers. I had grown especially friendly with two or three of the families, and the men had taken an avuncular interest in me. They were not symbols—they were people. The women were real; the children had names and faces and personalities. Some of the children I liked; some I disliked. One boy that I never knew well was believed by whites and blacks alike to be the smartest boy in the neighborhood. I do not know what became of him.

The outbreak of southernism at my segregated white school at first amused me. I tried to join in the spirit of the thing, in much the same way that I had tried to learn smoking and crap shooting behind the tennis courts. But I quickly learned that I had no taste for it. For one thing, my roots to the Civil War were very shallow. Unlike my elders, Carter, McGill, and Ashmore, I almost never heard talk of the war at home. Even the old people spoke of it only when asked, and then with what seemed to be reluctance. Like McGill, I had ancestors on both sides, but none of them was ever portrayed as romantic. I had no sense of being the heir of a Lost Cause. When my schoolmates shouted slogans and talked with apparent sincerity of the injustices of Reconstruction and the nobility of the Confederacy, I felt like an alien in their midst. I also felt a little ashamed and bereft. But finally I took no part in the game, for whatever reasons. I had no consciousness of it at the time, but I now believe that the main reason was my personal relationship with my father's black customers. The easy racism from the boys who did not share that experience simply made no sense to me.

I include this personal note to make clear where my own history of the South lies, and to suggest that a journalist's predispositions may rise from the most obscure and parochial past. Southerners share a common region and to some extent a common history. But it is clear from those who have shared their lives with the public that there are also large and significant differences within the clan.

Bibliography

Ashmore, Harry S. *An Epitaph for Dixie*. New York: W. W. Norton, 1957.
———. *Hearts and Minds: The Anatomy of Racism from Roosevelt to Reagan*. New York: McGraw-Hill, 1982.
Ayers, H. Brandt, ed. *You Can't Eat Magnolias*. New York: McGraw-Hill, 1972.
Carter, Hodding, Jr. *Southern Legacy*. Baton Rouge: Louisiana State University Press, 1972.
Egerton, John. *The Americanization of Dixie: The Southernization of America*. New York: Harper's Magazine Press, 1974.

Frady, Marshall. *Wallace.* New York: World Publishing Company, 1968.

Kneebone, John T. *Southern Liberal Journalists and the Issue of Race, 1920–1944.* Chapel Hill: University of North Carolina Press, 1985.

Liebling, A. J. *The Earl of Louisiana.* Baton Rouge: Louisiana State University Press, 1970.

McGill, Ralph. *The South and the Southerner.* Boston: Atlantic, Little, Brown, 1959.

Martin, Harold H. *Ralph McGill, Reporter.* Boston: Atlantic, Little, Brown, 1973.

Morris, Willie. *Yazoo.* New York: Ballantine, 1972.

Watters, Pat. *The South and the Nation.* New York: Pantheon, 1969.

Southern Personal Essays

Between Defiance and Defense

Owning Up to the South

JAMES M. COX

I t wouldn't be right for me to begin an essay on southern autobiography without first acknowledging—even proclaiming—my ignorance of the subject. To be sure, I have worked long enough on the
subject of autobiography to know some of the problems that attend the
study; I have even gotten to the edge of the thicket of theory that has
grown wildly about the subject in the last twenty years. I have acquired
enough beggar lice in that thicket to enable me to doubt profoundly
whether there is such a thing as American autobiography, let alone
southern autobiography. About all we can say with reasonable assurance is that there is such a thing as autobiography, whether or not we
can agree on its definition, and that there has been much autobiography
written both in America and in the South.

The adjective "southern" has particular force because the South,
of all the regions in the country, has a particular distinctness. Like
Texas, it was once a nation, but it lost much more than Texas did in
the process of ceasing to be one. Being a southerner, and I am one,
is not only to feel the loss but to feel the defensiveness and defiance

that attend it. The unconditional surrender of the southern nation to
the triumphant union left within every southerner a region of feeling,
association, and knowledge more defensive than the analogous inner
regions of nonsouthern Americans. Put it this way: the southern conviction of region carries with it a convictedness not present for New
Englanders, midwesterners, and westerners.

That convictedness—let us say simply "conviction" with a full sense
of the double meaning of that charged word—goes back to the moral,
social, and political loss the South experienced in the Civil War. Since
its society came increasingly to be predicated on slavery and since
slavery became increasingly the moral and political issue dividing the
nation, the South became more and more a fixed image in the northern mind, and subsequently in the national mind, of a society divided
into planters and slaves, with a middle-class refuse of illiterate whites
making up the remainder.

Against that oppressive stereotype all southerners are, I hope, in
rebellion. If they are defensive in the face of it, surely they must be defiant. The defiance is usually concealed or restrained, yet there, ready
to ambush not merely the other, the majority, but also the self. This
defiance, so familiar in the civil rights marches, often takes the form
of political resistance by conservative white southerners. But it is also
present in the minds of liberal southerners whether they stay at home
feeling themselves a minority within their native region or go north to
prove their fair credentials among the majority. However they seek a
truce with America, their thought retains a hostility not only to the
conservative political and social traditions within the South but also to
the distortions of the stereotype aggressively imposed from without.

The writings of Thomas Wolfe are probably the greatest written effort
to utter the drama and anguish of southern liberalism. No wonder *Look
Homeward, Angel* was published in 1929, the same year that saw *The
Sound and the Fury* come into print. In October of that year the rest
of the country entered the depression that the South had been in since
1865. Nor is it surprising that the book is intensely autobiographical,
so much so that Eugene Gant seems always to be Thomas Wolfe writ
large. It is well to remember that Wolfe's manuscript actually began
with the moment when Eugene's father, as a boy, had witnessed southern soldiers marching toward Gettysburg. Just as Walt Whitman had
sought poetically and autobiographically to hold the country together

in an imaginative embrace in 1855, Thomas Wolfe left home to find in Brooklyn and Manhattan a current of prose that would at once express and bridge the mortal division he felt within himself. Faulkner recoiled into the South to invent a world that would save all the loss of his region and its history. Saving that loss was his great imaginative economy during the Great Depression, the period when he did his finest writing. Whereas Wolfe could not lose himself in his quest to express the country he had left and the one he sought to reach, Faulkner lost himself to the deeper fictive country into which he determined to draw the world. Faulkner has, of course, become the dominant writer for the country, yet a fiercer comparison of these two southern writers than any I have yet seen might achieve a contrast between them sufficient to disclose a richer region of the southern mind.

Having opened such a possibility, I want to retreat from it back to the slave and the planter, those two classes that have preempted so much of the history and image of the South; and I want to retreat from the world of the novel to the two unmistakable yet strong autobiographies that represent what I believe are the fates of the lives of those two classes: Frederick Douglass's *Narrative of the Life of Frederick Douglass, an American Slave* and William Alexander Percy's *Lanterns on the Levee: Recollections of a Planter's Son*. They were published almost one hundred years apart, the first in 1845, the second in 1941. Wishing both of these texts to be a pretext for my own life, I shall make no intensive analysis of either. What, after all, are autobiographies for if not to serve as such pretexts?

For Douglass, life is the heaven of freedom lying ahead of him in the narrative of his experience; at the same time, his polemical perspective is grounded in the victorious freedom he has reached—the freedom to *write* his life. The true spiritual life of freedom he has achieved is equated with the actual power to write of his triumphant escape from the hell of slavery. I use the terms "heaven" and "hell" simply to emphasize the relation of Douglass's narrative to Christian conversion narrative. Such narration goes directly back to Saint Augustine. But Saint Augustine set the climax of his conversion, his baptism, in the ninth book of his thirteen-book account of his life. He devoted the tenth and eleventh books to an account of his consciousness of memory and time, conducting his analysis in the form of a prayer. It was no ordinary prayer but what might have been, in the pagan world in which Augustine had been a master rhetorician, a Socratic dialogue. That prayer, with all its questions addressed to God who remains silent, is literally the form of Saint Augustine's intelligence pursuing the light that his conversion has enabled it to see. His pursuit is both his journey into and his exploration of his soul—a soul that is itself upon its journey toward God. Books 12 and 13 take Augustine through the problem of form and matter, concluding with an interpretation of the opening verses of Genesis. Indeed, book 13—the very number reflecting Augustine's transcendence of the twelve books of the *Aeneid*—reveals Augustine in the true imperial *act* of reading Genesis, the Creation. His reading of Genesis, forecast at the moment of his conversion by the voice that had said, "Take up and read," is fatally allegorical, disclosing Augustine's true relation to original creation as parabolically elliptical.

Augustine recognizes from the beginning of his narrative that if his negative or unregenerate life forms the antithetical background of his conversion, it nonetheless *narratively* leads to his conversion and therefore can figure, no matter how negatively, as a cause of that conversion. The last four books are in their way Augustine's attempted denial of such a causal relationship. Actually, his entire narrative is a prayer denying the implications of his narrative sequence, just as the narrative itself is the adventure of a new epic hero who leaves the lusts of Odysseus behind in order to enter a kingdom greater than any Rome that Aeneas could find or found.

To touch upon Augustine's narrative is to gain a perspective on the narrative of Frederick Douglass. It too is a conversion story leading from slavery to freedom; it is possessed of a moral intensity directly relating it to autobiographical narratives polarized around evil and good, sin and salvation. Yet it is utterly different because it is relentlessly secular and social. It takes place in history, in time and place. Slavery, its hell, though the world of the devil, is yet an oppressive social institution capable of being removed; freedom, its heaven, actually exists in the states of this world, not merely in a state of mind. Then, too, Douglass's escape from slavery is much more a self-willed act of courage and persistence than a result of God and Providence. If we sought to relate Douglass's vision to that of Saint Augustine, he would come out largely a Pelagian, diametrically opposed to the free grace that comes arbitrarily and undeserved to originally sinning and unregenerate man. If we sought to relate it to Bunyan's *Grace Abounding* in its simplicity and in its pilgrim's anxious efforts to escape the repeated threats of slavery that thwart his progress toward freedom, we would see little more than occasional references to Providence somehow coming to his aid. The secularity of Douglass's vision moves much more toward self-reliance than toward faith in God. If the Bible is the master text for both Augustine and Bunyan, *Columbian Orators* is the work that has at once inspired and moved Douglass. He has learned to read not from the Bible or the *New England Primer* but by enlisting his free white playmates as teachers, just as he learns to write by peeping at and copying the school notebooks of his master's son. James Olney is surely right in seeing that the true precursor of this book is the Declaration of Independence rather than Puritan autobiography. I would only add that the strong oratorical tone of the book recalls Patrick Henry. Institutionalized religion is for Douglass as much a tyranny over the mind of man as it was for Jefferson; it threatens to enslave him as much as the hated constitution authorizing slavery. In light of his narrative it is not surprising that Douglass feels compelled to append a lengthy statement insisting that it is institutionalized Christianity, not the true spirit of Christ, that he is attacking. Despite this declared intention, Douglass devotes almost the whole of his appendix to a renewed attack on the churches of America.

The negation so characteristic of Douglass's narration brings us back to the problem of his antithetical narrative. James Olney has written of the rigid convention of the slave narrative, rightly calling it a master plan and rightly seeing Douglass's book as both the finest example and the most complete fulfillment of the convention by virtue of the incontrovertible fact that Douglass wrote his own book. Being able to speak as an orator in the cadences of Columbian oration is Douglass's first move toward achieving genuine equality among the abolitionists; being able to write his own life seals his true freedom in this harsh convention.

The freedom, defined almost totally out of the antithetical polemic against the experience of slavery, is as rigid as the convention. Experience of slavery is, after all, the very ground of Douglass's denunciation of the institution that has fatally aroused his determination to be free. It is not too much to say that this determination—surely the word for Douglass's spirit—carries with it an irony that is all but beyond the means of his extraordinary rhetorical skill. In the great moment of the book when he recounts his fight with the slave-breaker Covey, he tells of how the two of them seized each other and could not let go. That interlocked struggle could stand for Douglass's rhetorical situation. He has taken such a hold of slavery, it threatens to possess his mind in his freedom to write about its horrors.

Failure to see the latent irony in this fiery determination to be free—a determination always at the threshold of being enslaved to the principle of freedom—seems to me a failure to see the ultimate terror of slavery, which, beginning with the father who disowned the son by owning him, ends in the son's determination to master a life in language all but in bondage to the principle of freedom.

There will, of course, be southerners who resist the idea that Douglass's book is a southern life; others will deny that the book is literature. In my context the book is certainly southern, not merely because the total ground of Douglass's experience is southern to its very core but also because it is so defiant. If Emerson had sought to live in self-reliance, Douglass lives in self-defiance. He is, in writing, defying the experience of slavery that has been his life; defiance organizes, inspires, and relentlessly animates his account of that experience. In my view, Douglass represents the old southern defiance in the face of absolute rule. Surely such rebellious defiance is not to be casually ceded to the North. To those who would exclude the book from the realm of literature, I could only ask whether they wish to exclude the Declaration of Independence or *Notes on Virginia* from that realm. What true southerner, seeing the eloquent spirit of defiance that took Douglass away from the South, could read of his departure without a sense of both political and literary loss?

To think of loss is to come sharply in relation to Percy's *Lanterns on the Levee: Recollections of a Planter's Son*. Whereas Douglass's book begins with the formulaic "I was born"—that problematic statement that begins so much autobiography—Percy opens his narrative with this sentence: "My country is the Mississippi Delta, the river country." How much is there. First, there is the metaphorical possession, and not just of a house or land or county but of a country. At the same time, this ownership separates the possession from a larger world. The implications of this sentence unfold themselves throughout Percy's narrative. There is the assurance of ownership, the confidence of class, the ease that comes from leisure and cultivation. Evident throughout the book is the quality of charm that Walker Percy speaks of in his introduction to the 1973 edition of the book. Here is a man who, beginning with "his" country, can draw himself through his childhood, reflect lovingly on his relations both direct and collateral, and affectionately regard the blacks who are so much a part of his world. He does not boast of his breeding precisely because he is sure of his family. He has the generosity and geniality that go with true cultivation; and he has a directness and modesty of style sufficient to allow these qualities clear visibility. Formally educated at Sewanee and later at Harvard Law School, he returns to his native Greenville, Mississippi, to take his place in his father's law office. He has, and can convey, sufficient learning and culture not to be proud of them. If he is not rich, he has enough means to be free. His father has sent him to Europe without his having to refer to the cost of the trip; he has chosen to go to Harvard without writing of having applied for admission. Beyond these attributes, he has courage, having distinguished himself in the fire of World War I, having faced the violent politics of Vardaman before the war and the reborn Ku Klux Klan after it, and having served his community with efficiency and decision in the great flood of 1927.

Yet for all the grace, clarity, and assurance of Percy's narrative, it is profoundly defensive in character. If there is a touch of defiance in the "my country" of the opening sentence, there is also implicit defense. It is quickly clear that Percy's country is losing ground to encroachments from without. His life is, in effect, a holding operation; his vision is of a world inexorably deteriorating; his retrospective survey of his people has a constant elegiac note. There has, as he observes, been the Civil War that ruined his South, followed by World War I that has ruined his world, leaving it open to a return of the vicious element of the Klan. Decline is always present. Part of this defensiveness is that of a man looking upon mortality. Only the river is eternal, and even it is a current mortally threatening as well as sustaining the country with a beauty at once powerful, haunting, and lonely. The levees are themselves the mute and frail defenses against its power.

But mortality is only half the story. There is also a powerful social force encroaching upon the borders of Percy's country and his mind. It is not too much to say that this force is the spirit of Frederick Douglass, forever at the gates of Percy's physical and mental reservation in all its sure conviction. Percy is quickly at pains to assure himself and his readers that he loves the blacks who are so profoundly present in his country. Claiming their presence as a concrete fact and a personal social reality rather than as the ideological abstraction that they become in northern liberal vision, Percy emphasizes his affectionate relation to them throughout his book, from his memory of fifteen-year-old Nain, who took care of him as a child, to his tenderly humorous trials with his chauffeur, Ford, who finally leaves him to go to Detroit. This love of blacks comes at the cost of the poor whites, who have, for Percy, no redeeming traits. Here Percy engages in the old, familiar moral economy, not restricted to the South, that, in its sympathy toward blacks, invariably robs and even brutalizes the white trash. They may be as brutal as they are poor, yet I never cease to be troubled by these evaluations of them. They become the "evil" element residing in Percy's country—a violent and implacable and growing presence always at the threshold of political power in the figures of Vardaman and the Klansmen, who are ready to trample on the refinements, courtesy, and affection that, for the truly cultured man, run both publicly and secretly across the color line between the gentlefolk and the blacks.

I often find myself a distinct minority in my concern. What troubles most readers, even as it troubles Walker Percy, are Percy's "outdated" attitudes toward blacks and sharecropping—outdated precisely because the realities of history have made Percy's genuine claims of personal association merely one more part of the mortality of his country. The history that has outdated Percy is nothing less than the living embodiment of the spirit of Frederick Douglass, which not only has prevailed but shall prevail down all the future we can see. Surely every southerner who reads these two lives knows this reality to the bone.

Actually, Percy—and this is the deepest strength of his book—knows it too, and knows it all the more as he moves toward the end of his life. At the end of his book he writes of his servant Ford leaving for Detroit. Since Ford calls him from time to time asking for money, Percy would like to think that the calls are evidence of Ford's reliance upon the personal relationships possible in a paternalistic society in the face of the anxieties he experiences in the impersonal world of free labor. Yet Percy knows better; he knows that Ford's departure is but a confirmation of the whole drift of history toward freedom. Left increasingly alone, Percy turns to the wisdom he has gleaned from his garden. Finally he comes bravely to his true home, where, walking among the graves of his townsmen, he concludes:

Here among the graves in the twilight I see one thing only, but I see
that thing clear. I see the long wall of a rampart sombre with sunset, a
dusty road at its base. On the tower of the rampart stand the glorious
high gods, Death and the rest, insolent and watching. Below on the
road stream tribes of men, tired, bent, hurt, and stumbling, and each
man alone. As one comes beneath the tower, the High God descends
and faces the wayfarer. He speaks three slow words: "Who are you?"
The pilgrim I know should be able to straighten his shoulders, to stand
his tallest, and to answer defiantly: "I am your son."

Here at last, after all the defenses against the true mortality of history
have proved defenseless, Percy proves himself a defiant son of Death.

To think of these two lives of a slave and a planter's son thrust
together, as I have arbitrarily thrust them, brings me to my own life. If
I knew more southern autobiography, I might seize upon another text
to provide a middle ground between the defiant and the defensive, the
adversarial and the elegiac, but my ignorance leaves me with my life. I
am southern, or at least I think I am; I have written a little, and finally
it is little writing. Of my sixty-four years spent on this planet, fully forty
have been spent outside the South, and those forty are about evenly
divided between the Midwest and New England. I loved the Midwest
enough to marry a midwesterner forty years ago. We are still together.
Can I say more? I loved New England enough to buy a house and
thirty-four acres and stay there twenty years. I deeded both house and
land to my wife when I decided to take early retirement at Dartmouth
and bring her to the Virginia mountain farm, twenty-eight hundred feet
above the sea, where I was raised and to the house where I was born.

I returned as much out of helplessness as out of free will. I couldn't
sell the land, not because it wouldn't sell, but because I couldn't sell
it. My grandfather had acquired it, I want to think, before the Civil
War. I haven't checked the deeds, believing that there is as much freedom in ignorance as in knowledge. His father must have helped him
get it. As far as I can make out, he owned three slaves, so I am close
to slavery, which yet seems far away. He joined the Confederate army,
was made a captain, and was struck in stride, I guess, by a minié ball
that went through both legs, in front of one thigh bone, out behind
the other. That was in the fall of 1861, early in the war, at the battle
of Gauley Bridge in what was then Virginia but is now West Virginia.
Brought home by wagon over two hundred miles of mountain roads,
he lived a semiparaplegic life until his death in 1906. He built a mill,

married, built a house, and sired eleven children, as if to prove that the war hadn't fixed him. Long after his death my father finally bought the shares of his six brothers and four sisters. Since my own brother was killed just before he turned twenty-one, I finally became both sole survivor and inheritor of house and 365 acres (I added 62 acres when an adjoining farm came up for sale). I knew none of my grandparents. The only one who survived my birth, my father's mother, died when I was two, so I was largely cut off from direct access to the past. My father died at home twenty-one years ago, as did his parents before him. My mother wanted to die there, and I've always regretted that I didn't command the doctors to grant her wish instead of weakly submitting to the order of the hospital. As her life was going, I was told to leave her room but didn't. I held her hand and watched her die.

That was more than eleven years ago, and I now am home for three-fourths of the year, struggling with resistant house and land. The struggle kills whatever sentimentality there could have been in returning. I cannot take a step on any part of the place that doesn't have associations with my childhood and adolescence. At one time or another I have walked with and worked with my father on every acre of the farm. But cutting briars and thornbushes, helping to build new fences to replace those that I watched being built fifty years ago, cutting and splitting locust posts for seasoning and future fences, sawing and bringing in firewood to feed three stoves—these are activities that, if they do not put memory to flight, at least put it firmly in its place. They mark my attempt to take hold of the land of my fathers, and they lie before me through every season of the year. It is futile to tell my colleagues in New England that there is winter in Virginia; they think that they have a monopoly on that season, just as they think that there are no fall colors except in the country north of Boston. Why should I claim that the climate in our county parallels that of Boston even though frost comes as late as the middle of May and as early as the middle of September, just as it does in Vermont?

Three men have particularly helped me. Paul Byrd has worked with me to clear land, get wood, and keep both yard and garden. He has helped my wife plant flowers and shrubs wherever she can want them. A strong student in his way, he knows gardening as well as the history of World War II and has many books about both subjects. And, true to his name, he knows all about birds—their calls, their nesting places, their seasons—and brings us books from his library. He claims relation to the great Byrd family of Virginia, scoffing with humorous contempt at my pathetic genealogical pretensions. Ever ambitious to expand his vocabulary, he seeks new words yet retains a deviantly recalcitrant streak in him that leads to violent mispronunciations. I pedantically correct him, lamenting all the while that my extraordinary tutorial efforts to make him respectable will exhaust the energy required for teaching my one term at Dartmouth. Two hours a day for three or four days a week we live together in the most profane vernacular as proof that we must have a religious spirit. I know that he does; his presence will save me if I am to be saved.

Then there is Johnny Wooten, a carpenter. I helped him build my bookshelves, insulate the house, and repair outbuildings. What a pleasure to be nothing but a helper. All last summer he came late in the day, after working a full shift with his crew, and we worked through the long evenings until dark. We would then come to the kitchen, the true living quarters for my wife and me. He would sit—and will, I dearly hope, sit again—for an hour or more to visit. He says that going to Galax, eighteen miles away, is about as long a journey as he can tolerate. He is absolutely at home in our county. Sitting with him in the kitchen, I have found myself watching his handsome, bearded, thirty-seven-year-old face turned slightly upward toward the light and thinking of Whitman's great poetic effort to reach the true heart and soul of the people of this land. For a long moment my restless thoughts have been stilled in blessed contemplation.

Finally, there is Neal Halsey, who rents my land. When he recently rented it he drove what seemed to me a pretty hard bargain, but he did so many things about the place that my spirit began to riot in exultation at having gotten out from under a long succession of three renters who had left the place running steadily down in the twenty years since my father died. Of course, a farm like mine is always running down, yet in Neal's genial presence I began to imagine a future order of resistant possibility. One day when we were clearing dead limbs at the border of a pasture, we took time out for conversation. He went to his long-bedded pickup truck and returned with a mason jar of homemade peach brandy, the peaches beautifully visible in the bottom of the jar. Leaning against the truck at the edge of a woodland, we could see a black church in the near distance (the church was, of course, actually white, not black, as if to remind me of the totalizing ruthlessness of present black-white designations of the races). As the conversation drifted to politics, I said I was thinking of voting for Jesse Jackson. Neal, a Republican, said that if he had known I had such sentiments he wouldn't have given me the peach brandy. I replied that it was the brandy that emboldened me to utter them, and we launched into an uninhibited talk of race and party politics.

I did not lecture him on race relations. Who am I, a white man, owning land out of all the past, to be sure I am not a racist, that word so easily hurled at all the world we would be free of? Part of Percy's problem in his southern defense was that he needed the blacks but did not need those southern whites he never could admire. He loved—and I do not doubt him—what he truly needed. Frost was right in his great poem "Two Tramps in Mud Time":

> Only where love and need are one,
> And the work is play for mortal stakes,
> Is the deed ever really done
> For Heaven and the future's sakes.

I love my wife because I need her, and I need her because I love her. I need the men I have spoken of. They somehow appeared amidst all the obscure succession of events making up the drift of life, and now I am, I hope, lightly held in that bondage—lightly held enough to call on the Yankee wisdom of Robert Frost, who, after all, was named Robert Lee Frost by his copperhead father.

The farm is heavier in its hold. I own it unencumbered, which means that *it*, and not any bank, is always at the threshold of owning me. The old legal language had it right in saying that such and such a man died seized and possessed of so many acres. Looking out the kitchen window to the hill due west of the house, I see the graveyard where my people are buried. They are Methodists, or nominally so, resting in a Baptist cemetery. My parents went to church but were remarkably free of true Methodism. My father was more Deist than anything else without being rigorously theological in his faith. He believed in Jefferson's version of the Bible and kept a pocket-sized copy near at hand. I have often wished that I had sent it with him to his long home. My grandfather gave the land for the original graveyard, reserving the eastern border for himself and his wife and their descendants; my father gave more land, and I have given more. At the vernal equinox, when day and night are in perfect balance, with the sun rising directly in the east and the trees still leafless, the granite gravestone of my grandparents flashes its reflection to the kitchen window in the early morning. As a child that sudden light as from someone holding a mirror fascinated me. I have come to look at it with more circumspection, as if the light might hurt my eyes, yet just before leaving the farm for my annual term at Dartmouth, I caught myself gazing directly at it in surprising concentration. The slaves, most of whom were freedmen by the time the graveyard achieved identity, lie beneath uninscribed fieldstone—with a single exception, Edmund Cox, who died a free man in 1883.

Saddle Creek runs through the very middle of the farm. It ran the mill until 1963, when a flood washed out the dam. The mill, which I myself operated for a whole summer and fall when I was fifteen years old, sits still with all its flour mill machinery and great millstones silent and unmoving. The creek has surely run through my mind all my life —at least I feel so when I walk beside it toward what was once the meadow but is now only pasture. Yet I could not be sure of its running so if I had not returned to it to be held again in the farm's fierce hold, a hold so attractive that it draws me out of my study to the never-ending tasks and possibilities I see through my study window. Colleagues and friends, knowing that I have gone back to it, congratulate me on having both place and time to write. If I ever thought the farm would provide such place and time, I was deluded. *The farm is against writing.* That is its wisdom. Its solid reality resists translation into language. Drawn to it, I more and more do not want to write. Writing, particularly writing autobiography, takes us away from body and nature even as we try to make language reach back to them in love and longing.

The future I dream in having come home to the South leans more and more toward an exchange of the freedom of writing for the freedom of not writing. Douglass could never stop writing autobiography; he wrote two more after his first one, losing in intensity what he gained in coverage and chronicle. Percy died almost as soon as he finished his. In the bondage of my land, I find myself in the freedom of not writing—a descent, if it is a descent, into ignorance and illiteracy, where, beside Saddle Creek, I can hear its fall over granite rapids rising in a measured roar. That is the South I would be truly lost in. Surely it is the South I could not give up, and, fated to own, I now own up to.

Uncles and Others

GEORGE GARRETT

A Confederate officer, himself as raggedy as a scarecrow, together with a few of his men, and most of them shoeless and all of them in tattered and torn and patched pieces of uniform, is on his hands and knees crawling down the long straight row of a cornfield. They all go very slowly, carefully, as quiet as they can. Above all they do not want the farmer in the log cabin, perhaps a quarter of a mile away, to find them here. For what they intend to do, the farmer could have them hanged. It is a capital offense in this army, and the commanding officer of these men and this officer would do it, too. He would hang them one and all for the sake of a discipline that has not broken yet. But, you see, they are starving. Truly. Since yesterday or perhaps the day before they have had nothing to eat and drink but a handful of acorns and muddy creek water. They have to risk hanging or die. Now, there are some skinny cows browsing a piece of pasture just beyond the edge of the cornfield. One, an old cow of not much use to anyone, is nearest the rows of corn. They plan to kill that cow. To cut it up and carry it off into the thick woods behind them where, at a safe distance, they will build a little fire and cook the meat. Young as they are (and some of these are scarcely in their teens, and the officer, my great-grandfather, is not yet twenty-one), they are experienced and hardened veterans of the war. By now, fairly late in the war as it will prove to be, they do not pray or plan or hope anymore to live through to the end of it. That will happen or not happen. But, among many other ways and means, they would rather not have to die hungry.

You can understand that.

It seems to be all clear ahead. The old contented cow has moved even closer to the cornfield. There is not even a thin feather of white smoke coming from the cabin's chimney. No sounds. No dog around, thank God, to bark and bite. Farmer is somewhere else at work, in another direction. They are still crawling along down the rows of corn when they hear something. The sound, unmistakable, of metal on metal. They hear that sound again, louder and somewhat closer. They freeze in place. Very slowly, even as a puff of light breeze teases the half-grown cornstalks, the officer turns his head to look in the direction the sounds came from. Light glints off something only a few rows away. It's a rifle barrel (what else?) and another one. There are armed men, uniforms of dark blue, so close by he could pick up a clod of red clay earth and chuck it and hit them.

What next?

Holding his breath he lowers his head and face to the earth. I lower mine, too, tasting, smelling the sweet odor of turned red clay in late springtime. I can hear the breeze rattling in the green cornstalks.

What next?

The Elizabethans, my forebears, with whom I have visited for many years, had themselves a proverb for almost every situation and occasion. One that I have kept in mind, as if blazoned in neon, is "There can be no play without a fool in it." Am I the fool of my own play? No good or happy answer to that question, but it led me toward a skinny and postmodern one of my own. Which might as well be "You can't write anything worth reading without an epigraph." And so here is my epigraph. It has the advantage of at least being economical since it is in my own words. Of course, I am fully aware of the dangers, even in autobiography, of depending on your own words. Wasn't it Raymond Chandler who said something wise like "When you use your own stuff for inspiration, you are already dead"? Anyway, dead or alive, coming ready or not, here is my text in brief and in part, a short poem called "Main Currents of American Political Thought."

Gone then the chipped demitasse cups
at dawn, rich with fresh cream and coffee,
a fire on the hearth, winter and summer,
a silk dandy's bathrobe, black Havana cigar.

Gone the pet turkey gobbler, dogs and geese,
a yard full of chickens fleeing the shadow of a hawk,
a tall barn with cows and a plough horse, with corn,
with hay spilling out of the loft, festooning the dead Pierce Arrow.

Gone the chipped oak sideboards and table,
heavy with plenty of dented, dusty silverware.
Gone the service pistol and the elephant rifle
and the great bland moose head on the wall.

"Two things," you told me once, "will keep
the democratic spirit of this country alive—
the free public schools and the petit jury."
Both of these things are going, too, now, Grandfather.

You had five sons and three daughters,
and they are all dead or dying slow and sure.
Even the grandchildren are riddled with casualties.
You would not believe these bitter, shiny times.

What became of all that energy and swagger?
At ninety you went out and campaigned for Adlai Stevenson
in South Carolina. Half that age and I have to force
myself to vote, choosing among scoundrels.

Autobiography, like any other form of confession, is finally, if not first
and foremost, a self-serving act. And what else could it be? At its most
sane and rational (that is, rarely enough) the autobiographical impulse
is most often a cry for mercy concealed as a nonnegotiable demand
for justice. What it amounts to, then, is copping a plea. And even on
its other, darker side, for the sake of whatever kinds of dark hungers
and satisfactions, autobiography remains much closer to the rhetoric of
fiction than to any objective arrangement of hard facts. It is a matter
of aesthetics most of all. And in any case there are some strict limits
to our contemporary shapes and forms of pleading. When the Book of
Common Prayer's latest version of the old General Confession dropped
the image of erring and straying lost sheep, presumably for the sake
of a more sophisticated urbanity, and cut as well (among other things)
the acknowledgment of ourselves as being "miserable offenders" and

the outright admission that "there is no health in us," all this added up
to something more than the simple and direct expression of the widespread contemporary desire to deal with God on some basis of equality.
It also represented a shift in the point of view of the praying narrator.
And so I ask you. When even our prayers partake of the art and craft of
fiction, why should autobiography be subjected to the vulgar claims of
credibility?

And southern autobiography has some other, special problems. It is
at least perceived by others as consisting of more things to confess and
to conceal. And even disallowing that notion—as I do, now and forever, though I recognize that it is widely held by many, at least some
of whom do themselves small honor and less justice by that kind of re-
flexive self-indulgence—even ignoring that problem, there is still the
matter of manners. It is generally thought, among my tribe, to be an
infraction, an exhibition of bad manners, to present oneself in any form
that is radically different from the expectations of others. Because this
is so, who knows, ever, how much of what passes for southern autobiography and humble confession is not, instead, purely and simply the
exercise of social charm?

I myself am the books I have written, whether you have read them
or not. And may I say here and now that even though for many years
it mattered to me, perhaps more than it should have, whether others
bothered to read the works, large or small, into which I had poured my
life, my self, as carefully and awkwardly as pouring from one bottle into
another, that although it was a matter of pride, and therefore of wounds
and blessings, for many years, it does not matter much to me now. It
is a desire that has waned. It is a hunger that I lived with so long and
intimately when I was young, so deeply, that it is now as strangely vanished as if it had been fully satisfied. And I would be ashamed of it, that
old hunger of my younger self, a hunger not for any kind of fame or any
measurable reward but for a kind of equity, a justice more outrageous
than either one, call it full acceptance as a legitimate craftsman of words
and fables, an honorable one among the many, living and dead. That
kind of acceptance, common enough in the lives of others, my friends
and enemies alike, did not arrive when I burned for it and cannot come
to me now when I have arrived at a place in my life where it is not,
really, left in the hands of others to accept or reject my work; a place in
my life where I, usually alone, have to act as my own judge and jury.

In that sense I am to be found, the life of me, in my work. But this is no kind of news. It is true of every writer, living or dead, whom I admire and respect and envy. The best of them held back very little. The best of all held back nothing at all and, in the end, were merely and enviably dry husks in the wind.

My autobiography is in my words and fables, though I must admit it has taken me most of a lifetime to recognize the simple truth of that, and I must also admit that much that is clear enough to me now will always be inaccessible to others. Which means, I reckon, that my life is written and printed in an unknown tongue. I seriously doubt that anyone, besides myself, could get to the bottom of it.

And I believe I am something more than the facts and events of my days. I do not mean to belittle the things that have happened to me or to make light of the things I have done that I ought not to have done and the things I have left undone that I ought to have done. But I do think that these things cannot mean very much to others. Probably should not mean much to others. Unless I were laying claim—which I am not—to a public life of great actions and events or even a closeness to such things.

I propose something else. The ancient and honorable image of the pebble that, when tossed in water, instantly vanishes but proves its existence by the slow spreading of concentric circles around an empty center. In addition to our works—which are there to be judged (or ignored) now or later—and in addition to the thin staining coat of facts and dates which is our reduced being, we are also all of those around us, our friends and enemies, those whom we love and hate. And we are also those we were given at birth, those we were given to, like it or not. We are our family, our tribe. And that is what I am thinking of here and now. Autobiography not precisely as a matter of inheritance, or as a ritual matter of tribal totem and taboo, but, anyway, as a matter of the self defined by blood, by kinship, by others who are not chosen, like friends or enemies, but *given* all at once, like it or not, like the mysterious gifts of some fairy godmother, benign or malevolent, at christening or wedding.

When I talk of the uncles and others around me, mostly ghosts already, I am also speaking of myself. From what they were I begin to learn who I am, where I have been, and even, sometimes, why.

The same is, of course, true of you and you, all of you, all of us. The lives of our blood kin are fables we are entitled to enter and inhabit.

Who are the uncles? Let us settle that right now. On my mother's side of the family there are her five brothers, from the eldest, Bill, named for his father, and including, in order, Courtney, Fred, Jack, and Chester. Bill was old enough to have been in the cavalry before the First World War. Chester is young enough to have served in the tank destroyers in World War II. My father had two younger brothers, Oliver and Legh. I never knew Legh at all except in photographs because he died before I was born. He was a mountain climber and a professional guide who disappeared forever (on Mount Washington? Mount Rainier? I cannot remember and nobody is handy here and now to ask) in a sudden and unseasonal snowstorm. There was more of that once upon a time in America. People just vanished. Not all of them died. Oliver came home, highly decorated, from the First World War to become first a newspaper reporter, an outstanding one, in New York and then, when silent pictures gave way to talkies, a Hollywood screenwriter. Very well— mountain climber and screenwriter on one side. On the other, Fred was a musician, Courtney was (among other things) a minor league baseball player, Jack was an outstanding PGA golfer, and Chester was a dancer, in Broadway musicals, in nightclubs around the world, and on the great ocean liners.

You can see that by the time I and others of the next generation came along, there was no special notice, neither blame nor shame, in the modest ambition to be a writer. There were writers already— my Aunt Helen Garrett, who wrote wonderful children's books, and my Uncle Oliver on the Garrett side, and on the other, a great-uncle, Harry Stillwell Edwards, of Macon, Georgia, a writer who won some prizes in the late nineteenth century, earned some money, and whose late short novel of Reconstruction, *Aeneas Africanus*, sold a couple of million copies and remains quietly in print.

Nobody would even notice another writer. It was, as my grandfather told me once, as good a way to be poor as any other.

In fact, if you think about it seriously (which none of us, in fact, did), being a writer was slightly more conventional and respectable, if a lot less rewarding, than what the majority of the uncles were up to. Certainly less adventurous. True, my mother's father and my own were lawyers, and very good ones, but each in his own way, as flamboyant performers in life and profession, trial lawyers when the give-and-take of the southern courtroom, equally urgent and dramatic in large matters and the smallest of things, was still one of the chief forms of entertainment and principal sources of public language in the South. My father had intended another kind of life. Went to MIT to be a mining engineer, ran out of money and became instead a miner, himself, in the Far West, becoming finally a charter member of the United Mine Workers. Then, partly crippled by accident and disease, made his way back home to Florida to some cousins there, aiming to go to South America but becoming a lawyer in Florida instead.

His father-in-law, my grandfather, originally from Charleston and McClellanville, South Carolina, was a licensed nautical pilot before he became a lawyer, drove his own trotters and pacers in high-stakes horse races. Served for a time as solicitor general of Georgia and ran, unsuccessfully, for governor of Florida. The story was and went that he made two huge and separate fortunes in his lifetime and spent three. I did not see him at his richest and most extravagant—the days when, for example, he had a ninety-foot steam yacht, the *Cosette*, as fast and nimble as anything in the Atlantic Ocean and which, with a minimal professional crew and his five sons, he handled himself. But I did see him in a couple of fine old houses, which he managed from the front porch with a nineteenth-century military megaphone. And later, too, when all his space was a rented room in the back of the post office of Naples, North Carolina, and later still in a plain and simple cottage next to the inland waterway in McClellanville where he died and his hound dogs crawled under the house and howled for three days before they came out. I remember his sister, Aunt Mamie, who had once enjoyed the society of Charleston, living, at her end, with a tall and solemn mountain man, Uncle Tom, who always wore bib overalls, in a dirt-floor log cabin, far gone in the North Carolina mountains. A well for water and an outdoor privvy and candles and kerosene for light. Spare and sparse and wonderfully neat and clean. Old family silver gleamed on the crude and sturdy dinner table where we ate (in summertime) cornbread and fresh vegetables and wild roots and berries, and mysterious and gamey stews, for Uncle Tom was a constant, seasonless hunter in the woods. It was, to me, an altogether happy place. Uncle Tom

taught me to shoot and to fish the mountain streams and where to find
blackberries and how to kill and clean and pluck a chicken. He also
taught me how to milk and to plow, too, with one mule or two horses.
Aunt Mamie seemed altogether happy, too. Couldn't have been more
so when she had lived with her first, handsome husband in a house on
the Battery in Charleston.

All of them on both sides were what we would call high rollers, seriously and sincerely wild spenders, never taking money or the getting of
it very seriously, often coming into money somehow, yet never seeking
for it, for its own sake, never doing things (or selling anything except
themselves) at the expense of others to get it. They all had honor, as an
ideal, and acted honorably. And they gave away, in common Christian
charity, as much as they spent; for service to others and to the community, the larger tribe, was an unquestionable duty. They were often
called generous by others, when they had the means to give and gave
freely to the less fortunate and the disabled and disadvantaged; but they
did not think of themselves as doing anything more (or less) than their
bounden duty. The American dream (not an expression I ever heard
from them or anyone except politicians) had nothing to do with upward
or downward mobility. It had to do with honor and liberty and fairness
(equity). When they were well-to-do they lived well. When they were
poor they worked hard at hard and menial jobs. They worked with hard
hands and without shame. They could, therefore, afford to be poor and
proud. Which is just as well, because that is how most of them ended
up, dirt poor in some cases; not in self-pity or spoken regret, but rich
in memories, anyway, and the laughter of recapitulation, stories of fat
times still preserved and repeated in the lean and plain and, at the end,
in what we would choose to call abject poverty. Fred, for instance, who
as a pianist had sometimes accompanied great singers and solo artists,
was a hermit and literally a beachcomber when he died. When asked
what he wanted, all he asked for was a set of teeth. Which he was
given. Chester, who had made thousands of dollars a week as a dancer
deep in the heart of the depression, came home from World War II to
find himself too old and battered and his way of dancing out of fashion.
Went through some bad times in New York before he got a job teaching at the newly founded Arthur Murray's. Where (his luck was always
pretty good) he sold two lifetime courses to a very rich, good-looking,
and recently divorced heiress, and then married her; they have lived

happily ever after since. On the other side, Oliver, in spite of several glamorous and very expensive wives, was about as rich as a Hollywood screenwriter can be. But when he died of a heart attack in a laundry across the street from his hotel, he was listed by the New York City police, who took him to the morgue, as "unidentified laborer."

A story. When cars, automobiles, were first coming in (a time when my grandfather was still in possession of one of his fortunes), my grandfather bought one at once. But by the time he had finished breakfast, his son Bill had already borrowed it. So he bought another, but one of his boys (my uncles) got to that one first, too. Finally, he had five cars, and yet when it came time to go down to his office in Jacksonville every morning, they were all gone and he had to take the old horse carriage, like it or not. He did the obvious thing—bought a sixth car, all his own. First time he drove it to work, it stalled on him on the big bridge over the Saint Johns River. He was blocking the way. Horns were blowing, harsh words were shouted, but the damned thing wouldn't start again (or, likely, he didn't know how to start it). So he got out, dropped the keys over the side of the bridge and into the river, and walked to work. "Never did find out what became of that damn car," he would say. "And if I never do, that will be soon enough."

Jack and Chester liked to remember that they were present (though they could not know it then, at the moment, only later, when they put time and two and two together), as the last two living at home, on the day that one of his fortunes, perhaps the last, turned from hard cash and assets into thin air. It was one of their birthdays, Jack's or Chester's, and after work he bought a sailboat as a birthday present, fifty dollars in cash from the last one hundred he had in the world; and the two boys and their father sailed it home on the Saint Johns in the fading twilight, tacking in the brisk warm wind an hour or so, until, just as the sudden dark was swallowing them up, he made a perfect stylish landing at the little dock below the house.

"I never saw the old man happier," they would say later. "He took off his coat and sailed that boat home without a worry in the world." It's a typical story, not a special one, an exemplum telling us in the tribe how to take the bitter with the sweet, with full awareness, certainty, that there will be something of both until the bitter end.

You will see that pride and honor mattered, but mainly as a matter of style, which in turn says that what is outward and visible, be it ever so bright and beautiful, be it ever so delightful, rich, or strange, is only costuming and camouflage. What is inward and spiritual is what truly and deeply matters. And it has nothing to do, really, with success or failure, good luck or bad.

I suppose this tribal code was good training for a writer, an American writer in our century. At least for this writer, myself, who has managed going on almost forty years now since my first published story, to go on working and performing with what I think I can fairly and objectively describe as a minimum of outside encouragement.

It was good training for them, too. Because some of them were wonderful, truly wonderful at what they did. Chester was a superb dancer who for a time had other dancers, including the great Fred Astaire, billed under him. You have never heard of him, that's for sure. Or my Uncle Jack either, though he won many a golf tournament, early and very late in his life, and a couple of times was a single stroke, one putt, away from the absolute top for the time. Other professionals, the old-timers, remember him. "Jack was the greatest golfer I ever saw," they usually tell me. But in an instant they are laughing and telling stories of bets he made and won or lost, all the tricks and jokes he pulled.

And only a true cinema buff, an antiquarian, would know about Oliver H. P. Garrett, though he wrote well over one hundred feature films, founded and was first president of the Screenwriters Guild, and wrote (and is now, at last, finally credited with it) the final shooting script of *Gone with the Wind*.

How can you write the final shooting script of *Gone with the Wind* and be unknown outside a small circle in the business? It's the kind of thing Garretts can do. And my mother's family as well. There are times when I think it is our doom, our destiny, that it is meet and right, that the Tomb of the Unknown American Writer should be quietly waiting for me.

There were virtues among the tribe also—good manners, expressed equally to all, regardless of station or status. How could we do otherwise? That bum or bag lady could just as well be one of us. There was an easy generosity. They withheld nothing from each other and, indeed, from anybody else who was not an enemy. Anyone who was an enemy, however, found them implacable, ruthless, passionately violent, and finally, in victory, magnanimous. Some of them, early and late, came to violent ends.

You could not, ever, even consider the notion of betrayal, of betraying any one of our own or any word or promise we had made.

Who taught us these things? you will justly ask. Who were the keepers of tribal history, the custodians of the tribal lore, the tribal virtues?

The women, of course. The aunts. They kept and tended the flames. And they made things easy for the uncles, who would not easily have dared to act any differently than they did.

Nor do I.

What are our vices? There is a pleasant laziness that often eases into a well-developed habit of procrastination. We tend to embrace the rigors of self-discipline (upon which our powers and virtues much depend) by fits and starts. And by the same token we have a tendency to cultivate all kinds of bad habits. There were and are too many drunks in the tribe. Some are, truly, greatly gifted, but they often take their gifts lightly and for granted, as if anything more than lighthearted acceptance would be corrupting. More seriously, although they are tolerant, even egalitarian, in their attitudes toward others, they can be very hard on their own. Within the tribe the casualty rate—dead, wounded, and crazy —is high. And although they are at once generous and compassionate, they are also damnably proud if pushed to be so and dangerously violent if challenged. Once challenged and fully engaged, they have been known to bear grudges over amazing distances of time and space, carefully cupped like water in their hands.

On the one hand, this is a source of shame and guilt because they are Christians and uneasy in their hatred. But, at one and the same time, in the secular world we have to live and die in, it means they can still be outraged by injustice or atrocity (at a time when, if you think about it, so few of us still are . . . at least for long). It renders our tribe more or less unfit for modern corporate life and the contemporary wisdom that anything under the sun is, finally, negotiable. Difficult for them, the uncles and others; but for a writer, to be given a constant dichotomy like that as a birthright is a great gift, even the continued inner conflict of it. Never quite to belong, outside the tribe, may not be comfortable, but it is helpful to the craft of fiction and especially so in a time, like our own, of ethical clichés and stereotypes.

Is there—has there—been any magic among us? Not much, I reckon. Some ghosts in the times gone by when ghosts walked about more freely. An aunt who could tell fortunes, by one means and another, with either amazing accuracy or amazing luck as the case may be. Dreams and visions. In my childhood, no death or disaster in the family ever took our women by surprise. They felt it just before it was known.

The aunts on both sides who were blood kin were formidable women, strong-willed, greatly gifted, sometimes difficult, if lighthearted. Some of the aunts by marriage were colorful enough. There was a German dancer who was one of Billy Rose's Long-stemmed Roses and was later with the circus. There were a Hungarian movie actress and even one aunt, whom I never met, from Bali. The sisters, it seems, never seriously begrudged their brothers' marital adventures.

Adventure was what it was all about. Uncle Bill could tell a tale or two about flying in the Great War, but he always said (and I believe) that nothing in the world could ever equal the pure excitement of leading a troop of cavalry flat out in a full-gallop charge. Bugles, the sudden thunder of hooves directly behind you, and the open space before you as, saber drawn and pointed, you rode your mount to its limit of speed and endurance and rode yourself to the limit of your courage.

Sometimes the source of writing (for myself at least) is uneasiness, the conflict of opposing, often contradictory powers. You can see that belonging to our tribe has often been an uneasy role. Especially when I was young and more painfully aware that there were many other tribes who thought and acted very differently than our own. At times it could be a burden, a sorrow even. It is nowadays another sort of tribal habit—from another tribe, the tribe of scribblers—to make more art from our wounds than from our blessings. I am as guilty of this as anyone. My family, my tribe, has appeared most directly in my poetry and short stories. I have not been fair or even accurate except in the summoning up of my own feelings. Which—true to my tribe—I try to do without flinching.

Here is a poem, "Child among Ancestors," which is precisely about all that.

> Dimensionless, they've left behind
> buttons, daguerreotypes, a rusty sword
> for a small boy to fondle, and the tales
> he hears without believing a word
>
> about the escapades of the tall people.
> The tight-lipped men with their beards

and their unsmiling women share the glint
of unreality. The facts he's heard,

how this one, tamer of horses, fell
in a flourish of flags and groping dust,
and one who met a dragon on the road,
and another, victim of his lust,

changed into a pig with a ring tail,
fail to convince or bear the burden of
flesh and his struggle for identity.
What he has never seen he cannot love,

though dutifully he listens.
Dismissed, he takes the sword and goes
campaigning in garden and arbor,
and in the henyard mighty blows

glisten in a tumult of feathers.
The hens cackle like grown-ups at tea
as he scatters them to the four winds.
The rooster, ruffled, settles in a tree

and crows an ancient reprimand.
"Let them stand up to me." The boy
thinks. "Let them be tall and terrible
and nothing less than kings." His joy

is all my sadness at the window
where I watch, wishing I could warn.
What can be said of the dead? They rise
to make you curse the day that you were born.

One way and another, poorly or sometimes very well, we were, one
and all, for as far back as I can learn, engaged in what were (at least
then) known as manly things—hunting and fishing; horses and boats;
physical sports, which, if not always "contact" sports, were always anyway the most risky and dangerous we could practice. Gambling, with
money and things, of course, but also with hide and hair and heart, was
good. To win was pleasure, to be sure; but losing was seldom a serious
pain (good gamblers shrug it off and bet again as soon as they can). And
losing was never a shame unless you had played things safely, withheld,
been miserly with energy, been stingy with the exposure of self. Victory was, could be, sweet enough, but not a gloating triumph when it

was earned over the full and honorable expense and effort of the defeated, of a beaten equal. In our tribe we would no more have danced in the brief, bright, end-zone joy of victory over a worthy enemy than we would have danced or pissed on the grave of a friend.

What you can see is that, whatever else, we were well prepared for war. Which is just as well because we fought in all the wars, from even before this was a nation until here and now. Not often as professional soldiers and sailors (of whom there were a few among us, but whose vocation was somehow as vaguely contemptible as it seemed unnecessary), but nevertheless as soldiers and sailors in all our country's wars —and thus in every generation from the beginning.

There are some things—simply left over, never preserved—from the old days. A rusty Civil War sword, a toasting fork presented by General Washington to an officer, an ancestor, who served him for a time. Various and sundry kinds of brass buttons and insignia. From later, from our own century, crossed rifles of the infantry, crossed sabers of the cavalry, crossed cannons of the field artillery, my Uncle Bill's wings as a flyer in the First World War. And more than these things, there have been voices, people to listen to, from my great-grandfather from Apalachicola, Florida, who fought out the long brutal years in the West, on down through the youngest cousins who fought and were wounded in Vietnam. We have all served our time. From them all came the gift of their stories, alike only in that they were always the kinds of stories told by combat veterans, which is to say, seldom if ever directly concerned with any kind of combat, or even suffering, but characterized instead by the exemplary anecdote, sometimes funny and almost always ironic. And usually paradoxical. Thus even the most innocent and inexperienced of us, thanks to tribal history, arrived wherever we were sent, that is, wherever we had to go, almost without expectations or illusions, which, in turn, meant that we were usually spared the common experience of disillusionment. Our concentration was not upon Cause or Causes or any other abstractions, which we deemed (long before we read any novels about any of it) irrelevant, having seen and known that the fighting qualities of soldiers, admirable or pathetic, have nothing at all to do with the justice or injustice of the Causes they are thought to represent. I should mention the paradox that in civil life we are often (as the first poem tried to say) passionate about political affairs, if never quite able to hew to any particular party line, and even though we do not, finally, believe that politics proves or settles anything under the sun. That is, we are free to care because it does not matter.

Ideally, there ought to be illustrations. In place of that let imagination and memory join together to create a slide show (or a sideshow) of illustrations.

Let us begin with portraits. I am thinking of those Brady portraits, his and his contemporaries. Thinking of those hard, odd, genuinely eccentric, and entirely individual faces, faces that we would call wild, if not savage and barbarous, if we did not already know many of the names that go with the faces and the deeds that go with the names. It may well be—it is at least a serious and debatable question—that American society was somewhat more homogeneous then. But judging by its recorded faces, we can easily surmise that, set against our own, the general gene pool then allowed for much more diversity and variety than the melting pot does now. Something has happened, and in a very short time, to the American face. Is there a single federal judge, coast to coast, who has a face as expressive and symbolic as that of the late Judge Learned Hand? Picture the famous profile of Major General William T. Sherman, the one with his collar buttoned and all the brass buttons on his dark uniform shining: close-cropped hair; dark, full, thick beard; the nose as sharp as an ax blade; one visible bright eye fixed in a thousand-yard stare; completely unsmiling. Summon up Grant and Lee, Jefferson Davis and Abraham Lincoln.

I know of only two contemporary faces to match any of the Civil War portraits—Shelby Foote and Alexander Solzhenitsyn, the latter having risen from the dead, one miracle from among uncounted and mostly unmourned millions, the former as the man who has lived longer and more closely with our Civil War ancestors than anyone else. Foote knows what they were looking for and looking at and what they saw.

Somehow the standard-issue American face has changed from its apparent material of cut stone, poured bronze, or whittled hardwood into something else, something much like molded plastic or (on a bad day) Silly Putty. And smiling. Almost always smiling. What is the smiling about?

Solzhenitsyn noticed it right away and mentioned it, earning some boos in response, during his Harvard commencement address of 1978: "But the fight for our planet, physical and spiritual, a fight of cosmic proportions, is not a vague matter of the future; it has already started. The forces of Evil have begun their offensive—you can feel their pressure —and yet your screens and publications are full of prescribed smiles and raised glasses. What is the joy about?" Which observation appropriately reminds us of a greater and deeper change, the change of what is *behind* the faces of then and now, as much as we can perceive and translate the things those faces seem to be saying to us. Of course, we always assume that what we read in a face is what was intended, that faces are saying no more and no less than they want to. We tend to praise and blame them for these very things, knowing full well that we make an outrageous assumption, knowing that no one alive, except perhaps a consummate professional actor, fully knows or is responsible for the expression of his face. And it is worth keeping in mind that the art of the actor is a mimetic derivation from the probably uncontrolled and irresponsible expression of authentic emotions by real people. But we judge anyway, bring a litigious and pharisaical generation of self-appointed judges. Judging ourselves gently enough, if not with very much mercy or charity. And judging these others, the dead, with an Old Testament rigor.

We do seem to feel compelled to judge our personal past, just as we so severely judge America's past and the South's, especially when family is involved and extends over several generations. Generations that openly embraced very different values from our own. Generations we regularly acknowledge as having been, in many things, ignorant, insensitive, and wrongheaded. We judge and condemn them, or we apologize for them, and hope to establish that we have improved and are better than they were, the scales fallen away from our eyes at last. This is so common a stance that I can't think of an autobiographical piece in recent years that does not (somehow) assume it. Or try to escape the problem by depicting our ancestors as innocent and lovable comedians.

I am not going to apologize for any of the values my family and ancestors may or may not have held. I am not going to apologize—or make light of the things they did that they ought not to have done and the things they left undone that they ought to have done. If I were being facetious, I would argue that the contemporary celebration of cultural relativism ought to be extended to include the dead. One of the characteristics of our secular society is the assumption that the living have not only the right but the duty to exhume and desecrate the dead. Saint Augustine was not strictly talking theology when he asserted his belief that the dead are beyond our capacity to wound or bless, to praise or blame. And that—best news of all—there is not and never has been any evidence that the dead *care* one way or the other what we think of them. Their attention seems to be focused elsewhere. (Well, in any case, we shall all be able to test the validity of his observations sooner or later, soon enough, won't we?)

Recently, in the *New York Times Book Review*, the point was made that Jefferson Davis never apologized for the Civil War, as, evidently, he should have. How do you suppose he would have framed his apology?

My family fought on both sides in that war, the worst war in all of modern history in terms of ratio of killed and wounded to general population.

And I knew some of those veterans in the flesh, by touch and by voice. As far as I know none of them apologized for it either.

And I am afraid I lack the necessary self-esteem to apologize on their behalf.

Hand in glove with the contemporary rush to judgment is the high-fever, hallucinatory joy of historical and personal guilt, self-righteousness turned inside out to display a wonderfully shrugging, worldlier-than-thou attitude which is sometimes confused by ignorant or innocent others as a posture of care, concern, compassion. I, too, must bear my burden of contemporary guilt like a student's obligatory backpack. But I flatly refuse to add to it one ounce, one feather's weight, of historical guilt for anything. I am not guilty of and for the actions of anyone but myself. Much that is autobiographical purports to be confession. I have yet to read any modern confession, in prose or in poetry, that is not so buttressed with mitigation and extenuation as to seem, finally, to ask more for reward than for punishment, that is not more a plea for love and understanding than a hope for judgment and forgiveness.

Still and all, dead and living faces do speak to us. Sometimes, as in the familiar Tudor court portraits by Holbein, the Elizabethan miniatures by Hilyard, they are, to our eyes, so masklike and enigmatic as to speak only mysteries in an unknown tongue. Sometimes, as in those Brady photographs, they do communicate some things clearly enough, some things in common. As different as they are from each other, those faces reveal an assumption that life is tragic and that pain, outward and inward, is a constant companion. They reveal the wish to be seen and known as courageous, strong enough to endure much, brave enough to seek to bear the best and worst without any wincing.

Above all, they do not wish to be taken as silly, foolish, laughable, or even as mainly clever. Wisdom and not shrewdness is their professed ideal. They do not plead for the love of perfect strangers. Look at the portraits of Henry James, or even those of Walt Whitman, that great poet and often profoundly silly man, who was surely wild for the love and admiration of strangers. See how he fell into the proper pose of the period. Consider that not one poet alive can even manage to make those expressions, not on a bet.

Something happened to our faces as we moved into this century. You can see it, conservatively enough, in the official faces of our presidents. Wilson, Harding, Coolidge even, though they already wore our own physiognomy, kept at the expression of hard seriousness they inherited from their fathers. Hoover began to lax and soften into inexplicable cheerfulness. And then, after Harry Truman, all of them, one and all, convey the foolish idea of wanting to be loved. Even Lyndon Johnson, who might have managed some nineteenth-century expressions if he had only known how. Next to our late-twentieth-century presidents, on the strength of faces alone, Rutherford B. Hayes, the nineteenth, and Benjamin Harrison, the twenty-third, for example, look like giants of the earth.

What is the message of the new face, the latest version? Think of our poets and novelists. Then go beyond the fragile arts and enter the worlds of the likes of Trump and Boesky, Iacocca and Icahn. It's all the same. Here are faces at once sly and shrewd (nobody would accuse them of expressing any wisdom except, perhaps, what used to be called worldly wisdom), ruthless and yet somehow sensitively vulnerable. Pitiless yet somehow self-pitying. There is an assertive weakness glossing over a dedicated and self-centered cruelty. They seem to beg for love and forgiveness even as they threaten to break your bones in two. And empty your pockets at the same time.

Contemporary man looks to be, by his own design and admission, a curious hybrid composed of almost equal parts of Woody Allen and General Manuel Antonio Noriega.

My generation, call them the cousins, is widely scattered geographically. As well as in the South, we are in Seattle and Santa Monica, Maine and Pennsylvania, New York City and New Hampshire. We are no longer likely to gather in strength and numbers even for weddings and funerals. This generation, however, remains tribal. I am typical in that I married into a family and tribe more or less like my own. Smaller and, in a sense, more distinguished. One that includes people like George Washington's Indian agent, Jasper Parrish, as well as (possibly) a famous Mohawk chief. Includes a prominent member of the Constitutional Convention, Nathaniel Gorham, and, farther back, the ship's carpenter on the *Mayflower*. Half of this family is southern, too, coming out of Alabama. And it is a tribe with values similar to our own, though more dignified, more calmly serious.

Much was probably wrong with old America and the early American colonists, and historians are busy telling us as much about their sins and follies as they can find out or imagine. But somehow, and simply, without special pride but without shame either, the old Americans created the place and the climate of social hope and political liberty which have attracted so many others from all over the face of the earth. This was their intention. This was their triumph. It cannot be revised away by anyone except a liar.

The newest generation of our tribe—call them, here, nieces and nephews, distant cousins and grandchildren—has almost uniformly married well outside of the tribe and its affiliations. The nation's suddenly self-conscious plurality is our own. The latest generation includes wide ethnic and even racial diversity. There are now blacks and Orientals who bear our family names and add hugely to its history.

We left my great-grandfather in a cornfield in Alabama or Georgia (most likely, in context, in Tennessee), having discovered that there were other armed men in those rows besides his own. Men in the blue uniforms of the enemy they had killed and who had tried to kill him and the others. What did he do? Well, from somewhere he produced a white handkerchief and, holding it, crawled among the Yankee soldiers until he met, face to face, his counterpart, a young Yankee officer crawling toward him on his hands and knees. Face to face like bookends, they held a whispered negotiation. This was, as he was, beyond grudges. Both groups had the same aim and idea—the old cow browsing nearby. Both had the same essential fear—hanging for the crime if the farmer caught them at the business of killing and butchering his cow. The two young veteran officers were good soldiers and reasonable men. They made an arrangement to work together and to divide the meat half and half. And that they did, spending what was left of that day doing it. So that all the men of both groups were, for once, well fed, full, and satisfied and lived to fight each other to the death on other days.

And he lived to hold me in his hands and on his lap and tell me that story.

And here and now I pass it along to you (like any other storyteller), claiming that I was there, even as I am here, and that at the center of the story there is something that speaks to you and me in the unknown tongue that we both understand.

Mosaics of Southern Masculinity

Small-Scale Mythologies

PAT C. HOY II

Nobody under forty can believe how nearly everything's inherited.

Reynolds Price

He simply wasn't there. My sister and two of her friends were comforting my Mom as we sat out front of our bus station in the 1943 sedan. As I scampered over the front seat into the back, I was stunned by her grief. It caught me in mid air, and as I toppled into the space between Ellisene and Dot, I stopped my squirming and snuggled down deep. He was gone, and he wouldn't be back. They were trying to help her through the ordeal, trying to stop the heaving and the suffering. And even though their words made no sense to me, I could feel her loss in my five-year-old bones. He was gone.

I saw him occasionally for brief periods over the next twenty-four years, but when he died at fifty-six of cirrhosis of the liver, I had not known him. I had no cause to miss him until I was thirty-five and it seemed my own marriage wouldn't survive. I missed him again at forty-three when Patrick left for college, and I began to wonder if I had done enough for him and his younger brother Tim, began to rummage around in my memories recalling signs of my father's influence, began, for the first time, to try to assemble a mosaic of my own masculinity.

I must have been seven or eight, sitting at my desk on the sleeping porch, working under the glare of a hanging light bulb, when my half brother, home on furlough, walked through the room and stopped to watch me do my arithmetic. I was absorbed in the figuring and could hear only the thud and soft glide of the iron as Mom touched up her dress for work. After a few minutes Willard interrupted me.

"Make a five again."

"Huh?"

"Make a five."

I made one. Starting at the bottom of the half circle, I moved the pencil around counterclockwise to the top of the curve, made a short vertical line straight up, and moved the lead point to the right, completing the horizontal bar, all without ever lifting my pencil from the paper. One smooth, natural motion. Easy. A five from the bottom up.

"Look at this, Mother," he exclaimed, obviously beside himself. "Have you ever seen Butch make a five? Pat Hoy! No one but Pat Hoy makes a five like that!"

I didn't understand his excitement, but I remembered the moment —my first conscious memory of my dad's influence, all the more interesting to me now because I know he didn't teach me to make fives. Neither did Miss Culbertson, nor Miss Barnes, nor any of my other teachers. It was a genetic remnant that came along with his smile lines, his love of fast cars, and his damning fascination with women. I knew none of this at seven.

The last time I drove Mom from Hamburg to Little Rock, she was eighty-five. I was forty-two. We had just left Monticello heading north for Star City, and I was stuck behind a log truck and a couple of straggling cars. When an opening came, I made my move, whizzed past the three vehicles, and eased back into my lane as a southbound eighteen-wheeler breezed by. I turned to Mom with a smile breaking on my face.

"Pat Hoy!" she said.

"What?"

"I've seen him do it a thousand times."

"Do what?"

"Turn to me with that look and a grin from ear to ear, wait'n for approval."

Three years later, in the fall of the year, I was at Fort Leonard Wood, Missouri, with two younger army officers. After two hard days of trying to teach high-ranking civil servants and senior officers to write more effectively, we needed sustenance. Leonard Wood had only a steak-and-fries restaurant on the strip and a small nightclub. We opted first for the mediocre food and then on a whim drove across the highway to the honky-tonk. We had spent six summer weeks with our traveling word show, laughing our way through airports, making students laugh while they learned in the classroom. We had a fairly good sense of each other's daytime habits. At nights we had gone our separate ways, visiting friends at each of the posts, army life being very much a small-town experience. The communities were separate, spread all over the world, but nonetheless of a piece. I was never a stranger in any one of them.

Our favorite pastime during the previous summer had been a Jungian game. We tried to second-guess each other's taste in women, tried to guess the nature of the woman in the other man's head. It was a game of images. We tried to predict "grid overlap," guessing when the woman in the classroom or the airport or on the plane would match the imagined woman in one of our buddy's heads. We joked about "anima seizures": spellbinding image overlap. The game was an older man's contribution to the summer fun.

The club across the street from the restaurant was small and close, but it felt friendly when we walked in in our khakis, polo shirts, and docksiders. The Missouri cowboys paid no attention, but the waitress seemed amused when she brought the beers. A Willie Nelson number drew couples out into the hazy space of the dance floor where refracting lights played softly around cowboy hats and occasionally found a patch of sequined hair. A strapping, lithe woman and her little man caught my eye. They were feeling their way around the floor, lost in the rhythms of those "lonely, lonely times."

Before I knew it, one of my buddies was on the floor, cutting in. The little man went back to his table, sat down, and tilted his hat forward just a bit. He sat with his back to us, but I could see him hook the heels of his boots over the bottom rung of the chair, slightly defiant.

The woman seemed unaware that she had changed partners. When she went back to the table, her man continued to stare at the door.

The vocalist didn't sound much like Anne Murray, but when she launched into "Son of a Rotten Gambler," I knew I couldn't sit there drinking beer any longer. I walked over to the strapping woman and asked her if she'd like to dance.

Reaching for my hand, she said, "I'd really like to, but I can't."

I asked her why not.

"He doesn't want me to dance with anyone else."

I looked over at him, sitting there immobilized, still staring at the front door. He might not have moved for three songs. They hadn't danced again. So I moved between them.

"Would you mind if I danced with your friend?" I asked, feeling my way into the protocol.

He didn't move his eyes.

"Look," I said, pulling up a stool from the table behind us. "I'm not after your woman. I just want to dance this song with her."

He cleared his throat but kept up his business with the door.

She reached up and put her hand on my arm, pulling me down in her direction as she said, "I'm sorry. I really would like to dance, but I can't do it tonight."

I made it back to our table as the singer slid into the last stanza. "He'd be the son of his father, / His father the teacher." But the teacher wasn't there to ask. I wondered what he would have done, wondered what the honky-tonk rules called for.

I remember his stopping by our house late one afternoon when I was about thirteen; he was on the way out of town, on the move as usual. I could smell vodka over Dentyne. Mom asked him where he was headed.

"Juking."

"Where to?"

"Chula."

I didn't know where Chula was, but I guessed it was the Howdy Club in El Dorado, miles away over the dump, a long stretch of suspended roadway flanked on both sides by the Ouachita River. I expected him to die there. But in those days, his life seemed charmed. Chula, I now suspect, was Xanadu. It was there he built his "dome of pleasure," there he "drunk the milk of Paradise." And perhaps, like me, as he listened to the "woman wailing," he "heard from far / Ancestral voices." I felt close to him that night in Missouri, very close, felt him in my bones again. And I felt too a painful advantage. He didn't have the wherewithal to distinguish the woman in his head from the one outside. Seizures carried him through life, and when the charms wore out, his liver couldn't carry the load.

The next morning at the post exchange, I saw the strapping woman. The image had dissipated; it couldn't hold up under the light of day. But she held up quite well. She apologized again, said her man had had a hard day, said he wasn't usually like that, said he was a good man. She thanked me for letting them be the night before. I liked her, liked my Dad. I think he would have left the cowboy alone too. He was good at that, leaving people alone. Until that morning, it had never seemed a virtue.

When my father began to reappear in my imagination, I turned to Erich Neumann for clarification. He claims that all of us have two fathers (as well as two mothers), one actual, the other archetypal, spiritual—a collective Father. Sons, in the decidedly patriarchal psychology of Neumann's *Origins and History of Consciousness*, must overcome both of the World Parents and both of the actual parents in order to gain independence and reach maturity. The son-hero initially fears the threat to "the spiritual, masculine principle," fears "being swallowed by the maternal unconscious," and needs help at the outset from the fathers. Because I had shut my real father out of my life and out of my imagination for so long, he was no help to me as a youngster. What independence I gained from the Mothers, I gained at the hands of the town Fathers who saw to my upbringing in a small southern hamlet that bears even today the indelible stamp of masculinity.

Neumann tells us, " 'The fathers' are the representatives of law and order, from the earliest taboos to the most modern judicial systems; they hand down the highest values of civilization, whereas the mothers control the highest, i.e., deepest, values of life and nature." Those gender differences ring true of my experience. The collective voice, the voice of the fathers there in that little hamlet called Hamburg, said this: you will be in the Boy Scouts; you will play football; you will go on the hunt; you will expose yourself to trials so that you can test your strength and independence; you will be a man and uphold the institutional values (never mind our own waywardness; what we represent, not what we do, that's what's important). The deepest voices said something different: you will be a gentle man; you will go to church; you will love and honor your mother and father (even if he has deserted you); you will avoid conflict and danger; you will remain always loyal to us, the deepest voices; you will never abandon us.

But there were ironic inconsistencies. The town fathers held up only part of their bargain. They understood too little of the myth they were unconsciously enacting. They pushed me into tests but did not draw me into community. My time on the hunt was limited to a day at a time, no weekends, no continuity, no time for fellowship. They forced Mom to let me play football, not because they were concerned about my development but because I was fairly tough and wiry; they wanted a winning team. The scouting activities were more satisfying; the men looked after our development. They drew all of us together, gave us their time and their guidance, took us in the woods, took us west to a national jamboree in California, taught us teamwork and responsibility. But always, at the end of those activities, the scoutmasters went home with their own sons. I could never confirm the experience, after the fact, with a man. The rituals never claimed me entirely. But, of course, no one knew that anything was missing. I certainly didn't.

There was yet another irony at work in my life long before I was aware of it. It was my mother, not my father, who sent me off to West Point, off to war—the same woman who, sending two sons to the last world war, had lost one, the same woman who had lost a young husband to an early death and a second to a woman in his head. Seduced by the spell of the old romance, unable to see the irony of what she was doing, she sent me away to redeem herself. She surely didn't know that, and neither did I, at the time.

Of another generation, I felt no deep yearning for the sound of the guns. Lead soldiers and toy cannons, "Dixie" and rebel flags had not moved my spirit. I had built my model airplanes in youth to commemorate the loss of my brother, one of the world war's ball-turret gunners. My electric train remains even today a reminder of my father's absence that Christmas morning, my sixth birthday. Had I been born a decade later, I might, like Sam Pickering, have decorated my model planes with flowers. But I came after the Agrarians and before the flower children. My sense of irony blossomed in a war foreign to both of them. When I left for West Point, the Old South had not claimed me. I wanted out, wanted to turn my back on the whole shootin' match. Northeast seemed like a good way to go. It was the only heroic thing left to do. The dragon still needed slaying.

Years later, after Vietnam, after my father's death, when I finally turned my mind south again, I began to understand what Allen Tate meant, in "A Southern Mode of the Imagination," about the change that took place after World War I, the change that turned the southern mind inward, causing it to "shift from rhetoric to dialectic," creating what he later characterized as a "literature of introspection" rather than a "literature of romantic illusion." I was not the "old Southern *rhetor*, the speaker who was eloquent before the audience but silent in himself." Rummaging around inside my head, I was discovering my heritage, recovering lost remnants of masculinity, developing a sense of irony. By that time, I had "slayed" the Mothers and saved my marriage, knew enough Jung to be dangerous, and had begun to make peace with the woman in my head. She was occasionally helpful as I moved into middle age, and the stories I began to tell myself in order to live seemed mythic. They began to reach beyond me into the world. I sensed that I could never be alone again.

In "A Lost Traveller's Dream," Tate writes of memory, her feminine nature, her free will. He writes of the difficulty of arresting the "flow of inner time." Memory, he says, has "its own life and purposes; it gives what *it* wills. . . . The Latin *memoria* is properly a feminine noun, for women never forget; and likewise the soul is the *anima*, even in man, his vital principle and the custodian of memory, the image of woman that all men both pursue and flee." Tate reminds us too that the "imaginative writer is the archeologist of memory, dedicated to the minute particulars of the past, definite things—*prima sacrimenti memoria*. If his 'city' is to come alive again from a handful of shards, he will try to fit them together in an elusive jigsaw puzzle, most of the pieces of which are forever lost." By the time I read Tate's words, my life had already confirmed them, but they still give me consolation. They point the way into a deeper myth.

But Tate's own notions about the southern myth seem to me a product of the very rhetorical mode he denigrated. He couldn't escape the story that the Old South told itself. Writing about Faulkner in 1968, Tate argues that "the Southern legend is a true myth which informed the sensibility and thought, at varying conscious levels, of the defeated

South." He goes on to add parenthetically that myth is "a dramatic projection of heroic action, or of the tragic failure of heroic action, upon the reality of the common life of a society, so that the myth *is* the reality." But when Tate illustrates what he actually means by the southern myth, he relays the old story about the curse of slavery, the invasion from outside, the destruction of a culture. Myth is historical, a story imposed on a culture from the outside, a way of accounting for what happened, rather than a story that embodies a culture's sensibility. Working from the outside, imposing a story on events, Tate buries the more powerful, stabilizing story that has always been there in the images and activities of family life.

Yet Tate knew that other story. In "The Fugitive," he tells us that he and his friends took with them to the university "a simple homogeneous background . . . a sort of unity of feeling, of which we were not then very much aware, which came out of—to give it a big name— a common historical myth." But wasn't the "common historical myth," as Tate's words suggest, a mere intellectual construct for what was and still remains an inherent sensibility? The southern community itself was there before the war: masculine and feminine; the higher values of law and order underscored by the deeper values of life and nature.

I'll Take My Stand seems in retrospect a colossal masculine effort to save a South that was not destined to disintegrate—a masculine, intellectual effort to stop the onslaught of industrialism. The manifesto was conceived in the old rhetorical mode. Tate explained that mode in the Faulkner piece, explained it in terms of Yeats's epigram: "It is the way we quarrel with others, not ourselves." The Agrarians undervalued the strength of the deeper values, the force of their cohesiveness. They certainly cherished those deeper values, but their faith was, I think, in themselves as rhetoricians. By a mere act of intellection, they would make one last-ditch rhetorical effort to save the South. It may well have been the last mighty beat of a dying aristocratic impulse—the heavenly, evangelical fathers saving a culture by a laying on of minds.

A child of the matriarchy, I was raised on the South's deeper values. My sense of law and order, skewed by my sense of the foibles of actual men, caused me to undervalue the archetypal Father just as the Agrarians, in the manifesto, inadvertently undervalued the Great Mother. I grew up in a house where dependence was more important than independence. So I grew up secure, seeing no need to hold my life together with stories. Life was just fine until I moved out of that southern hamlet into the world of conflict—into the mania of competition, war. Yet the remnants of masculinity passed on to me by the town fathers served me well enough when I moved east. I carried to West Point and later to Penn a sense of community that had shaped my imagination without my knowing it. I had a survival kit but had no sense of its inherent ironies, complexities, contradictions, strengths. I would not begin to understand that inheritance fully until nearly thirty years later, when I read Bill Berry's "Class Southerner." That essay gave me a sense of myself, a sense of what made me different from almost all my northern friends. When I read literature or read the history books, I, like Berry, "wanted more than brilliance." I wanted "the fleshed body of a living past." I looked too for the story that formed around the words, the personal myth that shaped the writer's vision.

Sitting here as I am, trying to fit the "handful of shards" together in the jigsaw puzzle that will constitute my own version of the city, I know that the masculine pieces are just now beginning to fit in place. Active all along, they have been influential in subtle ways. But my aversion to machismo—the boxing ring, the stench of the cadet gymnasium, the army's insistence on masculine standards even when such standards are inappropriate—has made me a maverick through my years of military service. Nevertheless, I have not left the army even when I have had the chance and the inclination to do so. I have been unwilling to turn the business of law and order over to the "real men." They spend too much time building monuments to their own magnificence. They spend too much time in the gymnasium. They undervalue the deeper values.

In the last few years, my imagination—working, I suspect, under some law of its own—has led me back into community with the South, into community with southern men: Roy Reed, George Core, Richard Marius, Bill Berry, Sam Pickering, William Humphrey, men whose work occasionally leads me to the telephone to talk with one of them about shared values, about a sense of place, about my own work.

I find Pickering's essays amusing. He's funny, and his deft affectations keep me interested, despite the fact that I know he's covering up an aristocratic impulse—the last Agrarian gone east. There is always the tension between the scruffy, doting, self-deprecating, rambling professor putting off his work so that he can perform ineptly but lovingly some family task—there is always the tension between that persona and the distinguished (but, of course, struggling, barely-making-ends-meet) man of letters: Sewanee, Cambridge, Princeton, Fulbright lecturer, world traveler. Even the titles of the early essays from *A Continuing Education* betray his pretense to commonality: "Man of Letters," "Pedagogica Deserta," and, a pair of ringers, "The Books I Left Behind" and "Reading at Forty," catalogs, albeit funny ones, of all the books he's ever read—a kind of Willie Nelson/Julio Iglesias tribute to a lifetime of intellectual promiscuity. But he just manages to pull it off, this Tennessee promoter of the deeper values. And when he turns himself into the pied piper of letters, I believe him, believe the fan mail from readers, believe the tributes from students as far away as Syria, believe that in the long run—all clowning aside—what's most important to him is family, in a larger sense, community. I resist the pretentious persona but surrender, finally, to Pickering and to continuity.

"Son and Father," from *The Right Distance*, begins with an informing image of his father, an image that made Pickering realize something about likenesses and the absurdity of repudiation. He walked into his father's room one evening to ask him about a book and found the older man asleep, "pajamas . . . inside out, as mine invariably are," found on the bed an older version of himself, positions identical: "Right leg pulled high toward the chest, and left thrust back and behind with the toes pointed, seemingly pushing us up and through the bed." During that moment of insight, "youth's false sense of superiority" fell away, and Pickering was bound to his father by "patterns of living."

The essay reconstructs a relationship even as it exposes threats to a "small-town world of particulars and familial relationships." Tracing with him the lines of his inheritance, I see why Pickering's persona is so intent on keeping his life simple, free from the entangling alliances of big money, great universities, corporations. Agrarian son that he is, he sees clearly where we seem to be headed, but instead of serving us the great sweep of history, the war and all that pomp, he gives us the most profound myth of all, the common, unabstracted patterns of a life of continuity and community.

In Pickering's discoveries about himself and his masculine inheritance, we discover the key to his literary sensibility. Like his father, who went to college "during the great years of Vanderbilt's English department—the years of the Fugitives and the Agrarians," he looks askance at criticism that abandons life, "shifting from the personal and anecdotal to the intellectual and the abstract." "In the sixty years that have passed since Father entered Vanderbilt," Pickering tells us, "criticism has become more rarefied, and the result is, as a friend and critic wrote me, 'we write books that even our mothers won't read.'"

Carthage, Tennessee, tied his father to a world of particulars and family values; it tied him to life. In turn he tied young Samuel to the same life. Samuel, looking back, claims that "Pickerings lived quiet lives, cultivating their few acres and avoiding the larger world with its abstractions of honor, service, and patriotism. For them country meant the counties in which they lived, not the imperial nation. . . . With the exception of the Civil War, the struggles of the nation have not touched us." He finds strength in this response to life: "We are soft and, in our desires, subconscious or conscious, to remain free, have become evasive. Few things are simple though, and this very evasiveness may be a sign of a shrewd or even tough vitality"—or perhaps a sign of the "great historical myth" recreating itself in human terms.

Pickering's sense of his family's shrewd, tough vitality reminds me of Roy Reed's stirring essay about the country folks in Arkansas's Ozark Mountains—rednecks, trash, survivors. Unlike Pickering, who recreates little southern hamlets wherever he goes, Reed left a prestigious London assignment with the *New York Times* and returned to his roots, returned to the land his father gave up when he moved to Hot Springs in pursuit of the dream. Reed returned, I think, to find out if he had what he calls the "Mother of vinegar—the few drops that contain the life of the entire line and from which a new batch of vinegar can be started any time." His rootstock comes clear in an epistolary piece, "A Letter to My Great-Grandfather." The wedding of his own son to an Ulster Catholic gives him occasion to write this spirited account of how the family line has been faring for the last hundred or so years. Reed writes half in jest about rednecks and survival, but he's concerned about folks marrying outsiders and those "leaving the hills and hollers" under the influence of Sears and Roebuck catalogs. In town, the men wear "themselves out on the pavement, running after the dream," and die young. The women with their washing machines fare no better. "They are," Reed tells his grandpa, "the unhappiest people I know."

The people in and around Hogeye are different, though. They're interested in a life of community, interested too in living close to nature. Coming to Reed's essays the first time, I was struck by their masculine power. I read *Looking for Hogeye* while working on an essay of my own about mother-son journeys of separation, a piece in which I was overvaluing the matriarchate. Reed's essays caught me up short, put me back on track, led my imagination through the mother to the father. In "Spring Comes to Hogeye," it is not a woman who is close to nature but a man. Reed writes lovingly of Ira Solenberger, whose life is so closely tied to the seasons that he, in concert with spring's late coming, knows intuitively to plant his crops late. Reed respects this old man's perception, cares about him. He makes us see that Ira dies in harmony with the seasons. His existence has followed a mysterious rhythm of ebb and flow.

In a larger sense, Ira is important to Reed because his death signals the loss of a special breed of hill people. Reed, like Andrew Lytle before him, understands the consequences of industrialism for the farming community. Lytle argued sixty years ago that "a farm is not a place to grow wealthy, it is a place to grow corn." He warned the South to "dread industrialism like a pizen snake." Reed's essays record the consequences, confirm the terrible loss. But he is not without hope. He relishes country folks' "plain damned meanness" and savors their sense of community: "Country people look after one another. . . . The trash take care of their own, not out of goodness but out of necessity. There is no one else to do it." Reed, like Pickering, refuses to give in to the disintegration. He is, after all, back in Hogeye recording the myth of community.

In "Fall," we enter the woods with a "bunch" of hunters, some old, some young. We might just be in the Mississippi woods with Faulkner tracking bear, but this ritual develops on a smaller, more accessible scale. The hunters' primary business is squirrel hunting. Reed's is the "exhilarating mystery that puzzles every hunter: the discovery that he can detect the presence of game by some sense that is beyond hearing, seeing or even smelling." Throughout this essay, Reed intersperses another narrative that begins in 1943 against the backdrop of war. It is a story about the "expectations that every Southern boy has a right to see filled at a certain time," a narrative of male ritual: the first hunt, the first drink, the first kill. That ritual "tied the boy not only to the uncle but, more importantly, to his father, and tied the two of them to the ancestral woods." But then, "the son lost his taste for it." Hunting became a "single ritual hunt each year," and the government flooded the land. The "bond was dissolved and the son set adrift from his own blood." "Fall" is a story of cultural disintegration embedded in a story of perpetuation, of renewal and mystery. Like Ira Solenberger, Reed's hunting neighbors live close enough to the land to live the myth.

Compare this to Allen Tate's view of the hunt: "One September day in the valley below Sewanee, twenty-five years ago, I shot a dove that fell into the weeds, and when I found her she was lying head up with a gout of blood in each eye. I shot her again. Her life had been given to my memory; and I have never hunted from that day." Tate explains his decision: "The feminine memory says: Here is that dying dove; you must really kill it this time or you will not remember it from all the other birds you have killed; take it or leave it; I have given it to you." One writer sees only the deeper values and not the highest. The other sees beyond the killing to the continuity, sees within the image of death itself the stuff of survival.

William Humphrey discovered the stuff of survival as a kid in Texas. In his memoir, *Farther Off from Heaven,* he resurrects a tough, wiry father every bit as wild as my own dad. He frames his memoir with his father's premature death. The fatal automobile wreck on the Fourth of July, 1937, was a strange, ironic emancipation for a boy of thirteen, but he survived because of a father's gift. Hunting was for the two of them an intimate, life-sustaining experience. The father himself had taken to the woods as a sanctuary from his tyrannical parents; he was, at first, the hunted. On his own in the woods, he learned to survive. He went there to verify the stories of danger told by outsiders; he went there "to see the dragons in their den." What he learned, he passed on to his son.

Reinventing years later the morning on which he and his mother accompanied his father's mangled body on the ambulance ride to Paris, Texas, Humphrey thought of the magic of those woods he shared with his father. He remembered the break of day, the pristine moment of first light, remembered that the "change seemed chemical, like a photographic print in the developer in the dimness of the darkroom, the image appearing out of nothingness, then rapidly becoming distinct, recognizable, familiar." He remembered his father's transformation in the woods, remembered that "old boyish wonder": "My oneness with him gave me some of his sense of oneness with that world." That world —their world, the world of the father and the son—was a world of trust and companionship, a world in which the two were on such intimate terms they could dispense with talk. Deep in the woods on an alligator hunt, Humphrey claims to have found "along with the deepening strangeness . . . a familiarity, as though one had been here before, but in another life"; he expected around one of the turns that the "long-forgotten, universal mother tongue" would come back to them; he thought they might very well reenter paradise. Telling this story, Humphrey reenacts Marlow's journey up the river to visit Kurtz, but these voyagers come back bound together for life. No need for Marlow's noble lie. They do not submit. They meet the alligator-dragon, subdue it, make it their own. They return, young and renewed.

Death, then, was not a new experience for the thirteen-year-old boy, but the sudden, revolting loss of his father was. Premature death shocked him because it left him alone. We can judge the severity of the jolt and the power of his father's influence by Humphrey's reaction on the night before the funeral: "My last night's sleep in Clarksville, with my father's body lying in the next room, would be my last ever, I vowed. No visits home for me, no reopening of wounds. It was a vow I was to keep for thirty-two years."

But finally, like a salmon's, Humphrey's "homing instincts" got the best of him, and he defied his vows. Back in town with a guide, he comes upon two boys playing in the cemetery; they offer to help him find the grave they think he's searching for: "Looking at either of them was like looking at myself through the wrong end of binoculars. I gave them half a dollar apiece, a token repayment for all the many nickels that men of Clarksville had given me in my time . . . thanked them; said no, we were not looking for any grave, what we were looking for was just the opposite: some spot where there was not any grave, where there was still room for one. Why? Was somebody dead? No; not yet."

The Texas Humphrey had come back to was changed, just as Cumberland, Hogeye, and Hamburg have changed. Lytle was dead right about the onslaught of industrialism. But something remains of place that is as timeless as those river bottoms Humphrey entered with his father, something deep. It calls us back wherever we are, calls us back into community. Whether our fathers were there or not, whether they took us literally on the hunt, whether they left us land or left us landless, there hovers about the place a presiding spirit, masculine, indomitable, inviolable.

There is mystery. My father, I used to think, simply was not there.

I have discovered, over time, that he was, still is. He's there, like the place; he's there in my bones. I know it by the fives I make. I know it by the cars I drive and the way I drive them, know it too by the smiling way I ask for recognition and confirmation. But I know it especially by my evolving relationship with the woman in my head. Like him, I know her power, know how easy it is to turn my life over to *anima*, seductress that she is, dancing there with her little cowboy in the starlight cafe. But I know too what he never seemed to learn. I know that she will not always stand up in the light of day, will not always stand up to the higher values. The real woman, outside my head, might, but the one inside is a different matter. She can lead me to destruction, or she can save me. Her duality is tricky business.

I have discovered that *anima* has a partner. *Anima*—soul, imagination, the woman in my head who is not a mere woman—*anima* and *animus* have been there all along in my psyche: a divine pair, a syzygy. James Hillman suggests, in *Anima: An Anatomy of a Personified Notion,* that to "imagine in pairs and couples is to think mythologically. Mythical thinking connects pairs into tandems rather than separating them into opposites." In my own acts of imagining, I recognize *animus* —a shaping, criticizing spirit. It has given me what Hillman calls "distance from mood." Perhaps it has given me what Sam Pickering might call the "right distance." I see more clearly now how the syzygy manifests itself in our time, how we can have "shrewd, tough vitality" on the home front, how the farmer can live in nature, how the intimacy of the hunt can match the intimacy of a good marriage. What I find in southern nonfiction and in my own imagination is a happy marriage of the highest and the deepest values, a mounting respect for the preservation of the community through close living, living so close to earth that we do not lose touch of her. I see there the myth of our time. And I hear from the bottomland of my imagination the deep cry of ancestral voices.

Class Southerner

J. BILL BERRY

O n my first day at Princeton, in 1967, I met my first southerner. I didn't like him—monogrammed dress shirt, bright red golf slacks shouting for attention, and washing (with the assistance of a black janitor) his new white Pontiac LeMans. He might, for all I could see, be ultimate Kappa Alpha. "Samuel Francis Pickering," he told me. His accent filled the air with molasses. I stirred it with a question. "Where are you from?" "Nashville," he responded. When I reciprocated, "Fay-etteville, Arkansas," he volunteered a prediction: "You're going to hate it here."

I had never lived outside Arkansas, or outside the twentieth century. At Princeton, I entered by the university gates a Gothic world where fierce gray gargoyles scowled from atop the great stone heaps I now called home. The medieval world that was the campus would have stretched the conservative principles of the most old-fashioned of men. I dived straight into the gargoyle's den, taking rooms at the graduate college, a particularly imposing example of Gothic architecture, laid out in quads, with well-groomed grounds and benefiting spring and summer from the refining and aromatic influences of the adjacent English formal garden. Over the green-tiled roof of the college, defining the skyline, soared Cleveland Tower, a larger but otherwise perfect replica of the main tower at Cambridge University. It was a fit symbol: we were in all ways possible an English outpost, a Cambridge on the western front, where the mind was never quiet, the tongue and pen, never still.

Nor had I ever seen a prettier town. Princeton was a postcard village then, with its imitation-English main street and square, its residential acres of flowering trees and shrubs where one grand house after another competed tastefully for attention. I had never lived among people of such diverse colors, features, accents, faiths, and customs and was at first a tourist of population. The green town-and-campus swatch that was Princeton reposed in the lap of industrial New Jersey, and Garden State factories had drawn millions of Italian, Slavic, and other southern and eastern European immigrants. The state, to this southern Protestant, seemed the western front of Rome and the terminus of a third diaspora. Ashkenazim and Sephardim—my mouth had never played with such syllables. Salvucci, Carlucci, and Tucci became familiar and easy, like Jones, and were twice as much fun to say—palpable and juicy as peaches to my tongue, with its fresh cunning.

Jews figured prominently in Princeton, and for the first time I lived among God's chosen: I didn't know anyone white could have such liquid eyes. The local Jewish community prospered, some active in Princeton businesses, law, or medicine. Others commuted daily to New York or Philadelphia, working hard at the trade of being highly successful and, like their non-Jewish counterparts, living the good life according to John Cheever.

What Princeton lacked was the poor or anything that could properly be designated the working class, unless one cared to call several hundred Italian and black workers, clustered in a small and dwindling neighborhood near the hospital, by a name more loosely fitting than a patient's gown. They were few, scattered in their working places, and permeated with the aspirations, styles, and manners of the encircling, prosperous community. While many of them managed to look as distinguished as the brokers and professors one met on the streets, some had experienced deprivation and no doubt knew it. But Princeton's poor had endured nothing to equal the bare, unremitting poverty of East Arkansas tenant farmers, or the Ozark mountain folk, whose memory trailed me to New Jersey.

Mostly, in this my new world (and never more than at the Graduate College), we observed the ancient forms of the English university. The housing manager was the porter, his office, the lodge; and I went that first day knocking at his gate (big brass knocker, heavy oak door) with almost superstitious awe. The head resident was the master of the

college (and a more charmingly crusty chap there never was); his apart-
ment, the master's quarters. The campus police were proctors, and I
am happy to say that I never saw the inside of their lodge and cannot
name its name.

The dining hall was a cathedral dedicated to the appetite, appropriate
to the scripture describing the body as the temple of God. Stained-glass
windows glowed in the gray stone walls, which rose to a vaulted ceiling
sixty feet at its peak. We did not drift into dinner casually but awaited
the appointed hour, when, on the more formal occasions, the organ,
with proper cadence and dignity, piped us in. We did not seat ourselves
one by one but waited for the master, or his appointed deputy, to offer
thanks, usually in Latin, sometimes in Hebrew, occasionally in Greek
—or else something exotic.

We could wear what we wanted. It did not matter: black academic
gowns, required even for guests, would cover whatever the costume
with which we had, during the day, profaned our persons. Be not de-
ceived: the ceremony was genuinely religious. But it had nothing to
do with God. It had everything to do with worship of the English university and its forms. Some of my new friends reveled in this worship
and delighted in being acolytes. Others resented it. A few took it as
a personal affront to which there could be no response—as though a
taxi driver, cab empty, ignored their hail and passed immediately beyond the range of their curse or raspberry. I had not been raised High
Church, in either religion or personal manners, but I knew enough of
ritual to understand its value. The ceremony had its points, especially
the gown. It saved on laundry, and I came to appreciate it as a sort of
fancy bib overalls.

The mysteries of ritual, I could penetrate. I had more trouble with the
way people talked. Everyone sounded so smart—"bright" or "clever"
being the words preferred at Princeton. Many had genius-level accents.
And I heard, for the first time, the twang, like a loose guitar string,
in my own voice. Everyone else heard it, too, and sometimes played
backup joker to my not so musical solos. My accent provoked good-
natured amusement and considerable curiosity. Upon meeting me, a
student in anthropology would ask, wonderingly, "What was it like,
growing up in Arkansas?" I was, I realized, her very first Samoan.

During my first dinner in Proctor Hall I encountered, from a gentleman soon to receive his Ph.D. in classics, the standard works of a

species of comedy that evidently owed its inspiration to "Beverly Hill-billies" outtakes:

> *Did I wear shoes to dinner?*
> Yes, and I wanted to thank him personally for the CARE package.
>
> *Did I grow up with indoor plumbing?*
> No, that's why Princeton was such an education for me.
>
> *Did I bring my pet pig to graduate school?*
> No, I was certain I could meet one here.

Perhaps my questioner thought nothing of the exchange. Or perhaps he derived a moral: white southerners, provided they're not violent, are almost as good-natured as black people.

Northeastern graduate students often considered Princeton a southern school located in a southern town. This view astonished me and other southerners at Princeton. "Somewhere in the greater Virginia area?" I asked a friend from New York City. "It's about like an Eskimo thinking 'Canada' and 'sauna' are synonyms," fumed Jim Tracey, a graduate of the University of Virginia. "Except maybe that makes the Eskimo think highly of Canada," I responded.

Most of my fellows had never visited the South, knew few southerners, and derived their perceptions of the region largely from newspapers, television, and movies. These sources, perhaps inevitably and regardless of their commitment to accuracy, passed over the typical, the humdrum routine and normal flow of southern life and highlighted and dramatized the romantic, the singular, the controversial, and the sensational. They magnified an impression, found among and fostered by southerners as well as northerners, that the South in basic ideals, traditions, and attitudes stood apart from the rest of the country—almost a separate civilization. These sources in their extremest expressions conjured images that verged on the fantastic and grotesque: the South as quagmire, miasmic and haunted and (after one scraped away the thin veneer of would-be aristocrats) peopled by brutalized but brave and endlessly enduring blacks; bland-brained but treacherous blue-eyed beauties and fading belles; scripture-spewing, hollow-souled, life-hating hypocrites; tobacco-spitting, paunch-bellied, graft-bloated sheriffs; inbred, bullet-headed, psychopathic idiots—a moral landscape worthy of the palette of some latter-day Hieronymus Bosch.

These images were not malicious fictions without foundation; they had basis in fact. Yet they were caricatures and increasingly dated as the South, for ill as well as good, had begun to merge in the common traffic of American life. Most of my colleagues did not subscribe fully to the stereotypes, but the images lingered and colored our relations. Perhaps a dozen acquaintances during my first year in Princeton questioned whether Jews would be safe in Arkansas, whether the mere circumstance of a northern accent or license plate would imperil life and limb. One colleague asked whether I had ever witnessed a lynching and had difficulty believing it when I said that there had never been a lynching in my hometown and that, so far as I knew, no one in my family had ever belonged to the Ku Klux Klan, the Knights of the White Camellia, or any other such organization. We didn't even belong to the Lions Club.

Some of my fellow students assumed that I was racially prejudiced and on occasion counted on it. One day, as I walked across the campus with a New York associate, a black teenager flew toward us on his ten-speed. Nearer and nearer he hurtled, then swerved around us, so close it might have been an afterthought. "Damn niggers!" my colleague exploded.

It had scared me, too, and I had a gift for anger. But here it pulled two ways. I stiffened visibly, and he noticed. "Should have kept every one of you in the South," he responded, trying to pass it off as a joke.

My colleagues were in most contexts swift to reprove stereotyping. Familiar with the tenets of cultural relativism, they might, with an airy wave of a platitude, dismiss any itemizing of the failings of Geronimo, Patrice Lamumba, or Eldridge Cleaver, while issuing a blanket indictment of the white neighbors who had taught me baseball, long division, and manners. I did not identify with Dixie, had not in Fayetteville and did not in Princeton. But from the beginning I defended my home and its people. My colleagues did not mean to insult me: I was all right, I had escaped, I fancied culture and was one of them. And wasn't I glad?

Captain Red Slacks fell in beside me a few days after our first encounter. His elegantly modulated voice poured out accent thickly, and I thought he was about to bow as he apologized for not "stopping round." "Lamentably remiss" he'd been in "virtues" imbibed from earliest childhood. I must forgive his not extending hospitality to me—a stranger in a strange land (a place lacking what he no doubt deemed the cardinal amenities). "But how are you finding it?" he asked.

It was New Jersey, and yet I stood in the awesome presence of the Lost Cause. "A southern gentleman of the old school," the Lost Causettes would have swiftly pronounced him. "HOW ARE YOU FINDING IT?" he repeated. I'd done nothing to invite it, but he mocked me all the same. The syrup chafed: from deep inside me rose an Ozarker's resentment of the aristocrat's condescension. "By the moss," I replied. "Grows thickest on the north side."

"That it does, Captain." He turned off at the bookstore and mounted the steps, singing a Roy Acuff classic:

Who did you say it was, brother?
Who was it fell by the way?
When whiskey and blood run together . . .

"I didn't hear nobody pray," I finished for him. Maybe he'd intended to turn back. "If you're not busy, I'll stop in before dinner," he said. "A touch of the native drink and a few of your records will mix nicely, I think." I didn't know I'd played my music loudly, hoped he'd bring the native drink, for I didn't know what it was. He arrived early, sherry bottle in hand, and, after an exchange of civilities, asked if he might pick out a record. He passed over Mozart, B. B. King, and the Beatles. Then his face lit up. He'd found Hank Snow, troubadour of tragedy and sorrow.

Four sorrows later, the Nashville gentleman shook his head. Dipthongs cropped out of the rich accent, and, insinuatingly country, he said, "That boy can get sorry fast. And ache mighty bad."

Is he taunting me? I wondered. "Like he has a twang pouch hid behind his palate," I dipthonged back.

"Rawest, best nasals west of New Jersey," agreed my guest. He glanced out of the window. The first berobed colleagues passed by on their way to high dinner. "It's warm in here, don't you think?"

"Barn hot," I responded.

From his seat in the window, he cranked open the casement that faced directly on the courtyard and the imposing bronze figure of Andrew Fleming West, distinguished founder and first dean of the graduate college. "Turn up the record to turn down the pain," my guest requested.

Hank Snow could speak as well as he sang, and, from time to time, he'd always talked a little in his saddest songs. He reached a talking part in "Shep," a mournful number concerning a sorrowing master and his miserably ill, ever-faithful best friend. There was nothing left for it, Hank told us. Had to shoot old Shep. All them good times, tough times, too. (Hank was getting to me like he always did, and the odd fellow opposite me seemed ready to cry.) Hank wouldn't stop but made us see it: how Shep muzzled up to his master's knee, soft brown eyes looked up like they were saying, "It's all right, we'll meet someday in heaven."

"Gott in himmel!" exploded the dapper little Austrian physicist, face pressed against the window screen, eyes darting. "Care for some sherry, Herman?" asked my guest. "Or taking the air? The air, I see," said my companion, as Herr Herman hustled on.

"He doesn't care for the arts?" I speculated. "But it is time for supper." We gowned and soon stood in line with the rest. The organ sounded magisterially. "Who did you say it was, brother?" sang Red Slacks and grinned. I still had questions, knew he was trouble, and knew Sam Pickering was one of my friends.

Despite the questions concerning Arkansas, birthplaces were not the first order of curiosity. Where are you from?—whether asked of me or of anyone else—meant, Where did you go to college? This seemed to me almost bizarre and based on a false assumption; and I continued, even after I understood local usage, to answer, "Fayetteville." No one was "from" a college. "From" was where you were born. "From" was where your people lived (or were buried), where you were taught whatever it was you could later reject or accept, however redefining the terms, and live by when you went off to wherever it was that not everyone knew you, your people, and what you had probably been taught to think about strange people who asked odd questions without apology or even apparent recognition that they were behaving oddly: Princeton, in my case.

But it wasn't odd, after all. Natives of Boston, New York, and Philadelphia didn't have hometowns. They might have neighborhoods or boroughs, often had ethnicity, sometimes had a church or a synagogue. But they did not have hometowns, home people, or fellow citizens. They might, often did, have smugness, but not civic pride. The city had shaped each of them, and deeply. But it had not (and could not have) assumed responsibility for nurturing, protecting, and enforcing standards—for good or ill—in the way a hometown assumed responsibility for its young. That's why they learned "street smarts" instead of manners.

Not all my new associates were from Philadelphia, New York, or Boston; but between Brotherly Love and Beantown, everyone who wasn't from the Big Three was a commuter or an industrial worker, a group of no interest to my questioners, except, occasionally, as an abstraction called "the working class" or "the oppressed." For my northeastern friends, college was their first hometown.

I answered that I was from Fayetteville out of principle. I was stubborn and constitutionally inclined to tease anyone whose shirt appeared the least bit stuffed. I was also defensive. The alumni of Harvard, Yale, and Columbia considered "the University of Arkansas" a confession of academic illegitimacy, and they brandished their degrees as beauties flash teeth. Many had schooled their accents at Andover, Exeter, Choate—places familiar to me only through the stories of Scott Fitzgerald, J. D. Salinger, and John Cheever. They were far more sophisticated intellectually than I. And looked it. By November I was one of two first-year history students who remained unable to punctuate profundity with a puff of pipe smoke. The other was female.

They had graduated from the *New Yorker* and moved on to the *New York Review of Books* at a time when I still thought New Yorker was a kind of Chrysler, or possibly a competitor of the *New York Daily News*. Later I would, in response to a taunt concerning southern finishing schools, suggest that the *New Yorker* was the city's substitute for charm school: it taught would-be sophisticates their cultural table manners. My gibe stung no one because no one saw it as aimed at himself; all were the genuine rather than the ersatz article.

I had acquired information in college. They had acquired "concepts," a familiarity with scholarly literature and trends, and an ability to dissect arguments—the tools of the trade upon which we were embarking. The scholarly trend at Princeton, although not all faculty subscribed, was toward the "new social history." The department chairman and other leaders emphasized quantification, group biography or "prosopography," and other methodologies at the cutting edge of the discipline. Not only the new social historians but others as well stressed the generation and elaboration of theories and models of historical change. While some faculty wrote admirably well, most would have dismissed as old-fashioned, romantic, and trivial a conception of history as narrative art. As serious scholars, their beau ideal was history as science.

My fellow students came to Princeton for specific professional reasons. They knew thoroughly and could place precisely in historiographical context the work of the faculty. They came to embrace the new methodologies, to study with Lawrence Stone or, with different approaches in mind, Arno Mayer, Cyril Black, or some other ranking figure who would teach them what they already knew they needed to know. They stepped off the train at Princeton Junction requiring no directions to their rooms.

Had I known what they did, I wouldn't have taken the train: I didn't know the new social history from the same old dance. I knew that James McPherson and Martin Duberman had inside angles on the abolitionists, but the nineteenth century, except for Andrew Jackson and the Populists, didn't interest me. I respected the scholarly achievement of Frank Craven and Arthur Link, who, as my Uncle Loyce would say, had "run their papers mighty high." I liked Arthur Link for liking Woodrow Wilson and Frank Craven for writing the most gracious letter of any representative of the schools to which I applied. What intrigued me more than any other historical issue (if it was an historical issue) was Crèvecoeur's question, "What, then, is this American, this new man . . . ?"

The question lay behind my interest in the Populists. Crèvecoeur's independent yeomen had become, by the late nineteenth century, the dispossessed—shunted aside by an industrializing nation. I hadn't the right but took that personally. It was family feeling, a birthright once removed: Daddy grew up on a forty-acre, hardscrabble Ozark farm his daddy homesteaded. Maybe I had a weakness for hard-fighting losers. Most southerners do, I soon would read. "It was the Civil War and the whole Spanish moss–dripping cult of the Lost Cause and its heroes that did it," I explained to Bob Curvin, a black classmate, who was no less skeptical than I was. Populist orator Mary Ellen Lease had charged her farmer audiences, "Raise less corn and more hell!" At my best I shared her fury for economic justice and broadened democracy. I accepted, too uncritically I now believe, C. Vann Woodward's argument that the Populists had tried to build a genuine alliance of poor whites and blacks.

Here at Princeton I encountered a picture that I didn't recognize: the Populists as Negrophobes, nativists, and anti-Semites; vicious, simpleminded folk who were possessed of a conspiracy theory of history; agrarian Luddites who struggled vainly to restore a mythic America of sturdily self-sufficient yeomen living simply but comfortably in bucolic democratic harmony. My earlier view was naive, but this was radically unfair. It made me mad, and I couldn't let it pass. Mustering my self-control, I commented, "This scholarship dismisses the Populist program as based on irrationality, bigotry, and gross ignorance. It allows the farmers no reasonable choice but to abandon their farms for the cities."

"That's an interesting suggestion," responded my teacher. "The more intelligent, forward-looking rural dwellers moved to the cities, leaving a less able, reactionary element behind." It was the first time my teacher had complimented one of my ideas.

The atmosphere teemed with abstractions, "conceptual schemes," theories. My colleagues could crunch through concepts like Fritos, swallow frameworks whole, order a theory for lunch, and rise to walk on air. Even Christ required the water. It made me uneasy. At supper one of my associates asked how I "conceptualized" a problem I'd finished explaining. Exasperated, I answered, "I don't. It's hard enough just to think."

"But really," he responded, as exasperated as I, "how do you conceptualize the matter?"

"I don't conceptualize," I repeated. "Know folks who'd break your jaw if you said it to their daughters."

Pickering said I was uneasy because I was southern, that southerners instinctively rejected the abstract and the theoretical. States' rights dogma had nearly done us in; and, let theory pound furiously at the door, we'd not open. The store was closed, now and forever. I didn't buy it. I was uneasy because I was American. Theory seemed foreign, and not simply because it might challenge existing institutions and beliefs. It took too much education for the nation of Jackson, Lincoln, and Truman, who had done quite well without conceptual schemes, so I thought. Theory was an impurity in what I deemed to be the national spirit: practical and accommodating and capable of the give-and-take and compromise essential for a democratic system and heterogeneous population. Being southern, if my friend were partly right, just made me more American. The trouble was also personal. I wasn't good at conceptual schemes, had little practice or natural bent. The folds of the cerebrum were none so high as to allow Mind to mount and gaze to far-off places, see not separate hills but a straight line running, and connecting the long range of the past.

Pickering said northern intellectuals were analytical, southern ones, anecdotal. That I partly bought—had heard too many stories not to and here met people who had never told or listened and had little ear, however great their curiosity or appreciation. This was a key, I since have realized, to a fundamental difference in the way my classmates and I approached learning. They looked for conceptual frameworks, supporting evidence, inconsistencies in argument, and paid little attention to any music in the author's mind and words. I read for argument also but held to narrative as the spine and essence of the craft. I listened chiefly to the author's voice, his sensibility and vision as revealed in the language that gave being to his thought. I was unpersuaded by any reasoning, however bright or erudite, that showed no humor or sense of beauty or tragedy, that conveyed no feeling for complexities of character and the tawny wash of attitudes, values, fears, and prejudices of time and place. Whatever the writer knew, he failed to understand. Nor could he evoke it for his readers, nor would he be long read, even by those in his own profession. Readers wanted more than brilliance; they wanted the fleshed body of a living past.

My vision of history did not derive from school or college. I defined it late but absorbed it early. It grew largely from the experience of listening to my father and his brothers (and later, as they came into their art, my own brothers, too) as they "storied" for hours, reciting the sayings and doings of funny-turned or notorious characters, endlessly detailing one funny, sad, wild, or violent tale after another from their own, our relatives', our friends', or the community's past:

> There was that time, it was the wake of Red Tom Clark, said Uncle Loyce. Put a whiskey bottle in Red Tom's hand, cigar in his mouth, someone lit it, now and then. Topped him off with his favorite hunting cap and propped him up at the front door, hand out, to greet his own mourners.
>
> It was the final killing in the Sims-Macklin War, said Uncle Vic. Your Great-Uncle Sol was there. He told me, your daddy, too. I remember it, like I was there—the sweat-stained hats, dark eyes deep-sunk like the Sure Pop Mine (Ain't scairt, that one, said your Great-Uncle Sol; Why not now, said Orton Jacks, eager, like he was drooling over pork loin, ready to carve).

And so it would go until I, too, saw, like it was yesterday, the wake of Red Tom Clark. Saw, too, Fice Sims and Velt Macklin, the very stump the two of them stood by, their story shaping, transforming the day and making it more than the others, demanding a voice by which they and their day would never be lost. These and other stories like them were for me the first history and the root of my interest in history ever since.

All of our graduate classes were seminars with heavy reading loads and an emphasis on critical discussion of scholarly literature and class presentations—thrust and counterthrust. My classmates had devastating self-confidence; I was not prepared for the fray. My undergraduate experience was with lecture courses. There, the lecturer might ask questions, and someone always responded, sometimes out of genuine interest or desire to impress the teacher, sometimes out of simple courtesy or because of the tension that developed when a question hung in the air, too long unanswered. But one did not respond at the expense of fellow students. To have done so would have been to forfeit membership in the tribe.

Here there was no tribe and certainly no one to race to the rescue of any fallen comrade. It was single sculls in open waters that boiled with sharks. Schools of pilot fish competed fiercely for any leftovers. I liked it, but not at first, and it was a long time before I loved it. Initially, I recoiled from what I perceived as academic carnivores, intellectual cannibals; seminars as bloody communions, discussions, in and out of class, as clacking moveable feasts, feasts of snakes. I had no choice. I had never seen exchange in which civility and personality were not more important than the substance of what was said. I had never seen impersonal relations. My first lesson was to cease to regard discussion as conversation.

The history department then required all entering students to take an introduction to social science theories and methods. The course brought together all first-year students in an experiment designed to encourage interdisciplinary approaches to scholarly issues. Four faculty regularly participated; a visiting, and most distinguished, French scholar frequently sat in; and professors from other departments and universities often served as speakers and discussion leaders. The class concentrated the mind as Samuel Johnson said only hanging could do.

One day the discussion turned to the American Civil War, and I could see that I knew more than the rest. The tide in the affairs of men had come: I summoned confidence, girded on armor, and, a proper Captain Carpenter, sallied forth to do argument. I sounded thoroughly professional, I thought, as I slashed through the wilderness, extended the line of reasoning, and prepared to close in: "The Yankees . . ." You'd have thought I'd said something funny: the entire class collapsed. My poise, my advantage, and my argument came tumbling after. A week later, no one could have remembered my point. But my innocent, accident-of-a-phrase hung in the air like an unanswered question.

Not everyone thought it was innocent. I was the class southerner and the only member of the class who did not from the beginning recognize me as such. My place was to supply special information and represent the southern point of view. I wasn't up to it. I had never taken a course in southern history and, except for my childhood interest in the Civil War, I had done little informal reading in the field. Nor had I come to Princeton with any notion of specializing in the area. I would be well into my third term before I seriously considered the possibility, and then in large part because I had to declare a specialty. But my first weeks pushed me toward doing special homework. It was read up or seem ignorant, inarticulate, or embarrassed about what my colleagues expected to come naturally, easy as my accent, which, without a command of the cultural heritage from which it was presumed to come, would have appeared to be so much false advertising. Whom was I trying to fool? Who did I think I was, anyhow? I resolved to be prepared for any questions referred to the class southerner.

I did have a potential rival but didn't know it: he refused to enter the lists. "I say, old boy," he wheezed one mizzling October morning when the skies looked up at Cleveland Tower. "I believe we grew up neighbors, at least in neighboring states." The trench coat–heavy fog had got him, I thought. Or maybe he was mocking me: I'd said something affected, or else had multiplied dipthongs astonishingly. But he stood too stolidly, two-quart-man pleasant and expectant of the warmth due a fellow countryman abroad.

"I'm from Arkansas," I stammered at last, unwilling to commit myself further.

"Mississippi," he responded as he extended his belle-smooth hand. You could have knocked me over with a fine-tooth comb, to quote the then carpetbag governor of the state of Arkansas. Neighbor Jones had summered at Cambridge University and, while there, had acquired Harris tweeds, an upper-class accent, and a number of idioms without which no English gentleman will appear in public.

He was the first of a series of what I came to recognize as a type: the southern exile, who—anxious to forget, embarrassed and eager to win acceptance, or afflicted with guilt and indignant over injustice— diligently distanced himself from the region of his birth. For some, the North and its ways were far enough, but not for Jones and other spiritual expatriates. Expatriates were by no means rare or in danger of extinction and might be of either sex, with only minor differences to distinguish the two. The females were more likely than the males to pass over England to light on the Continent, there to study French literature. They made, according to report, particularly thorny girlfriends.

Expatriates were fundamentally, inescapably unhappy—as full of sorrow as Irish writers without ale and in the bosom of the enemy. But they had their ethnic, cultural cake and ate it, too. They purged themselves of being southern without deserting to the enemy—the descendants of those who drove down Dixie, reviled her from generation to generation, and even now exercised (nose pointing like a finger) moral wardship over everything from Appomattox to Little Rock. Expatriates retained in revised form something of the South that they deemed worthy and superior: a sense of tradition, manners, an appreciation for what Richard Weaver called "the unbought grace of life." That retention was an anchor and, I now think, profoundly important. It allowed the expatriates to believe that they had not forsaken utterly the ways of the fathers, or betrayed the people who had taught them whatever it was that they now—where no one knew them, their people, or what they had been taught—so assiduously cleansed from their accents and attitudes, even washing away the memory of what they once had been.

The exiles and I got along at a distance. I wanted company but was not about to cross the ocean to get it. I could tolerate their rejecting the South; I repudiated much myself. But I could not abide their manipulating the image, firmly established in correct northern opinion, of southern ignorance, bigotry, and violence in order to win sympathy and respect for their having risen from the native mire. Now, spotless as the North Pole, they testified to how far they had come, how many, beneath them farther than sin was below God, they had left behind.

We could speak familiarly of commonly familiar things. I sympathized. But I could not understand such failure of pride, nor could I understand the inability or refusal to hear and follow the blood within that would have carried them back to their original pulse. They were ultimately farther from me than the several sons and daughters of eastern European immigrants I met in class, farther from me and less easy to befriend than the international students whom I would later, at a southern university, serve as foreign-student adviser. The expatriates were from no place.

I had always thought it was easy to make friends. You spoke and took it from there. Here I met people who had overlearned an early lesson: Don't talk to strangers. Don't even necessarily speak to people you know to be fellow graduate students, not even if you had class with them or sat at the same table in Proctor Hall the previous evening. Friendliness, civility—the theory seemed to be—were communicable diseases transmitted by opening one's mouth to those whose IQs and "where froms" had not first been medically certified.

One evening I answered the knock at my door to discover a female graduate student, intense as a laser and twice as bright, and her boyfriend, a Minnesota Nordic, blond as sunlight and fashionably casual from the soles of his earth shoes to the top of his turtleneck. I knew neither well, but we had a mutual friend. They had come, she said, because our friend had told her I had lots of blues albums. Would I play some? It was a weeknight, and I needed to work. But I had no choice; they had knocked, and a gentleman could only open. For the next two hours, I picked my way from cut to cut, while they said things off album covers and got cozy on comfort, funk, her eyes, my blues.

The next day I met him on the sidewalk and spoke cordially, only to have him walk by without a word. "The next time you see me," I yelled as I spun him around, "you speak or start swinging." The next time I saw him, I heard him first. "Hi, Bill, how are you doing?" boomed across fifty yards of campus. I was glad we had reached an understanding. We could fine-tune the arrangements later.

Most graduate students chose their friends predominantly, in many cases almost exclusively, from the members of their own departments. University student center, Graduate College breakfast room, or Proctor Hall—it made little difference. The departments huddled, conceptualized, and, along with the salt and pepper, sugar and tea, passed the bibliography. This was partly shyness and inexperience, an inability to make conversation or have fun outside their disciplines, partly obsession, a tabling of the seminar before the graded time resumed. It was at bottom primitive tribalism, an instinctive ring dance and ancient wariness that kept the heads up, ranks closed, columns unbent.

One evening Sam Pickering and I arrived late to dinner and took the remaining seats at what turned out to be otherwise a mathematics and physics table. We introduced ourselves and departments and, with a little effort, were able to elicit the same information from all but the most reserved of the company. We said that it had been a beautiful day. Meteorology was not their field. Nor was current affairs, the movies, good books, or hometowns. They responded only, and then without comment, to requests for salad, meat, bread, and whatever else was on the table.

They had a right not to know us. But we had a right to courtesy and the only chairs available. "Excuse me," I requested, "but would you pass the flowers, please?" They reached Sam, who needed no cue. He took daisies. I picked marigolds, and, with compliments to the gardener, we commenced.

No one laughed. No one smiled, looked surprised or sickened—ten faces, lost in mathematics, colleagues, salad bowls, or bread plates. We rejected the stems. They were, we explained, a little sour for the season.

I took my friends where I found them, be they schoolteachers, clerks, waiters, coaches, taxi drivers, a cop. Although raised staunchly Protestant, my social church here soon included Catholics, and a goodly number of them at that. We had a common vocabulary and shared fundamental categories of thought. The papists, unlike the northeastern Protestants I met, could speak without smirking of right and wrong as though the choice might, at least on occasion, be clear and certain, woven in a fabric of immutable truths. They did not doubt the reality of sin and, although they may have yielded as often as the rest, felt guilty, did not dismiss guilt as a sign of neurosis but regarded it as rational and healthy and pointing the way to reform and redemption, in this life, even if there were no other.

This outlook made sense. It lent coherence, meaning, and dignity to living. It imparted a cosmic sense of purpose and, in so doing, enlarged the dramatic possibilities of life and language. I accepted it in great part because of early training. But I also realized, as I began for the first time to study closely the history of the region, that the categories and vocabulary offered appropriate terms for understanding the southern past.

I took to these Catholics, discovered, as Flannery O'Connor found in her evangelical Protestant neighbors, a deep spiritual kinship under the cloth. Robert Atwan, a free-lance writer and former altar boy, who grew up tough-minded in a New Jersey industrial town, became a particularly close friend. We shared a multitude of interests: baseball, history, writing, sin, even country music, and once, the divine afflatus descending, we co-composed an unsettling lyric, "Are You Selling Your Soul to Satan?" more a confession, perhaps, than a question or accusation and, unfortunately, never to be number one on anyone's chart.

My friend had theology and talent, both hard to find among academics. He also had a first-rate ear for cant, was at war with it, and could be ruthlessly clever in exposing pretension and shelling the vulnerable flanks of currently fashionable ideas. It did not always make him popular. It did make him fun. We planned, but other diversions prevented our writing, *The Book of Wrong Attitudes*, a frontal assault on contemporary cant, particularly the cult of self and mental hygiene, and targeting every pop psychology that arrayed itself in the field.

Half of the southerners in graduate school were expatriates or closet southerners, little fun and no use in a difficulty. The remainder drew together, as did the equally small groups of women, blacks, and foreign nationals.

We did not feel persecuted or excluded—victims of Jim Crow for white southerners—and had no lack of nonsouthern friends. Nor did we always or inevitably like one another, any more than we would have had we met on native grounds; and some could be offended by the assumption, occasionally manifested by one of our number, that all sons and daughters of Dixie were by birth and history destined to be friends. This seemed at best presumptuous, at times preposterous, and could easily mask an attempt to take advantage of any misguided sense of loyalty and obligation. A North Carolinian, with whom I had little in common, insisted on calling me "cousin," although there was between us no blood tie or, prior to Princeton, a single shared acquaintance. I did not challenge him. The alternative, Jim Tracey warned, might be "Bubba."

Being backward had its benefits. Classmates, expecting little, might be easily impressed. I once won praise simply by demonstrating a basic grasp of social Darwinism. When I mentioned the little episode to Bob Curvin, he only grinned. Even our friends viewed us, or so it sometimes seemed, as a sort of ethnic group—fun loving, amusing, and often interesting, but provincial, not quite up to the mark. They looked at us and saw our region, viewed us not as individuals but as representatives of the land of cotton, old times there not forgotten. Upon our shoulders rested responsibility for the reputation of our families, communities, states, and region.

Playing the southerner entertained our northern friends, who incited us at times and might provide cues and props. Two northeastern friends triumphed over fact and took me for a southern aristocrat. From an area discount store they bought a Rhett Butler planter hat they insisted I wear to a Graduate College Christmas party. A black friend from Philadelphia liked the hat but not the way I wore it. The afternoon of the party, he set me straight—tilted the hat low over my brow and cocked it jauntily to the side, then had me practice my walk until he pronounced it "street corner cool." It worked. Everyone laughed—except one rugged fellow who approached, as stiff-legged as I was loose, and, chest out, shoulders back, demanded, "Take it off." I laughed. He didn't. "Take it off," he repeated, this time showdown inches from my face. "You gotta problem?" interposed Bob Curvin, Jim Tracey moving in beside him. "You do, and we'll work it out." He didn't and withdrew politely. "Get your own fights," I instructed my protectors and laughed. A planter hat given to me by Jewish friends, a walk taught to me by a black militant, and an Arkansas twang had almost brought me to blows with a Boer from South Africa.

Anthropologists and psychologists, as well as parents and moralists, tell us that games may be very serious matters indeed. The game of southerner was serious enough. We played with the idea of the South. We examined the manners, traditions, attitudes, and values of the people from whom we came and whose image we saw reflected in the expectations of our new neighbors. We explored what it meant to be a southerner, what we wanted our region and ourselves to become. We sought the true, individual shape we could, with art and will and labor, release from the rough stone of the expectations of our neighbors, north and south, and in which we might otherwise remain permanently lodged and buried. We hunted ground on which to take a stand and assert our loyalty, however much we had changed and were changing, to the people and finest traditions of the place of our birth and childhood.

My parents were well educated and had done their best to teach me manners. But neither their backgrounds nor their values were aristocratic. Gentility was for them a code of conduct, not a pedigree. Their manners did not stem from their sense of station or depend on their perception of the station of others. Rather, they flowed from a democratic faith that everyone was entitled to courtesy and respect. Further, everyone was "as good as anyone else."

My parents' commitment to democratic ideals was especially strong, but the principles they instilled were deeply rooted in my family's past, which was in turn rooted in the southern past. My Great-Uncle Troy, one of many schoolteachers in the line, once told me, "Your people took democracy for granted, assumed it. As much a reflex as a principle."

"Marion County, and likely the places before, didn't give us any options," said my Uncle Loyce.

"No wonder in the end so many took off for the cities," I responded. My father laughed but didn't let it drop, for I needed as usual to see the lesson pointed. "Mark Twain called it 'Sir Walter Scott disease.' The South had quite a bout."

"Still has it," said Loyce.

"Comes back like morning sickness or malaria," admitted my father. "Even so, the South is mostly democratic. And mostly has been. As much so as the rest of the country. In some ways, more." I thought he meant its politics. But he meant its manners and, beyond that, the very personalities the South produced and, though he would not have said so, he and my uncles embodied.

When I stressed the strength of the South's democratic traditions, I provoked hot disagreement. Nor was I effective in explaining my idea of democratic manners, even apart from my effort to place it in a southern context. My friends for the most part agreed with Trollope that democracy undermined class and other distinctions upon which manners depended. An eastern European émigré and friend saw clearly, even though she had not heard my argument. She chuckled at a comment I made one evening: "How quintessentially American. My dear, you are the most American person I have ever met." It was condescension I accepted as a compliment.

I liked it here—this emerald, tidy pocket of prosperity where merit mattered more than color, where intellect and culture were coin of the realm, where Brotherly Love and Bagdad were but fifty miles in opposite directions. Yet I missed what Sterne called "the small sweet courtesies." I could not get used to the brusque, insistent trample of daily life, the impersonality that turned clerks, waitresses, and janitors into functional units without biography or desire and having but a single cause: a menial task, a commercial exchange, the customer's will.

I missed the poor and would tolerate slower "units." I missed farmers, missed the sight of the world's most perfectly designed garment, bib overalls. I missed people whose lives depended on the weather and its fluctuations. Here the weather affected nothing but moods and the speed of transportation.

I could not regard as a community a place without the poor, a place that did not and could not in any degree provide for its own feeding and that had no understanding of the lives and work of those who did supply the table. Out for a walk one evening, I turned to an elegantly suited gentleman who waited with me for the light and invaded the solitude that northeasterners sometimes wore like an additional layer of clothing: "Boy, my beans and tomatoes sure could use rain." He stared at me as though I were from another planet and, with the change of the light, bolted for the next galaxy.

The next galaxy didn't interest me. Home did. Categories and ideas; my place and people; the sources of who and what I was (or wanted to become); what I valued in those who had formed me, made me ready, and sent me here to learn and be whatever I would without them— did not grow suddenly clear but at least became accessible and capable of subtler definition and articulation. Home had tongue, and, although not always certain of its choices, point of view, and vocabulary, spoke to find a language of true expression. I owed this emerging sense of who and what I was and wanted to my northern friends. Especially to their occasional self-righteousness: it made me define what I had to defend.

I tarried here in Princeton, would leave and come again to serve on the faculty. But I wanted to go home. And be at home—not on the terms posed by the George Wallaces, Ross Barnetts, and Billy Bob Bozarts; not slumbering in the arms of some daughter of the white camellia, nor drunk on bourbon mixed with milk of magnolia. Such elements and images, for southerners as well as northerners, had for too long dominated the conception of the South. They had in my childhood worked powerfully on me. They were emblems of what my parents taught their sons not to be. The images had for me and others obscured more fundamental, worthier ideals: traditions of civility, neighborliness, and charity, a commitment to democratic principles so thoroughly embedded in regional manners that an honored native son would remain Plains "Jimmy," President Jimmy though he was.

As a child, I had failed to recognize that the worthy ideals were no less characteristic of the South than the unworthy ones. That's why it took twenty-one years and New Jersey to teach me what I should have known all along: I was a southerner. It was time to return and take my stand.

Notes on Contributors

ROBERT ATWAN of Seton Hall University has written critical essays on literature, psychology, and American culture and is the founder and series editor of *Best American Essays*. He reviews for the *New York Times, Los Angeles Times,* and other papers and journals. He is the coeditor of numerous textbooks and anthologies, including *Popular Writing in America: The Interaction of Style and Audience* and *Harper American Literature*.

J. BILL BERRY is a member of the history department and vice-president for academic affairs at the University of Central Arkansas. He earned his Ph.D. in history from Princeton University, where he also taught for two years. His essays and reviews have appeared in *Journal of Southern History, Sewanee Review, Virginia Quarterly Review, Arkansas Times,* and elsewhere.

MARILYN R. CHANDLER of Mills College has written widely on American and comparative literature. Her articles and essays have appeared in *Studies in Jewish American Literature, Notes on Mississippi Writers, Walt Whitman Review, Women's Review of Books,* and elsewhere. She has been guest editor of *A/B: Auto/Biography Studies* and is the author of *A Healing Art: Autobiography and the Poetics of Crisis*.

GEORGE CORE, who has edited the *Sewanee Review* since 1973, is also adjunct professor of English at the University of the South. The editor of two books and the coeditor of three others, he is the author (with Walter Sullivan) of *Writing from the Inside*. He is a regular contributor to the periodical press, writing for such quarterlies as *Hudson Review* and *Virginia Quarterly Review* and reviewing for *Book World* in addition to his own magazine.

JAMES M. COX of Dartmouth College is the author of *Mark Twain: The Fate of Humor* and *Recovering Literature's Lost Ground: Essays in American*

Autobiography. He has written extensively on southern fiction and on auto-biography, and his essays have appeared in *Virginia Quarterly, Yale Review, Southern Review,* and elsewhere. His numerous honors include a Guggenheim Fellowship and the E. Harris Harbison Award for Distinguished Teaching from the Danforth Foundation.

ELIZABETH FOX-GENOVESE is the Eleonore Raoul Professor of the Humanities and director of women's studies at Emory University. Her publications include *Within the Plantation Household: Black and White Women of the Old South* and, with Eugene D. Genovese, *Fruits of Merchant Capital: Slavery and Bourgeois Property in the Rise and Expansion of Capitalism.* Currently working on a collection of essays, *Feminist Interventions: Politics, History, Culture,* she is also editing, with Carol Bleser, a series of nineteenth-century southern women's diaries.

GEORGE GARRETT of the University of Virginia is the prolific author of books of criticism, poetry, and fiction, including the critically acclaimed *Do Lord, Remember Me, Death of the Fox, The Succession: A Novel of Elizabeth and James,* and *The Collected Poems of George Garrett.* He is also a productive editor and a member of the editorial boards of several leading journals. He has served as a writer for CBS television and a screenwriter for Samuel Goldwyn, Jr., at Goldwyn Studios.

WILLIAM HOWARTH of Princeton University is the author and editor of many books and essays, including *The Book of Concord, Thoreau in the Mountains, Nature in American Life,* and *Twentieth-Century Interpretations of Poe's Tales.* He has published extensively on autobiography and is a regular contributor to the periodical press, writing for quarterlies and magazines such as *Sewanee Review* and *National Geographic.*

COLONEL PAT C. HOY II of the United States Military Academy at West Point was for five years the managing editor of the *Doris Lessing Newsletter.* He is the author of *Writing Essays: A Persuasive Art* and coeditor of *Prose Pieces: Essays and Stories* and *Women's Voices: Visions and Perspectives.* His reviews and autobiographical essays have appeared in *Sewanee Review* and elsewhere.

JAMES OLNEY is editor of the *Southern Review* and Voorhies Professor of English, French, and Italian at Louisiana State University. One of the seminal scholars of autobiography, he is the editor of several collections, including *Autobiography: Essays Theoretical and Critical* and *Studies in Autobiog-*

raphy, and the author of three books, *Metaphors of Self: The Meaning of Autobiography*, *Tell Me Africa: An Approach to African Literature*, and *The Rhizome and the Flower: The Perennial Philosophy—Yeats and Jung*.

ROY REED of the University of Arkansas, Fayetteville, has served as both foreign correspondent and national correspondent for the *New York Times* and was that paper's chief southern correspondent during much of the civil rights era. He has written for *Atlantic, Time, Southern*, and other journals. He has also published a critically praised volume of personal essays, *Looking for Hogeye*.

SALLY WOLFF is assistant dean of Emory College, Emory University, where she received her Ph.D. in English. She collaborated with David Minter on the recent Norton Critical Edition of *The Sound and the Fury*. Other work includes "Companion Collections: Eudora Welty and Elizabeth Spencer," "Eudora Welty's Nostalgic Imagination," "A Matchless Time: William Faulkner Composing *The Sound and the Fury*," and "The Wisdom of Pain: Chekhov's 'Ward Number Six.'"